D0151536

Blake and His Bibles

LOCUST HILL LITERARY STUDIES
NO. 1

Blake and His Bibles

Edited by
David V. Erdman

with an Introduction by
Mark Trevor Smith

LOCUST HILL PRESS
West Cornwall, CT
1990

PR
4148
.B52
B57
1990

© 1990 David V. Erdman
All rights reserved

Library of Congress Cataloging-in-Publication Data

Blake and his bibles / edited by David V. Erdman ; with an
    introduction by Mark Trevor Smith.
        237p.   cm. -- (Locust Hill literary studies ; no. 1)
        ISBN 0-933951-29-9 (lib. bdg. : alk. paper) : $30.00
        1. Blake, William, 1757-1827--Religion. 2. Religious poetry,
    English--History and criticism. 3. Bible in literature. 4. Bible-
    -Illustrations. I. Erdman, David V. II. Series.
    PR4148.B52B57 1990   89-14052
    821'.7--dc20   CIP

Printed on acid-free, 250-year-life paper
Manufactured in the United States of America

Contents

v

CONCORDIA COLLEGE LIBRARY
2811 NE HOLMAN ST.
PORTLAND, OR 97211-6099

About the Contributors

Mark Trevor Smith is Associate Professor of English at Southwest Missouri State University. He is a member of the team that compiles the annual *Romantic Movement: A Selective and Critical Bibliography* (also published by Locust Hill Press) and has published articles on Mary Shelley, Percy Bysshe Shelley, and Alexander Pope. He is in the throes of shaping his obsession with the coincidence of opposites, especially as found in neo-classical and Romantic poetry, into a book.

J.M.Q. Davies is a Lecturer in English at the Northern Territory University in Darwin, Australia. He has published articles and reviews in *The Durham University Journal*, *Philological Quarterly*, *Modern Languages Review* and *Review of English Studies*, and translated an anthology of *German Tales of Fantasy, Horror and the Grotesque*. Currently he is completing a book on the Milton illustrations to be published by the University of Western Australia Press.

Florence Sandler is Professor of English at the University of Puget Sound in Tacoma, Washington. She writes on Spenser, Milton, Blake and others, in their different political and biblical contexts.

John E. Grant is Professor of English at the University of Iowa. He is co-editor of the Norton Critical Edition of *Blake's Poetry and Designs* (1979) and the author of many articles on Blake's poetry and pictures.

Mary Lynn Johnson, Assistant to the President of the University of Iowa, is co-author of *Blake's 'Four Zoas': The Design of a Dream* (1978) and co-editor of the Norton Critical Edition of *Blake's Poetry and Designs* (1979). Her most recent essay is "Feminist Approaches to Teaching Blake's *Songs*" in *Approaches to Teaching Blake's Songs of Innocence and of Experience*, ed. Robert F. Gleckner and Mark L. Greenberg (1989).

Sheila A. Spector is Assistant Professor of English at Kennesaw State College in Marietta, Georgia. As a result of the research completed for this study, she has been able to complete several other articles dealing with Blake's Hebrew, published in *BIQ* and *Philological Quarterly*.

David V. Erdman, the editor of this volume, is Emeritus Professor at the State University of New York, Stony Brook.

Abbreviations

B   (with catalogue number, followed by plate number) Martin Butlin, *The Paintings and Drawings of William Blake*, 2 vols. (New Haven: Yale Univ. Press, 1981)

BIQ   *Blake, An Illustrated Quarterly*

E   (with page number, e.g., E275): David V. Erdman, ed., *The Complete Poetry and Prose of William Blake* (Garden City: Doubleday; Berkeley: Univ. of California Press, 1982) (some errors of pagination)

Essick   Robert N. Essick, *William Blake: A Catalogue* (Princeton: Princeton Univ. Press, 1983)

IB   *The Illuminated Blake*, ed. David V. Erdman (Garden City: Doubleday; Oxford: Oxford Univ. Press, 1974)

PL   John Milton, *Paradise Lost*

Blake's illuminated works are referred to by plate and line numbers, e.g., *J* 49.50–52.

A   *America a Prophecy*

ARO   *All Religions Are One*

Eur   *Europe a Prophecy*

J   *Jerusalem the Emanation of the Giant Albion*

M   *Milton a Poem*

MHH   *The Marriage of Heaven and Hell*

NNR   *There Is No Natural Religion*

Ur   *The Book of Urizen*

Other Blake works:

DC	*A Descriptive Catalogue*
EG	"The Everlasting Gospel" (in Blake's Notebook)
FZ	*Vala, or The Four Zoas* (cited by Night, page, lines)
NT	*Night Thoughts*; Blake's illustrations to Young's poem
VLJ	"A Vision of the Last Judgment" (E554–66)

Versions of the English Bible:

KJV	King James Version (1611)
NEB	New English Bible (1970)
RSV	Revised Standard Version (1952)

Introduction

Mark Trevor Smith

In his diary Crabb Robinson records that Blake once "warmly declared that all he knew was in the Bible." Taken aback, Robinson clarifies Blake's hyperbole (or perhaps adds Blake's own explanation): "but then he understands by the Bible the Spiritual Sense" as opposed to "the natural sense" (*Blake Records* 322). Distinguishing between Blake's spiritual understanding of the Bible and a natural understanding is the business of the six essays in this volume.

The key to our project may be found in Northrop Frye: "one of the most striking features of the Bible ... [is] its capacity for self re-creation" (*Great Code* 225). Blake, by re-creating the act of re-creation already performed by the Bible, raises the art of re-creation to its highest level. Blake's power of re-creation is more startling than Coleridge's secondary imagination, which is "a repetition in the finite mind of the eternal act of creation in the infinite I AM," because Blake's is not merely "an echo" (304) of God's creation; Blake is co-creator with God and invites us likewise to assume our full human divinity.

In this sense Blake re-creates the Bible in two opposing ways: he rewrites by repeating, imitating, honoring, but he also re-writes by denying, contradicting, making new. This simultaneous acceptance and rejection is stated most radically by Thomas Altizer when he defines *Jerusalem* as a "re-creation directed to effecting a coincidence of the opposites, a drawing together of all or most of those antinomies which our history has established" (167-68). Leopold Damrosch, Jr. similarly emphasizes Blake's attempt at inclusiveness: "Rather than accepting one or another of the compromises that have been developed over the centuries, he aspired to put the entire structure of Western thought together again" (114).

It is Blake's very relationship to the Bible which makes him the revolutionary artist, satisfied with no less than a complete and continuing redefinition of God and man. Such fervor pits him of course against all complacent religious and literary stances: "his reading of the Bible certainly convinced him that the symbolic artist operates in conflict with received values rather than codifying and confirming them" (Damrosch 68).

Given its fundamental importance, Blake's attitude toward the Bible has received surprisingly little attention. Michael Tolley's unpublished dissertation, *William Blake's Use of the Bible* (London, 1974) contains a detailed listing of all biblical allusions he could find. It should be consulted by anyone who wants to be sure of knowing the Bible references in any part of Blake. The only published book-length treatment is Leslie Tannenbaum's *Biblical Tradition in Blake's Early Prophecies*. In that book Tannenbaum insists on the historical context of Bible interpretation in Blake's day as he defines the importance of the Bible for Blake: "The Bible is the great code of art because it contains and inculcates the highest form of mimesis, the *imitatio dei*, which for Blake is the imitation of the actual process of vision ... to transform the reader-viewer-auditor into the body of Christ" (85).

This volume of essays, in its consideration of Blake and the Bible, is central to the more general issue of literary criticism and the Bible. The most recent entry in this field, Robert Alter and Frank Kermode's *A Literary Guide to the Bible*, while reminding us that "the Bible is probably the most important single source of all our literature," points out that "the Bible, once thought of as a source of secular literature yet somehow apart from it, now bids fair to become part of the literary canon" (2-3).

Each essay in this collection defines in a different way and through a different medium Blake's enormous capacity for creation, re-creation, and self-re-creation, above all his re-creation of the Bible.

Three of the essayists interpret Blake's illustrations: John E. Grant interprets those for Young's *Night Thoughts*, J.M.Q. Davies those for Milton's *Nativity Ode*, and Mary Lynn Johnson those for David's Psalms. The other three essayists interpret Blake's words: Florence Sandler those in the annotations to Watson, Sheila A. Spector those in Hebrew, and Mark Trevor Smith those in *Jerusalem*.

Each essay pursues the very Blakean project of using minute particulars to confront mass assumptions, to consolidate error, to find a spiritual understanding of Blake's Bible. In their varying approaches, each captures Blake's exuberance, what Davies in his essay calls the "extraordinary buoyancy of his temperament, the tenacity of his faith in the dignity and potential of man."

Florence Sandler, in "'Defending the Bible': Blake, Paine, and the Bishop on the Atonement," establishes illuminating historical backgrounds. We should know, for example, that in historical context Bishop Watson was a champion of latitudinarianism and had even opposed banning Paine's *Age of Reason* despite his strong disagreement with it. Sandler points out that Watson always offered brotherly reconciliation to his opponents. But as we know from Blake's frustrations with William Hayley, good intentions often mask repressive forces. Corporeal friends can be spiritual enemies, and spiritual enemies may obscure the spiritual sense of the Bible.

Paine's anti-Christian Deism ironically makes him a better Christian than the Bishop in Blake's view. Nevertheless, although Paine's stand is to be preferred to Watson's, Watson and Paine are both ultimately allied with the God of This World who demands morality and therefore death. Paine essentially wanted to preserve Natural Theology and the Urizenic God as Watson did, Sandler concludes.

Blake's irritation in his annotations to Watson is finally for Sandler an issue of canonicity. Whether the text is the moral law of the Bible or the natural law of the Newtonian universe, Watson and Paine both advocated closure, while Blake insisted on constant re-creation.

Mary Lynn Johnson, in "David's Recognition of the Human Face of God in Blake's Designs for the Book of Psalms," part of her continuing labor on the magnificent series of Bible illustrations that Blake painted for Thomas Butts, shows how Blake redefines David and interpolates Christ in certain illustrations to the Psalms. She agrees with Northrop Frye that Blake shakes the Bible upside down and makes it say something not intended by its human authors.

Johnson early takes on one crucial question: if Blake is so gruff and blasphemous in his words against Watson and others, why is he so apparently mild and orthodox in his Bible paintings? Johnson's answer includes a kind of subterfuge: "Blake ... emphasizes meanings compatible with his own ideas while keeping up appearances as a guileless visual translator who refrains from ruffling the tranquil surface of familiar texts."

Most important, Johnson places these illustrations to the Psalms in the context of all Blake's Bible illustrations. She sees them as marking a turning point in the progression from fall to reunification. Specifically she discusses three christological designs in terms of their visionary and historical content. Johnson's narrative sequence from the need for Jesus' presence, through the fulfillment in the incarnation, and finally to the installation of Mercy as the judge of humankind insists on the triumph of the spiritual over the natural.

"David Delivered out of Many Waters," for example, blends Psalm 18 and Psalm 69 by "superimposing upon his [David's] worst fantasies his genuinely imagined visions." The iconography of "Mercy and Truth are Met together, Righteousness and Peace have Kissed each other" emphasizes the reconciliation of separations. The unfamiliar pose of Jesus forces attention as he "marries" heaven and earth.

In "Blake as an Eighteenth-Century Hebraist," Sheila A. Spector continues her valuable work as a Hebraist and student of Kabbalah to dismiss false premises and lay careful groundwork for further study. Even though her conclusions are tentative, her work invites further speculations.

She establishes two starting points: first, the variety of possible sources of Hebrew and possible attitudes toward Hebrew in Blake's time, and second, the precision of Blake's artistry. This combination of social forces and individual trait makes it clear that Blake could write correct Hebrew, so that when he writes incorrect Hebrew, he is probably not making a mistake, but is rather using the "error" as part of his meaning.

Among her examples is an ambiguous reversal of a letter in the negation in "thou shalt *not* commit adultery," which Spector interprets to mean that "the subject is too complex to be reduced to a simple either-or." This method, in Blake and in Spector, encourages the reader to look beyond the obvious, to find the spiritual in the natural.

J.M.Q. Davies, in "Apollo's 'Naked Human Form Divine': The Dynamics of Meaning in Blake's *Nativity Ode* Designs," contrasts Blake's and Milton's visions of the birth of Jesus to show how Blake's designs are more dramatically counterpointed against the ode than has been previously recognized. In "The Descent of Peace," for example, certain details reveal that Blake is more optimistic about the pending redemption of Nature than is Milton.

Complicating Davies' approach are Blake's two different series of designs, similar but displaying marked differences. Davies focuses especially on "The Overthrow of Apollo," the climax to Blake's visionary progression. The design in the Whitworth series and the one in the Huntington series contain the greatest differences of any two paintings in the two series. The Apollo in the former series is much more favorably portrayed than the one in the latter, leading Davies to ask: "If this design is simply a celebrative tribute to Milton's vision of paganism eclipsed by Christianity represented by the Star of Bethlehem, why did Blake present an Apollo not only majestic but triumphant?" Davies concludes that Blake wished to "distinguish his own vision of man's redemption from Milton's by transforming Apollo into a redeemer." Blake thus reverses Milton's intention and incorporates the pagan into the Christian. The apparent act of exclusion is therefore an act of inclusion.

John E. Grant, in "Jesus and the Powers That Be in Blake's Designs for Young's *Night Thoughts*," shows that Blake reshaped not only Young's vision but also "Young's conception of himself as poet." Grant emphasizes Blake's impatience with Young, his insistence on fighting his adversaries.

Blake refocuses the divine vision in Young by redefining Father and Son and Satan. Jesus especially becomes redefined as a fraternal figure replacing the paternalistic God of Young. Grant is adamant in his stand against any "charitable ambiguity" which might allow "what is wrong" to be mistaken for what is right. Above all, Christ and anti-Christ need to be distinguished.

At one point Grant raises an important issue that lurks behind all six essays: the extra difficulty of interpreting illustrations as opposed to interpreting the kinds of directly stated opinions that we find in, for example, the annotations to Watson. The difference, however, is not as great as one might think, for interpreting Blake's direct statements, such as the one which heads this introduction, can be no less difficult.

Mark Trevor Smith, in "Striving with Blake's Systems," explores two episodes in *Jerusalem*—Reuben's crossing the Jordan and the birth of Jesus—to point out the impossibility of a simple separation of the spiritual and the natural. Although the two realms are often seen as mutually exclusive, the real difference between the two is that the spiritual includes the natural, while the natural excludes the spiritual.

Focusing on Los's declaration, "I must Create a System," and following in the lines of Michael Cooke's *Acts of Inclusion* and Hazard Adams' *Philosophy of the Literary Symbolic*, Smith insists that creating a system is not simply a matter of choosing right from wrong. It must include creating its contrary and even its negation, or it will fall into the destructive vision of the Sons of Albion, who try to separate good from evil and eliminate the latter. In *Jerusalem* Los discovers the impossibility of such a project, and so must we. Blake's re-creation of the Bible works because it contains no element of revenge that is not redeemed by forgiveness, no element of self-righteousness that is not blasted by self-annihilation.

The biblical traditions into which Blake fits are those of imagination and poetry. As Robert Alter points out in his "Introduction to the Old Testament" in *A Literary Guide to the Bible*,

> the very pinnacle of ancient Hebrew poetry was reached in Job, the biblical text that is most daring and innovative in its imagination of God, man, and creation; for here as elsewhere in the Hebrew Bible the literary medium is not merely a means of "conveying" doctrinal positions but an adventurous occasion for deepening doctrine through the play of literary resources, or perhaps even, at least here, for leaping beyond doctrine. (15)

Clearly Blake leaps beyond doctrine, both theological and literary, by writing, as does the writer of Job, the best poetry about the most daring reaches of religious belief. The essays in this volume extend our understanding of such Blakean biblical play.

Works Cited

Adams, Hazard. *Philosophy of the Literary Symbolic*. Gainesville: Univ. Presses of Fla., 1983.

Alter, Robert, and Frank Kermode. *A Literary Guide to the Bible*. Cambridge, Mass.: Harvard Univ. Press, 1987.

Altizer, Thomas J.J. *The New Apocalypse: The Radical Christian Vision of William Blake*. East Lansing: Michigan State Univ. Press, 1967.

Bentley, G.E. *Blake Records*. London: Oxford Univ. Press, 1969.

Coleridge, Samuel Taylor. *Biographia Literaria*. Ed. James Engell and W. Jackson Bate. The Collected Works of Samuel Taylor Coleridge, 7. Bollingen Series LXXV, Princeton: Princeton Univ. Press, 1983.

Cooke, Michael. *Acts of Inclusion: Studies Bearing on an Elementary Theory of Romanticism*. New Haven: Yale Univ. Press, 1979.

Damrosch, Leopold, Jr. *Symbol and Truth in Blake's Myth*. Princeton: Princeton Univ. Press, 1980.

Frye, Northrop. *The Great Code: The Bible and Literature*. New York: Harcourt, 1982.

Tannenbaum, Leslie. *Biblical Tradition in Blake's Early Prophecies*. Princeton: Princeton Univ. Press, 1982.

Tolley, Michael. *William Blake's Use of the Bible*. Unpublished dissertation. Univ. of London, 1974.

Blake and His Bibles

Apollo's "Naked Human Form Divine": The Dynamics of Meaning in Blake's *Nativity Ode* Designs

J.M.Q. Davies

The ode *On the Morning of Christ's Nativity* is considered Milton's first major tribute to his Saviour in his new-found vocation as poet-prophet of Albion, a lyric prelude to *Paradise Lost* and *Paradise Regained*. And it has long been admired for what Blake would have regarded as its visionary qualities—its swift expansive movement from the Nativity scene itself dwelt on by Catholic poets to the effects of the Incarnation: the descent of Peace, light and celestial harmony, the redemption of Nature, the demise of the pagan oracles and the binding of the "old Dragon" (line 168)—in a vision which both embraces and transcends the whole of human history from Creation to Apocalypse. Blake's two sets each of six illustrations to Milton's hymn, the larger in the Whitworth Art Gallery (B 538: 1-6; pls. 660-5), the other in the Huntington Library (B 542: 1-6, pls. 666-71), are the shortest and superficially least prepossessing of his watercolor sequences illuminating Milton's major poems.[1] But recently there has been a growing recognition that his answering vision in another medium and a new philosophical key more than matches the imaginative range and iconographic sophistication of his prophetic precursor's achievement.

The precise extent to which it is a dissenting vision, however, and the celebrative impulse behind the illustrations qualified by criticism, are hard to determine because of Blake's scrupulous fidelity to the letter of Milton's text. In the *Nativity Ode* designs, as in all the Milton sequences, he seems to have regarded this both as one of the constraints of his task as illustrator and as a test of his interpreters. And to a degree at least, a critic's reading both of the designs and of *Milton* will be affected by wider variables—by whether for instance he concurs with Northrop Frye's influential distinction between Milton as a radical and Shakespeare a conservative artist, or tends toward, say, C.S. Lewis' view of *Paradise Lost* as a *summa* of traditional Christian wisdom.[2] In an important essay on both *Nativity Ode* sequences, Stephen C. Behrendt has argued persuasively that Blake's principal concern is to illuminate the Christocentric nature of Milton's vision, to celebrate his rejection of classical culture, and to "liberate the poem from ... misguided criticism."[3] And neither Leslie Tannenbaum's recent discussion of Blake's Christocentric typology, which clarifies how Blake could deny that art is progressive yet find fault with his precursors, nor Morton D. Paley's explorations of Blake's evolving attitude to the classics have diminished the plausibility of this point of view.[4] But the celebrative hypothesis tends to see Milton as the prophet, Blake the scribe, and to assume that what is radical in one revolutionary era is necessarily so in the next. It also underestimates the extent to which Blake was the intellectual heir to enlightenment skepticism.

It is true that by 1809, the date of the Whitworth *Nativity Ode* designs, Jesus had assumed a crucial role in Blake's thought. But it is hazardous to assume that the mere fact of his presence at the center of the *Nativity Ode* would have been enough to secure Blake's unqualified approval. For Jesus is not a static symbol in Blake, a "Ratio" (*MHH* 5, E35) as he felt he tended to be in Milton. And his various manifestations as "secret child" (*Eur* 3.2, E61), as rebellious prophet, as the seventh "Eye of God" (*M* 13.17, E107) or historical advance in man's conception of the divine, as love and friendship, and as the imagination, though related must be kept distinct since they function differently in different contexts. In *Europe*, which as Michael J. Tolley has demonstrated is richly counterpointed against Milton's hymn, Blake presented the rebirth of energy at the Nativity as merely a prelude to Apocalypse, followed not as in Milton by a catalogue of its miraculous effects, but by a nightmare vision of "Urizen unloos'd from chains" (*Eur* 3.11, E61), the "night of Nature" and the "Eighteen hundred years" (*Eur* 9.3-5, E63) of Enitharmon's sleep which preceded the American and French Revolutions.[5] In this context the fact that Moloch worship seems to be in full swing in the design traditionally titled "The Flight of Moloch" (figs. 9-10) may be significant. And while the way the series closes by returning to the opening scene with the stable in the foreground (figs. 1-2, 11-12) does indeed suggest that "the 'time' elapsed is visionary," as Behrendt (p. 68) astutely observes, it could also signal an abortive Apocalypse, a return to the *status quo* in a perennial round of revolt and repression.

1809 was also the year in which Blake, roused perhaps by the beginning of the Peninsular War, wrote some of his most scathing attacks on the classics. Since he felt that "Shakspeare & Milton were both curbd by ... the silly Greek & Latin slaves of the Sword" (*M* 1, E95), he is likely to have been aware of the conventional nature of the youthful Milton's dismissal of the pagan gods. And he was probably also conscious that even in *Paradise Regained* Milton's reasons for rejecting classical wisdom were essentially theological, and thus closer to Dante's than to his own. But it nonetheless seems likely that he would have wished to illuminate the importance of so central a truth, however conventionally perceived. Another puzzling particular in the series, however, suggests that he chose not to do so in any obvious way. In the Huntington version of "The Overthrow of Apollo and the Pagan Gods" (fig. 8), the pedestaled statue of Apollo with its serpent-entwined stele is shown, in Jean H. Hagstrum's words, "amid the ultimate apocalyptic destruction ... dumb, frozen, and helpless," his departing spirit plunging to the waves below.[6] In the Whitworth version by contrast (fig. 7), Apollo though still on a pedestal has no supporting stele and looks very much alive; indeed he is presented in the act of vanquishing a quite formidable-looking Python. How is this to be understood in relation to his departing spirit, which still suggests the notion of his overthrow? Such apparent incongruities seem to hint that Blake's pictorial commentary may be more dramatically counterpointed against Milton's hymn than has been recognized. In the ensuing discussion of the dynamics of Blake's meaning in the series, I shall attempt to show that they are in fact bold but coherent departures from Milton, quite in keeping with what we might expect from the author of *Europe, The Marriage of Heaven and Hell,* and *Milton.*

A preliminary word, though, about the order of composition of the two sets and the arrangement of the individual designs within each set. The Whitworth designs done in pen and brown wash for the Rev. Joseph Thomas in 1809 are as large as the Huntington set of *Paradise Lost* designs (B 632-43) that Blake had painted for him two years earlier. And partly because they are more articulate iconographically—in the context of Blake's vituperations against chiaroscuro in his *Descriptive Catalogue* (E547) the same year, they seem defiantly linear—they have usually been assumed to be the later set. But Martin Butlin has proposed that the smaller undated Huntington set painted originally for Thomas Butts, which is highly finished in pale, misty luminous tones, should on stylistic grounds be grouped with the *L'Allegro and Il Penseroso* (B 672-83) and *Paradise Regained* (B 684-95) designs, which are both watermarked

1816 and on the same intimate scale. He contends that "the strongest argument for placing the Butts series first is that the first design, 'The Descent of Peace,' follows the more imaginative idea of the tempera 'Nativity' of *c*. 1799-1800 (B 502)," which shows Christ miraculously suspended in mid-air. But "Blake could equally well have reverted to the earlier composition after showing the Nativity in a more conventional way in the Thomas version of 1809."[7] Blake does mention the *Nativity Ode* in a letter to Butts dated 6 July 1803 (E729-30) in connection with the prospect of illustrating Cowper's Milton, but only the *Latin and Italian Poems* was to eventuate and the letter may indicate no more than that Blake contemplated such a series at the time. Butlin's hypothesis, moreover, helps explain why iconographically both sequences seem equally felicitous but in quite different ways, and, unlike the two completed sets to *Paradise Lost* (B 632-56) done within a year of one another, do not obviously suggest a process of revision and refinement in one direction or another. If the Huntington set was indeed executed around 1815-16, several years after the Whitworth set, then the sometimes radical differences between them could simply reflect two closely related but quite independent responses to the *Nativity Ode* at different times. The survival of preliminary sketches for individual designs in both sequences (B 728, 730-31) is consistent with this notion and may indicate that Blake did not have access to Thomas' set at Epsom when he came to do the second set for Butts. Some though never all the particulars in four of the six designs are reversed in the two versions. In the opening design (figs. 1-2) Peace descends and Nature lies pillowed to the left of the stable in the Whitworth series but in the Huntington to the right; in the second (figs. 3-4) the central shepherds are shown in the same attitude but they gaze heavenward in opposite directions; in the third (figs. 5-6) the starry extension of the Dragon's tail has likewise been reversed; while in "The Flight of Moloch" (figs. 9-10) only the presiding spectre's position remains unchanged. These variants, for some of which I shall suggest possible explanations, are quite compatible with the notion that Blake worked the second set up from memory, but they do not illuminate which came first. This discussion will not resolve the problem—though despite what I consider to be the greater iconographic daring of the Whitworth series I think Butlin's hypothesis is right—but it may help us gauge the probabilities with more confidence.

If, as the recurrent image of the stable implies, the designs are to be read serially like the sequences of Hogarth, their internal ordering is obviously important. Of the various proposed arrangements Behrendt's is undoubtedly the most purposeful.[8] Influenced by Arthur E. Barker's account of the tripartite structure of the hymn, Behrendt (pp. 67-9) argues that if "The Old Dragon" (figs. 5-6) is placed in fifth instead of third position, the stable recedes and reappears by regular stages, revealing the "intellectual and artistic symmetry" (p. 68) of Blake's visual commentary more clearly.[9] And this arrangement has the further advantage of locating the binding of the Dragon in the same approximate position as in Revelation (20.2). But against this we must consider that the *L'Allegro and Il Penseroso* and *Paradise Regained* designs numbered by Blake follow the order of events in the poems.[10] This is also the case with the unnumbered but trimmed *Paradise Lost* series, which broadly speaking have one design for each of the poem's twelve books, and with the *Comus* illustrations (B 616-31), although there Blake is especially apt to conflate more than one image or episode within a single design. Blake probably developed this methodical habit when illustrating Young's *Night Thoughts* and Gray's poems in the 1790s, where he was obliged to follow the order of the text by its presence offset within his exuberant designs.[11] It is true that he experimented with the arrangement of the *Songs* and the full plate illustrations to the *Book of Urizen* in various copies, but there his own text provided adequate internal control over the meaning of the work. In the absence of unequivocal evidence to the contrary, therefore, it seems prudent to assume that the *Nativity Ode* designs also follow the order dictated by the text.

Blake's strategy in the opening design, "The Descent of Peace" (figs. 1-2) (B660), is characteristic of his method in the sequence generally. He focuses on the first three verses of Milton's hymn and draws in images from other points in the poem, while also discreetly introducing his own iconographic controls. No direct allusion to Milton's proem is made, but some of its functions are taken over by Blake's personification of Peace, a figure resembling his later heavenly messenger, the ascending Lark in *L'Allegro and Il Penseroso* 2 (B 673; cf. *M* 35.54f., E135). As Christ's "ready Harbinger" (49) she descends through the three concentric circles of the "turning sphere" (48), which forms a magnificent vortex like that expanding behind Milton as he descends from Eternity in Blake's epic (*M* 15.21f., E109). Her splayed palm and encompassing gesture—which Behrendt (86) sees as a redemptive echo of Urizen's dividers on the *Europe* frontispiece (*IB* 156)—indicate that like Milton in the proem she is introducing, indeed revealing, the Divine Vision opened to the spectator and to nature beneath her. The visual continuity established by her vortex with the "Globe of circular light" (110) in the next design (figs. 3-4) im-

Figures 1 and 2. The 1805 Whitworth version (above) of Blake's watercolor illustration, "The Descent of Peace," is less jubilant than the 1815–16 (?) Huntington version (right), with its light-radiating Christ-

child, but in both versions Nature (foreground) seems more likely to be redeemed than Milton suggests—*Whitworth Art Gallery; Henry E. Huntington Library and Art Gallery*, respectively.

plies that like the angel of the Lord in Luke 2.9-14, she also acts as herald to the angelic choir. Her function as spiritual nuncio is emphasized in the Whitworth version by the resemblance of her wand to Mercury's caduceus. The Nativity itself takes place within a stylized gothic stable oddly reminiscent of the tombs in Westminster Abbey Blake engraved for Gough's *Sepulchral Monuments* (cp B 4, 9, 18, 23, 26), and not unlike the winged ark on *Jerusalem* 39 (*IB* 318) and the Ark of the Covenant in his engraving of Raphael's "Joshua passing over Jordan."[12] Prompted perhaps by Milton's description of Peace's "Turtle wing" (50) and olive crown (47), and his later allusion to the rainbow (143) and Osiris' "worshipt Ark" (220), Blake has recalled the stable's function as a refuge from tyranny in the Gospel story, by presenting it as a Beulaic ark in which the Divine Vision is kept afloat in time of trouble.[13] Hence perhaps the two oxen in lieu of the traditional ox and ass in both versions, and the addition of a window in the Huntington design. The Nativity scene in the Whitworth version is more conspicuously Beulaic, in that Joseph and Mary are shown tending a passive Christ-child, "meanly wrapt" (31) in swaddling clothes, his head surrounded by a modest aureole—an inauspicious figure altogether reminiscent of the "secret child" in *Europe*. Commenting on the opening plates of that poem, Tolley (119) writes that "the birth of Christ represented the crucial challenge to Urizen's compasses; by circling Him tight round with swaddling bands, by the very milk of His mother's breast, Urizen and Enitharmon, forces of mortality, attempted to control the Infinite." In this context the Whitworth design seems less than jubilant, as though in 1809 Blake were convinced of the symbolic importance of Christ's birth, yet reluctant to endorse Milton's view of it as an event of unique historical and eschatological significance, and more than ever aware that in the ensuing 1800 years Jesus had become Jehovah (cf *MHH* 5, E35).

The Huntington version by contrast, with its naked energetic Christ-child radiating light as he leaps from the swooning Mary's lap, seems redolent with hope. The image is unprecedented apparently in the iconography of the Nativity, though a source has been proposed in a Roman bas-relief of the "Birth of Dionysus," and within Blake's canon such exuberant modulations of "Glad Day" (B 331-2) recur repeatedly.[14] But since Blake follows his tempera "Nativity" (B 502) in including Zacharias, Elizabeth, and the young John the Baptist opposite Joseph and Mary (though in reverse), his portrayal may also have been inspired by Elizabeth's vivid account in Luke 1.44 of how "the babe lept in my womb for joy" at Mary's news that she was with child by the Holy Ghost. Evidently Blake wished to illuminate the spiritual rather than the historical significance of Christ's advent here, and he has emphasized this by presenting it as an epiphany, a Divine Vision the spectator is invited to share with the subordinate figures. Christ's cruciform gesture also establishes a much firmer line of continuity with the Cherubim raising their arms exultantly in the next design (fig. 4) and with the sacrificial child in "The Flight of Moloch" (fig. 10).

In both versions Blake also seems more optimistic about the pending redemption of Nature than Milton, who leaves her ultimate fate at the Last Judgment an open question, and whose emphasis on her "foul deformities" (44) would have given Blake little cause to revise his view that Milton never entirely freed himself from nature goddess Enitharmon's doctrine that "Womans love is Sin!" (*Eur* 5.5, E62). And in both versions an intimate relationship is suggested pictorially between her and Peace. She lies in the lower foreground pillowed against a stone, her hair divided about it in token perhaps of her original "fall into Division" (*FZ* 4.4, E297), and she "hid[es] her guilty front with innocent Snow" (39). And as Irene H. Chayes observes, Blake also seems to have associated her with Eve, placing her appropriately in subordinate position beneath Mary as the Second Eve, since her recumbent position resembles that of Eve in the eleventh *Paradise Lost* illustration (B 642, 655), and her snowy covering recalls Eve's fleecy garment in *The Angel of the Divine Presence Clothing Adam and Eve with Coats of Skins* (B 513).[14a] In the Whitworth version she even crosses her legs in a gesture Blake consistently used to express repressed desire, and in *L'Allegro and Il Penseroso* 11 (B 682) modulated in one of his portrayals of Milton himself. But other signs are more propitious. For whereas the lapsarian Eve in the *Paradise Lost* design faces outward, a traveler "from Eternity, pass[ing] outward to Satans seat," Nature by contrast, like those other "travellers to Eternity" (*Mil* 17.29-30, E111) Milton on the *Milton* titlepage (*IB* 217 and Los on the frontispiece to *Jerusalem* (*IB* 280), is facing inward. Moreover unlike Eve she is awake and looks up responsive to the Divine Vision, listening even perhaps to the first strains of the angelic choir, and against the surrounding blizzard is evidently humanizing. In the context of the embracing figures in the series of *Last Judgment* paintings, (B 868, 870-74) Blake had recently completed, she seems in the Whitworth version to be about to ascend and join with Peace on the side of the redeemed. Their position is reversed in the Huntington version, where Nature's legs are no longer crossed and her snowy covering less pronounced, possibly to emphasize that, unlike Eve and Milton's Nature, she is innocently unconcerned about her "naked shame" (40). But there too the pictorial relationship between them implies that Peace will descend to Nature, Nature be restored to Peace, that a "happier union" between "Heav'n and Earth" (108) is imminent.

In "The Annunciation to the Shepherds" (figs. 3-4), Blake again responds creatively to several images in the central verses of the *Nativity Ode* (vii-xv), while concentrating appropriately on the climactic moment of the epiphany to the shepherds:

> At last surrounds their sight
> A Globe of circular light,
>> That with long beams the shame-fac't night array'd,
> The helmed Cherubim
> And sworded Seraphim
>> Are seen in glittering ranks with wings display'd,
> Harping in loud and solemn choir,
> With unexpressive notes to Heav'n's new-born Heir.
>   (109-16)

Reverting to a motif he had originally adapted from Bryant in the *Night Thoughts* series, Blake depicts the Cherubim advancing above the distant stable which has been extended laterally, their interlocking arms upraised in a gesture perfectly expressive of harmonious jubilation.[15] Within their globe of light they recall the passage in *A Vision of the Last Judgment*, where Blake distinguishes between the natural and visionary suns: "What it will be Questiond When the Sun rises do you not see a round Disk of fire somewhat like a Guinea O no no I see an Innumerable company of the Heavenly host crying Holy Holy Holy is the Lord God Almighty" (E565-6). And in relation to the borders of the designs the angelic choir forms a squared circle, a motif which in *Milton* 47 (*IB* 263), "Ezekiel's Wheels" (B 542), and elsewhere Blake associated with fourfold vision, as Edward J. Rose has shown.[16] Very similar figures appear again in a fourfold context in *Job* 14 (B 710), where if we follow S. Foster Damon the "morning stars" are used to symbolize the imaginative realm.[17]

What this seems to imply is that Blake has effected a bold reversal of Milton's priorities in the first two designs. For whether or not Milton intended the angelic choir as the aesthetic center of his poem, there can be no question that doctrinally its importance is hierarchically subordinate to that of the infant Christ whose praises it sings. But in Blake, I propose, we move from a Beulaic vision in which Christ as the spirit of truth and love is born and cherished in the stable, to a fourfold Edenic vision of the choir as an emblem of harmony among men who in the aggregate form the Divine Body of Jesus. The effect is of an expanding "Vision of Light," analogous to that Blake described in a poem to Butts (E712-13), which was to form the nucleus for the extended moment of *Milton* and to reappear greatly condensed on plate 34 of *Jerusalem* (E180). In the Whitworth series the notion that this heavenly light, which now illuminates the shepherds and floods out into the world, originated in the stable is suggested by the fact that Mary and Joseph are now alone. The way the Cherubim in the Huntington set echo Christ's cruciform gesture implies, less cryptically, that the Divine Body itself has as it were increased and multiplied. In the context of *Europe* this "humanized sphere," as Pamela Dunbar rightly calls it, supersedes the stellar globe of "Newtons Pantocrator" (*M* 4.11, E98), and represents a millennial state in which the redemption of Nature begun in the previous design has been fulfilled.[18] Milton's "helmed Cherubim / And sworded Seraphim" also provided convenient emblems of the vigorous imaginative intellectual activity in the pursuit of truth and the rejection of error Blake termed "Mental Fight" (*M* 1.13, E95). In the flatter Whitworth globe the rather regimented leading angels are more effectively delineated in that their upraised arms do not obscure their neighbours' faces. And the circumambient figures equipped with lute and harps to make their "stringed noise" (97) number a round apocalyptic eight. In the Huntington version Blake may have wanted to inhibit any confusion of these mental warriors with the avenging angels of Milton's "dreadful Judge" (164). For there the leading angels are all youthful, naked, and (save their helmets) unarmed, and advance with a lither, less military step, and the central figure in cruciform position stands out more prominently against the receding ranks, giving the globe a more three-dimensional appearance.

The humble recipients of this sudden revelation of man's and nature's potential are the shepherds. In both versions (though in reverse) the central figure is shown in a less dramatic modulation of the position adopted by other inspired figures in Blake's canon, such as William and Robert in *Milton* (*IB* 248, 253), or Job in "Job Confessing his Presumption to God who Answers from the Whirlwind" (B 538). Surrounded by their watchdogs and sleeping flocks, his companions all either participate in or are wakening to the Divine Vision. In the Whitworth version all the shepherds appear to be male, but in the Huntington design Blake has made them more explicitly representative of the family of man. He has also increased their number from six to eight, a hint perhaps that they represent the millennial state in which Moses' prayer cited in the Preface to *Milton*,

Figures 3 and 4. In both the Whitworth and Huntington versions (above and right, respectively) of "The Annunciation to the Shepherds," Blake reverses Milton's priorities: the angelic choir supersedes the infant Christ

whose praise it sings (and whose diminutive stable sits in the distance)—
Whitworth Art Gallery; Henry E. Huntington Library and Art Gallery,
respectively.

"would to God that all the Lords People were Prophets" (E95), will be fulfilled for all mankind, rather than merely for the elect that Milton had in mind when he quoted it in *Areopagitica*.[19] In the Huntington version pyramid-like tents have been included, emblems of the state of bondage from which the shepherds have been delivered.

In the demonic sequel to this Divine Vision in the next two designs, "The Old Dragon" (figs. 5-6) and "The Overthrow of Apollo and the Pagan Gods" (figs. 7-8), both Blake's appreciation of the apocalyptic dimension to the *Nativity Ode* and his determination to illuminate it on his own terms emerge more clearly. The immediate subject of the first of these is Milton's account of how with the advent of Christ

> Th'old Dragon under ground,
> In straiter limits bound,
>   Not half so far casts his usurped sway,
> And wroth to see his Kingdom fail,
> Swinges the scaly Horror of his folded tail. (168-72)

And Dunbar (100) suggests a further identification of Blake's terrifying beast with "Typhon huge ending in snaky twine" (226). Several particulars indicate that this design bears an intimate relationship both visually and thematically to "The Annunciation to the Shepherds." The most immediately apparent link is of course the stable, which again appears with lateral transepts, but surrounded now by slumbering flocks. The entrance is guarded by two Cherubim, the two perhaps from the Ark of the Covenant, who Blake tells us in *A Vision of the Last Judgment* (E562) appear above Christ as reminders that he has opened the temple and rent the veil, here standing aside to reveal the infant Christ. Further, by placing the stable above the Dragon, in the position of the Throne of God in his "Last Judgment" paintings, Blake endorses the significance of the Nativity at least insofar as it was regarded by Milton and Christian tradition as a symbolic victory of peace over war, truth over error, and, especially in the Huntington version where the three kings kneel before the entrance, spiritual over temporal dominion.

But continuity is also established by the starry extension of the Dragon's tail above the stable. This is an obvious allusion to Revelation 17.4, where the Dragon's "tail drew a third part of the stars of heaven" down, immediately before the battle in heaven, but in the context it also serves a very precise iconographic function. For the line of descent it indicates, considered in conjunction with the way the Dragon and his crew gaze generally heavenward and not just at the stable, clearly implies that they have been routed in an encounter with the Cherubim in the previous design. Indeed this dark Ulro world of discord is a demonic parody of the Edenic harmony within the globe of light—a contrast which is reinforced visually by the way both scenes are foregrounded but in opposite segments of the two designs. In the Whitworth version the Dragon's vigorously swingeing tail shows that they have plummeted on the side of the damned in Blake's "Last Judgment" paintings. This endorses the earlier suggestion that Nature is preparing to rise on the side of the redeemed in the opening design. The line of their descent has been reversed in the Huntington version, and their underworld is less like the Dragon's cave in the "Last Judgment" pictures. But Blake has intimated that they are victims of a mental war in heaven with the Cherumbim by making the figure pointing directly upward on the right do so with both hands, and by placing the stable much further back.

Here too then Blake's emphases are subtly different from Milton's, and may be accounted for in terms of his post-enlightenment attitude to the events in Milton's hymn. For though Blake also went through a period of optimism about the prospect of an imminent millennium, unlike Cromwell's Latin Secretary and many of his contemporaries 150 years earlier, he never believed it would come about through a miracle of divine intervention of the kind envisaged in the hymn. And by alluding to the war in heaven again in this design he seems to be insisting that if "God becomes as we are, that we may be as he is" (*NNR*, E3), it is through emulation of Christ as mental warrior and "bright Preacher of Life" (*J* 77.21, E232) that mankind will be redeemed, rather than through worship at the shrine of the Nativity. The Dragon's six heads in the Whitworth version indicate that Blake was specifically thinking here of Jesus as the seventh "Eye of God," further evidence of the close relationship between this set and *Europe* with its explicit historical time-scheme. And the way he is bound by his own tail suggests that these manacles are "mind-forg'd" (E27), self-imposed. In the Huntington design the Dragon has his traditional seven heads, implying that the millennium is at hand, and Blake has sharpened the contrast with the unarmed Cherubim by giving him both sword and sceptre. The looseness of the greenish tethers round his ankles however is a sobering reminder that the banishment of corporeal war can be achieved only by ceaseless imaginative effort. The reversals here and in the opening design make the connection with Blake's "Last Judgment" pictures rather less intimate than in the Whitworth series, and it is possible that they reflect an uneasy attempt on Blake's part

Figures 5 and 6. In both the Whitworth and Huntington versions of "The Old Dragon" (above and right, respectively), the dragon and company gaze not just at the stable, but heavenwards, suggesting that they are

engaged in mental war with the heavenly cherubim of figs. 3–4—
Whitworth Art Gallery; *Henry E. Huntington Library and Art Gallery*, respectively.

to dissociate his vision more clearly from Milton's religion of atonement with its ferocious day of reckoning.

The subordinate devils in the two designs are sufficiently different to support the hypothesis that the Huntington set was done without access to the Whitworth, but in both cases individual figures are hard to identify with confidence. Seated appropriately at the Dragon's right hand in the Whitworth version is the Great Whore, a voluptuous figure in several of Blake's other paintings and illustrations (B541, 584, 868; *Night Thoughts* 345), but here shown "desolate and naked" as in Revelation 17.16, exposed like Spenser's Duessa as the hag she really is. The fiend diagonally opposite her could be Satan bidding them "Awake, arise, or be for ever fallen" (*PL* I.331), since he somewhat resembles Blake's portrayals of him in the *Paradise Lost* series, and in *A Vision of the Last Judgment* (E556-8) he and the Dragon are kept distinct. If the Cherubim in their globe of light represent fourfold man, the four principal male devils could be the four fallen Zoas or Elements, and the subordinate figures, with the Whore as Vanity, the "Seven deadly Sins of the soul" (*Ur* 4.30, E72). In the Huntington version the flames are localized around Satan, there is a scaly amphibious creature in the lower foreground, and an earthbound female like the worm-encircled mother beyond Death's Door in *The Gates of Paradise* (E267) has replaced the Whore, but one would expect all the Elements to be male as in the 69th *Dante* illustration.[20]

In "The Overthrow of Apollo and the Pagan Gods" (figs. 7-8), the differences between the two versions are more fundamental than at any other point in the series. In both sets Blake has incorporated several particulars from Milton's account of the flight of the pagan deities, while focusing on stanza nineteen of the ode:

> The Oracles are dumb,
> No voice or hideous hum
> > Runs through the arched roof in words deceiving.
> Apollo from his shrine
> Can no more divine,
> > With hollow shriek the steep of Delphos leaving.
> No nightly trance, or breathed spell,
> Inspires the pale-ey'd Priest from the prophetic cell.
> > (173-80)

The central figure, as has often been remarked, is based on that neoclassical touchstone of sublimity and grace, the Belvedere Apollo, and Blake may well have been familiar with the tradition which "held that Augustus

Figure 7. "The Overthrow of Apollo and the Pagan Gods": With Christianity ousting him, why does Apollo appear so vigorous?—*Whitworth Art Gallery.*

had had it taken from the site of Apollo's oracle at Delphi."[21] The Whitworth Apollo (B663) however is essentially a free imaginative modulation of the classical prototype, quite different from the statue in the Huntington design where Blake adheres to it more closely. By adding masculine strength to the slightly feminine grace of the original, and showing Apollo strangling an obviously puissant Python rather than shooting one present only emblematically, he has also created an altogether more dynamic deity, with attributes that recall not only Apollo but Hercules and Christ, as Behrendt too (85) has registered.

If this design is simply a celebrative tribute to Milton's vision of paganism eclipsed by Christianity represented by the Star of Bethlehem, why did Blake present an Apollo not only majestic but triumphant? The obvious explanation that he wished to show Apollo forsaken by his indwelling spirit at the very height of his powers seems at first attractive. And the hypothesis could be supported by analogy with the "Death of the Strong Wicked Man" in the illustrations to Blair's *Grave* published the previous year.[22] But this would not resolve why Blake, who had depicted the strong wicked man *in rigor mortis* so expressively, and was to present Apollo as a very convincing statue in the Huntington design, should have chosen not to do so here. Indeed Blake seems to have deliberately enhanced the sense of Apollo's vitality and vigour by counterpointing him against the rigid idol petrifying on the hill behind him. Furthermore, Blake can scarcely have been unconscious of the parallel with Hercules his portrayal would suggest, as a surviving pencil sketch where he depicts "The Infant Hercules Throttling the Serpents" (B 304) tends to confirm. And if so he must also have been aware that, as Hercules was a traditional type of Christ, the parallel in the context of Apollo's demise would be ambiguous.[22a]

One must therefore consider the more problematic hypothesis that, with the same imaginative daring as he was to display when illustrating *L'Allegro and Il Penseroso* and *Paradise Regained*, Blake has exploited these parallels to distinguish his own vision of man's redemption from Milton's by transforming Apollo into a redeemer. When this design is contemplated in relation to the iconographic continuities already established, it becomes possible to see it as the appropriately placed climax to a visionary progression again analogous to that in Blake's ecstatic poem to Butts, where he describes how

> My Eyes more & more
> Like a Sea without shore
> Continued Expanding

The Heavens commanding,
Till the Jewels of Light
Heavenly Men beaming bright
Appeared as One Man (E683)

We have moved, I would urge, from the birth of Christ in the first design
to a vision of the Divine Body as a "Multitude of Nations" (*VLJ* 76,
E557) in the globe of light, and now as if stepping back to view the general contours of Blake's lost "Last Judgment" painting, we perceive
Apollo as a macrocosmic image of renovated fourfold Man.[23] Inspired
perhaps by Milton's own allusion to Christ as "mighty Pan" (89) or to
how "the chill Marble seems to sweat" (195), Blake has shown Apollo
come dramatically to life, a symbolic event comparable to Albion's
awakening and "Resurrection to Unity" (*FZ* 4.4, E301) in the prophecies.
Like the redeemed Milton at the close of Blake's brief epic, and like
Christ on the pinnacle in "The Third Temptation" from the *Paradise Regained* series (B 693), this Herculean Apollo has "cast his Spectre into the
Lake" (*J* 37, E184; cf. *M* 39.10-11, E140). He has achieved a decisive
victory over Python, a classical counterpart of "that old serpent, which is
the Devil, and Satan" who in the previous design lay bound, but only for
"a thousand years" (Revelation 20.2). The crucial difference between this
Last Judgment and those envisioned by Dürer or Michelangelo or Milton,
however, is that Apollo's is an act of self-purgation, for "whenever any
Individual Rejects Error & Embraces Truth a Last Judgment passes upon
that Individual" (*VLJ* E562). This accomplished, Apollo stands like the
risen Albion in "Glad Day," another fourfold vision based on classical
statuary, unselfconsciously displaying his "Naked Human form divine"
(*EG* 66, E522), as earlier Nature had begun to do.[24] The serpent's victory
over Adam and Eve, who had sought to hide their naked shame, is thus
reversed.

The priests as "Guardian[s] of the secret codes" (*Eur* 12.15, E64) are
none too pleased, but the vestals are learning their "own humanity ... to
adore" (*EG* 72, E520). A distracted Pythia is seen behind them, her hair
on end like Pride's in *Night Thoughts* 302, in straiter limits bound within
her cavern. Blake would probably have recognized this deliverer of noto-
riously ambiguous oracles as a pagan counterpart to "Mystery Babylon
the Great" (Revelation 17.5) in the previous design, and as an appropriate
consort for Python as her name implies. Above a classical colonnade
ominously like the trilithons in Stukeley's reconstructions of Abury and
Stonehenge, other pagan deities representing all the superstitions that
have enslaved mankind are seen departing.[25] A horned "Isis ..., and the

Dog Anubis" (212) and a winged solar disk with double-headed serpent adapted from Bryant can be specifically discerned above the bolts of lightning.[26] The shipwreck like that in Dürer's woodcut illustrating the opening of the Seventh Seal (cf. Revelation 8.9), and the tiny figure retreating before the rising tide, imply that the old order is on the point of being cleansed by flood, as in "The Old Dragon" it was purged by fire.[27] The Star of Bethlehem, which significantly did not appear above the stable earlier and is omitted from the Huntington version of this scene, thus signals that it is with Apollo's exemplary triumph that man's salvation lies, rather than with the birth of the secret child as Milton and his age believed. Its function in the last design (fig. 11), where it appears as the flickering "Handmaid Lamp" (242) of "Heav'n's youngest-teemed Star" (244), is to lighten our way during the intervals when the Divine Vision is asleep.

I have presented this reading of the Whitworth version without pausing to consider objections in the interests of clarity, and to show that a redemptive interpretation of Apollo does seem to fit organically into the internal iconographic structure of the sequence. What makes it problematic of course is that the series was executed during precisely the period when Blake was perfecting epic poems which rejected classical models for "the Sublime of the Bible" (*M* 1, E95), and working toward the philosophical conclusion that "The Classics, it is the Classics! & not Goths nor Monks, that Desolate Europe with Wars" (E270). On the subject of classical sculpture specifically, he wrote in the *Descriptive Catalogue* to his abortive one-man exhibition of 1809 that of "the Greek statues ... perhaps the Torso is the only original work remaining; all the rest are evidently copies, though fine ones, from greater works of the Asiatic Patriarchs.... Those wonderful originals seen in my visions ..." (E531). But Blake's attitude to classical philosophy and art was a complex one, as all investigations have concluded. Peter F. Fisher pointed out that "the positive influence of the classical tradition was assimilated without comment, and Blake obviously agreed with the Platonic theory of ideas which were essentially his own imaginative 'Forms'—the 'Existent Images' of eternity."[28] Moreover his assimilation of the great works of classical sculpture from casts in Pars's drawing school, engravings, and neoclassical imitations was so complete that as Joseph Burke has observed, "an eidetic image ... appeared to Blake, not merely as a kind of living sculpture, but in a shape suggested by antiquity."[29] And the many instances of indebtedness to classical models which Paley (171f.) has been able to trace in Blake's later works indicate that his reservations about the rationalist abstractions of classical philosophy and the warrior code that "Turnd Love into a Boy" (E479) did not lead him to abandon the habits of a lifetime.

The specific objection that as a solar deity and symbol of reason Apollo is unlikely to have appealed to Blake as a redeemer is a real one, despite Milton's allusion to Christ as a "greater Sun" (83). And later of course he was to present Apollo negatively in *L'Allegro and Il Penseroso* 3 (B543: 3, pl. 674), naked but sceptered and wearing a spiked crown within his solar orb, and dominating a diminutive Milton's vision in the background. Virgil's fourth Messianic *Eclogue*, where the return of the golden age is associated with a renewal of Apollo's reign, provided an important precedent, but one Blake could well have reacted to negatively.[30] As an illustrator however Blake was always a great opportunist, and within the constraints of literal fidelity to Milton he had to improvise with what he encountered in the hymn. Moreover the difficulty begins to recede when one recalls Apollo's humanist credentials as physician, lyrist, Python-slayer, and leader of the Muses, albeit the "Daughters of Memory" (*M* 1, E95). Blake also alludes to him positively in his note to the now lost painting of those "naked civilized men," "The Ancient Britons":

> It has been said to the Artist, take the Apollo for the model of your beautiful Man and the Hercules for your strong Man, and the Dancing Fawn for your Ugly Man. Now he comes to his trial. He knows that what he does is not inferior to the grandest Antiques. Superior they cannot be, for human power cannot go beyond either what he does, or what they have done, it is the gift of God, it is inspiration and vision. (E544)

> The Strong man represents the human sublime. The Beautiful man represents the human pathetic, which was in the wars of Eden divided into male and female. The Ugly man represents the human reason. They were originally one man, who was fourfold; he was self-divided, and his real humanity slain on the stems of generation, and the form of the fourth was like the Son of God. (E543)

This is by no means the only occasion in the *Descriptive Catalogue* where Blake reveals that he shared the general enthusiasm for classical art that events such as the arrival of the Elgin marbles and the opening of the Townley galleries were currently generating.[31] But Blake's explanation of his painting is of special relevance to the Whitworth design in that it presents Apollo and Hercules in close association as two facets of fallen man. It is only a step imaginatively to reverse this symbolism and present a Herculean Apollo as a fourfold image of the eternally "Divine-Hu-

Figure 8. "The Overthrow of Apollo and the Pagan Gods": Feminine, stonelike, weak—Apollo in his demise more traditionally rendered than in Blake's Whitworth version (fig. 7)—*Henry E. Huntington Library and Art Gallery.*

manity" (*J* 38.19-20, E185). Blake's association of these famous statues with his own archetypes also illuminates why in the redemptive last plate of *Jerusalem* (*IB* 379) he should have modelled the central figure on the Farnese Hercules, but endowed him with something of the Belvedere's grace.[32] How Blake could use both models in redemptive contexts and yet fulminate against the classics without inconsistency is best understood however by thinking of them not as Apollo and Hercules Farnese but as representing those "wonderful originals" seen in his visions. Moreover the Greek and Roman delight in the human body, which Winckelmann too was aware Christianity had neglected, is clearly another facet of classical culture which Blake silently assimilated.[33] From this point of view, what more appropriate corrective to the transcendental dualism of Milton's religion than to place Apollo's Naked Human Form Divine at the visionary climax of the sequence?

The Huntington Apollo resembles the Belvedere statue much more closely, and this may well be a consequence of Blake's having studied it afresh in 1815 or 1816 when he was making sketches from casts in the Royal Academy for illustrations to Flaxman's essay on sculpture in Rees's *Cyclopaedia*.[34] If so this would corroborate Butlin's dating. Paley (172) is surely right to interpret Apollo here as a negative emblem more in line with Milton's hymn. His vacant eye and statuesque appearance leave little doubt that this is Apollo turned to stone, and that as with the strong wicked man his spectre swooping up out of him and startling the tiny figure above the water signals his demise. One may assume that here he is specifically Apollo as rationalist sun-god, a fallen version of the triumphant figure in *L'Allegro and Il Penseroso* 3, his locks bound up, his arrow spent, his dwindling fires consuming the last remnant of a sacrificial ox, his vestals cowering in terror.[35] He has been eclipsed by the "more bright Sun of Imagination" (E655) represented by the angelic choir, as pagan wisdom and pagan oracles were superseded not by the Nativity but by the voice of inspiration in the Gospels. For "What Jesus came to Remove was the Heathen or Platonic Philosophy which blinds the eye of Imagination The Real Man" (E654).

Since this conception seems less inspired iconographically and makes for less of a crescendo, if Apollo is indeed a redemptive figure in the Whitworth series, why did Blake abandon his original idea? For one thing the Huntington solution is in some respects intrinsically more satisfactory. It gives greater emphasis to the importance of rejecting pagan error, and creates a nicely balanced contrast between this design and "The Old Dragon," where the errors of Judeo-Christian culture are cast out. And it may also, like the reversals in fig. 2 and fig. 6, represent a move away from traditional Last Judgment iconography to avoid the danger in the Whitworth image of being misconstrued in terms of Milton's vengeful doctrine of at-one-ment. But whether or not this was the case, it is entirely consistent with the mixture of praise and censure of antiquity we find in the *Descriptive Catalogue* that Blake should have used the Belvedere Apollo in the way proposed in 1809 and become more resolutely anti-classical by 1815. Blake was also an inveterate experimenter, and need have felt no more compunction about rejecting the Whitworth model in the fourth design than in the first. It is always tempting in such cases to speculate about the influence of individual purchasers, in this instance Thomas Butts. Could Blake not have relinquished his more radical interpretation in deference to the piety of his most loyal patron?

In both versions of the next design, traditionally titled "The Flight of Moloch" (figs. 9-10), Blake's epiphanic vision of a man-centered millennium in the globe of light and in the Whitworth Apollo is replaced by an archetypal scene of human sacrifice, which in the historical context of the Nativity was of course a gruesome reality. I would urge that it represents a brilliantly improvised contradiction of Milton's account of how

> sullen Moloch, fled,
> Hath left in shadows dread
> His burning Idol all of blackest hue;
> In vain with Cymbals' ring
> They call the grisly king,
> In dismal dance about the furnace blue.
> (205-10)

For all the particulars indicate that the cult of Moloch here is very much alive. The scene corresponds to the moment in *Europe* immediately after the Nativity when Urizen is "unloos'd from chains" and his sons "Seize all the spirits of life and bind/ Their warbling joys" (*Eur* 3.11-4.4, E60). Both scenes are related to John's prophecy that after the binding of the Dragon and immediately before Jerusalem's descent, "Satan shall be loosed out of his prison" (20.7) for a time. As his close resemblance to Blake's Accuser in the Epilogue to *The Gates of Paradise* (*IB* 279) and his scarlet hue both indicate, the powerful bald and bat-winged figure above Moloch is evidently not his expiring spirit but Satan himself, his arms extended in a gesture Blake consistently associated with dominion. He departs to his own place leaving Moloch not exactly "rejoic[ing] thro the Land" (*J* 68-38, E222), but evidently reinstated for a further eighteen hun-

Figures 9 and 10. Like the not-so-vanquished Apollo of fig. 7, Moloch and his cult are still going strong in both the Whitworth and Huntington versions of "The Flight of Moloch" (above and overleaf respectively). Above Moloch is Satan himself, not Moloch's expiring spirit (cf. Apollo's

expiring spirit in figs. 6–7). The parents in fig. 10 are perhaps not
delivering their child *from* the furnace but, rather, abandoning it to the
flames—*Whitworth Art Gallery*; *Henry E. Huntington Library and Art
Gallery*, respectively.

dred years, his furnaces blazing, his priests and vestals dancing around him in frantic jubilation.

Hagstrum (123) sees his most prominent victim as "a fiery Orc who leaps out of the furnace," but in both versions he is being abandoned to the flames by his reluctant parents. Blake's iconic frontal presentation perhaps leaves this a little ambiguous, but it is certainly expressive of the child's resistance. Since Moloch and Nebuchadnezzar would have been typologically related in Blake's mind, and the child is shown in cruciform position, there is almost certainly an allusion here to Daniel 3.25, which Blake cited in the passage from the *Descriptive Catalogue* quoted above. But this promise that man will eventually be delivered from the fiery furnace appears to be subordinated to the negative implications of the crucifixion image, amounting to an inversion of Milton's pious reflection that "The babe lies yet in smiling Infancy,/ That on the bitter cross/ Must redeem our loss" (151-3). For what Blake's pictorial commentary is asserting is that, taken literally, this cornerstone of Milton's faith was itself a remnant of druidism, the Father's sacrifice of his only begotten Son a travesty of true self-sacrifice—"allegoric and mental signification" turned into "corporeal command" (E543). The point is made more explicitly in the Huntington series, where the cruciform Infant in "The Descent of Peace" and the sacrificial victim here form positive and negative mirror images of one another. Analogously, in *Night Thoughts* 121, which draws on the iconography of the Passion and the Harrowing of Hell, Blake had foregrounded the suffering adult Christ crowned with thorns and pierced by huge nails, while invoking the redemptive promise of the Daniel episode by showing him striding through billowing flames.[36]

Several other redemptive motifs encountered earlier are recapitulated in demonic form in both versions of the design, indicating that from the first Blake conceived this as a turning-point, a massive negation of the millennial vision that had gone before. That "mighty Angel" Peace (*M* 36.12, E135) has been displaced by Satan as harbinger of discord, who like God appearing to Moses reveals only his "back parts" (Exodus 33.23). The choric globe of angels where the sexes were commingled (cf. *J* 69.43, E221) has become a segregated band of priests and virgins, "drunk with unsatisfied love" (*J* 68.62, E222) and locked in a dance of death. Plying their trumpets and cymbals, they recall Milton's description in *Paradise Lost* of

> Moloch, horrid King besmear'd with blood
> Of human sacrifice, and parents' tears,
> Though for the noise of Drums and Timbrels loud

> Thir children's cries unheard, that pass'd through fire
> To his grim Idol.[37] (I. 392-6)

Youthful dynamic Apollo in the Whitworth series has been replaced by a
hoary slothful Moloch, whose name "betokeneth a king."[38] He is the
perennial tyrant to whom Christ as Orc or Love or Truth or Imagination
or the Eternal Divine Humanity is perennially sacrificed, an aggregate of
such historically pertinent figures as Herod and Nero. In the Huntington
version he bears some resemblance to Blake's satirical portrait of George
the Third wearing a papal crown on *Europe* 11 (*IB* 169).

The furnace of Moloch's throne on its druidic circular dais has multi-
ple openings as described in Banier, formed in both versions by gothic
arches which parody the peace and spirituality of the simpler gothic stable.[39] Again prompted perhaps by Milton's mention of Osiris' "worshipt
Ark" (220), in the Whitworth version Blake has presented Moloch's
throne as a demonic ark, a pompously ecclesiastical perversion of the Nativity stable on which the crowned and sceptred Moloch sits like a monstrous Covering Cherub. This effect is relinquished in the Huntington design where Moloch's position is reversed and he now holds a spiked
poignard with which to dispatch his victims. But the gothic openings to
the furnace are topped by battlements, together suggesting the twin powers of Church and Caesar to whose interests humanity is sacrificed. In the
Whitworth design the druidic nature of all such ceremonies is also perhaps
emphasized by the surrounding mountains. Stukeley, Mallet, Davies, and
others comment on the fact that stone circles occur on high ground in
open places, and that both in earliest antiquity and among northern tribes
such sacred edifices were not roofed over for fear of presuming to confine
the deity.[40] But perhaps the most poignant contrast in both sequences is
between the innocent Divine Family in the opening designs and the distracted parents sacrificing their offspring for king and country in the foreground here. A similar scene occurs in "A Little Boy Lost" from the
Songs of Experience, where the priest took the child "in trembling zeal"

> And burn'd him in a holy place,
> Where many had been burn'd before:
> The weeping parents wept in vain.
> Are such things done on Albion's shore. (E29)

In the first design the converging figures of Nature and Peace had anticipated a time when "Heaven, Earth & Hell, henceforth shall live in harmony" (*J* 3-10, E144). Here the way the parents fall apart reinforces the
sexual message of the segregated dancers—like them, their relative posi-

tion has been reversed in the Huntington version—and brings home that all has again been plunged into division.

In purely artistic terms the way Blake's final design, "The Night of Peace" (figs. 11-12), in both sequences balances his first seems to pay gracious tribute to the symmetry of Milton's hymn, without however reproducing the abruptness with which Milton bids us adieu. And unlike the previous designs it confines itself to the details of Milton's final stanza:

> But see! the Virgin blest,
> Hath laid her Babe to rest.
> Time is our tedious Song should here have ending;
> Heav'n's youngest-teamed Star
> Hath fixt her polisht Car,
> Her sleeping Lord with Handmaid Lamp attending:
> And all about the Courtly Stable,
> Bright-harness'd Angels sit in order serviceable. (237-44)

But doctrinally Milton's lines are merely neutral, whereas in the iconographic context Blake has established it is clear that we are here presented with a scene of armed neutrality, or more aptly guarded optimism. As mooted earlier, the modulated repetition of the opening scene also serves to emphasize that, with the reinstatement of Moloch and the divine right of kings, the cycle of revolt and repression Blake explored in the Lambeth prophecies has come full turn.

But all is not lost. One of the remarkable things about Blake, despite the poignant *Notebook* entry for "Tuesday Jan. 20, 1807, between Two & Seven in the Evening—Despair" (E672), and his fear of perhaps being too passive, is the extraordinary buoyancy of his temperament, the tenacity of his faith in the dignity and potential of man. And here the Holy Family should be taken as principally an emblem of man's sleeping humanity, preserved in the arkite stable against his resurrection. In the Whitworth version Joseph remains awake: perhaps like the prophetic eagle *cum* Michelangelesque thinker *cum* watchman on *Jerusalem* 78 (*IB* 357), his function now is to keep the "Divine Vision in time of trouble" (*J* 44.15, E191). The guardian angels surrounding the stable, whom Behrendt (90) rightly associates with the Cherubim in their globe of light, correspond to the Angels of the Divine Presence who watch over Milton's slumbering humanity in *Milton*. In the Huntington version they are again more youthful and have been increased from four to eight, and the thatched transepts of the Whitworth stable have been eliminated, creating a more precise mirror image of the stable in the first design. Promise that Satan

Figures 11 and 12. "The Night of Peace": A return to the quiet opening
scene of each sequence (figs. 1–2), but armed with guardian angels this
time. In the Whitworth version above, the angels' inattention to the
Christ-child (especially that of the angel with the lamp at the top of each

illustration) suggests a more pessimistic vision than the Huntington version above does, where most (open) eyes focus on the source of deliverance—*Whitworth Art Gallery*; *Henry E. Huntington Library and Art Gallery*, respectively.

has been loosed but for a season, that harmony will return and man once again ascend the "Fiery Chariot of his Contemplative Thought" (*VLJ*, E560), is held out by the harping angels and "Heav'n's youngest-teamed star." Blake indicates that the star has come to rest above the stable by depicting the two horses reposing charmingly upon a bed of cloud. The Whitworth version seems a shade more pessimistic though, for both they and their mistress with her "Handmaid Lamp" are seen against a sky filled with Urizenic stars, and they look round as if expecting deliverance from elsewhere. Judging from the glum expressions of the guardian angels and the mass of fodder Dunbar (112) notices, they all anticipate that before the dawn a long dark night still lies ahead. In the Huntington version the stars have been eliminated as have the cattle, and the two guardians in the foreground and two of the three figures in the sky all gaze upon the Christ-child reverentially. This seems entirely consonant with the greater importance Blake appears to have attached to him in the sequence as a whole. Where in the Whitworth series he seems to have had the Nativity as a historical event principally in mind, in the Huntington version he has concentrated on the symbolic significance of Christ's advent. In both series he has traced its wider implications from a post-enlightenment perspective, acknowledging the high seriousness of Milton's theme, but exposing the negative implications of some of his most central orthodoxies, and simultaneously presenting his own more truly humanist answering vision with marvellous imaginative ingenuity.

Notes

1. Grateful acknowledgment is made to the Killam Foundation for initial sponsorship of this research, and to the Whitworth Art Gallery, Manchester, and the Huntington Library and Art Gallery, San Marino, for permission to reproduce the *Nativity Ode* illustrations in their collections. I am also indebted to John E. Grant and Michael J. Tolley for valuable suggestions and criticism. References to Blake's illuminations and text are to the works of Butlin, Erdman, and Damon—using the abbreviations listed above (B, D, E, and *IB*).

2. Northrop Frye, *The Return of Eden* (Toronto: Univ. of Toronto Press, 1965), pp. 89ff.; C.S. Lewis, *A Preface to Paradise Lost* (London: Oxford Univ. Press, 1942), pp. 82f.

3. Stephen C. Behrendt, "Blake's Illustrations to Milton's *Nativity Ode*," *PQ*, 9 (1976), p. 91; see further his *The Moment of Explosion* (Lincoln: Univ. of Nebraska Press, 1983), pp. 38-41. Alexander N. Hutchison in his "Blake's Illustrations to Milton's *On the Morning of Christ's Nativity*," *British Columbia Library Quarterly*, 36 (1972-3), pp. 9-10, also holds the view that

"Blake does not take liberties with the text of the *Hymn* ... he subordinates his desire for revision to the delight he took in exploiting the imaginative possibilities of Milton's verbal imagery."

4. Leslie Tannenbaum, *Biblical Tradition in Blake's Early Prophecies* (Princeton: Princeton Univ. Press, 1982), pp. 86-123; Morton D. Paley, "'Wonderful Originals'—Blake and Ancient Sculpture" in *Blake in His Time*, ed. Robert N. Essick and Donald Pearce (Bloomington: Indiana Univ. Press, 1978), pp. 170-97; see also his "The Truchsessian Gallery Revisited," *SIR*, 16 (1977), pp. 155-78.

5. Michael J. Tolley, "*Europe*: 'to those ychain'd in sleep,'" in *Blake's Visionary Forms Dramatic*, ed. David V. Erdman and John E. Grant (Princeton: Princeton Univ. Press, 1970), pp. 115-45.

6. Jean H. Hagstrum, *William Blake: Poet and Painter* (Chicago: Univ. of Chicago Press, 1964), p. 27.

7. The fact that both sets are signed "W. Blake," a form Butlin has discovered Blake tended to adopt in preference to his monogram around 1806, also argues against an early date for the Huntington set; see Butlin, "Cataloguing William Blake" in Essick and Pearce, pp. 82f.

8. If one includes W.M. Rossetti's probably random ordering in his "Descriptive Catalogue" of Blake's work in Alexander Gilchrist's *Life and Works of William Blake*, 2nd ed. (London: Macmillan, 1980), II.222, five different arrangements and a formidable array of different titles for the *Nativity Ode* designs have been proposed. Details are given in Behrendt's article, pp. 68, 93, n. 11.

9. Arthur E. Barker, "The Pattern of Milton's *Nativity Ode*," *UTQ*, 10 (1941), pp. 167-9.

10. See Adrian van Sinderen, *Blake, the Mystic Genius* (Syracuse: Syracuse Univ. Press, 1949), where Blake's notes accompanying the *L'Allegro and Il Penseroso* designs which he numbered 1-12 are reproduced; and David Bindman, *Catalogue of the Blake Collection in the Fitzwilliam Museum Cambridge* (Cambridge: Heffer, 1970), pls. 25-34, where Blake's numbering of the *Paradise Regained* designs is visible.

11. See *William Blake's Designs for Edward Young's Night Thoughts*, ed. with a commentary by John E. Grant, Edward J. Rose, Michael J. Tolley, and David V. Erdman (Oxford: Clarendon Press, 1980), to which all ensuing allusions to individual designs in the series refer; and Irene Tayler, *Blake's Illustrations to the Poems of Gray* (Princeton: Princeton Univ. Press, 1971).

12. See Roger R. Easson and Robert N. Essick, eds., *William Blake Book Illustrator* (Normal: American Blake Foundation, 1979), Vol. 2, XVI. pls. 1, 9; XX. pl. 5.

13. See Nicholas O. Warner, "Blake's Moon-Ark Symbolism," *BIQ*, 54 (1980), pp. 44-59; Jacob Bryant, *A New System, or, an Analysis of Ancient Mythology* (London, 1775), II.59f., 198f.; Paul Henri Mallet, *Northern Antiquities*, trans. Thomas Percy (1770; rpt. London, 1847), p. 98; Edward Davies, *Celtic Researches* (London, 1804), pp. 24f., 157, 309, 316; and *The Mythology and Rites of the British Druids* (London, 1809), pp. 90f., 154f., 293. In the *Descriptive Catalogue* Blake writes that "the British Antiquities are now in the Artist's hands" (E533), and the arkite symbolism Warner has found in his epics makes clear that he was familiar with the kind of parallels these synchretist mythographers were drawing between Noah and other heroes such as Osiris, Perseus, Dionysus, and Deucalion, who were exposed in arks but returned to renew civilization. Further pictorial support for an arkite stable here can be adduced from the fact that Noah in the "Epitome of James Hervey's Meditations among the Tombs" (B 967) and Moses leaping from a rather different ark in "The Finding of Moses" (B 533), appear in similar postures to the Christ-child in the Huntington design. *A propos* the stable's resemblance to the tombs Blake sketched in the Abbey, it is interesting to find Bryant writing that "as the confinement during the deluge was esteemed an interval of death, the Ark from thence was represented as a bier or coffin" (II.328). Conceivably Blake was also familiar with the traditional association Gertrud Schiller has drawn attention to of the Ark of the Covenant with "Mary, in whom the divine Son was hidden," *Iconography of Christian Art* (Greenwich: New York Graphic Society, 1971), I.109.

14. See note on B cat. 401, and C.H. Collins Baker, *Catalogue of William Blake's Drawings and Paintings in the Huntington Library*, 2nd ed. (San Marino: Huntington Library, 1969), p. 26.

14a. Irene H. Chayes, "Fallen Earth and Man in Nature: William Blake in Iconographic Tradition," *Studies in Iconography*, 10 (1984-86), pp. 186f.

15. See Geoffrey Keynes, *Blake Studies*, revised ed. (London: Oxford Univ. Press, 1971), p. 27.

16. Edward J. Rose, "Mental Forms Creating: 'Fourfold Vision' and the Poet as Prophet in Blake's Designs and Verse," *JAAC*, 23 (1964), pp. 173-83.

17. Damon, *Blake's Job* (New York: Dutton, 1966), p. 38.

18. Pamela Dunbar, *William Blake's Illustrations to the Poetry of Milton* (Oxford: Clarendon Press, 1980), p. 98.

19. See Christopher Hill, *Milton and the English Revolution* (London: Faber, 1977), pp. 159-61; and Michael Fixler, *Milton and the Kingdoms of God* (London: Faber, 1964), pp. 127, 134, 153.

20. See Albert S. Roe, *Blake's Illustrations to the Divine Comedy* (Princeton: Princeton Univ. Press, 1953), p. 134 and pl. 69; and Milton Klonsky, *Blake's Dante* (New York: Harmony Books, 1980), p. 153 and pl. 72.

21. Francis Haskell and Nicholas Penny, *Taste and the Antique* (New Haven: Yale Univ. Press, 1981), p. 148.

22. See Damon, *Blake's Grave* (Providence: Brown Univ. Press, 1963), pl. IV.

22a. In the most recent study of the Milton designs, *Blake's Vision of the Poetry of Milton* (Lewisburg: Bucknell Univ. Press, 1986, p. 26), Bette Charlene Werner sees both Apollo and Hercules as types of Christ who are now superseded by His advent. This fits intellectually but does not resolve the visual ambiguity of the design.

23. For a discussion of Blake's extant "Last Judgment" paintings and sketches see W.J.T. Mitchell, *Blake's Visions of the Last Judgment*, a booklet published by *BIQ* for the MLA Blake Seminar, 28 December 1975.

24. See Anthony Blunt, *The Art of William Blake* (New York: Columbia Univ. Press, 1959), p. 34 and pls. 6-7.

25. See William Stukeley, *Stonehenge, a Temple restor'd to the British Druids* (London, 1740), pls. XII, XIII, XV, XVI. In *Abury, a Temple of the British Druids* (London, 1743), p. 67, Stukeley writes that Phut, whom he equates with Apollo, "planted the country about the mountain Parnassus, where he built ... a great serpentine temple, like ours at Abury, at the bottom of that mountain, by the city of Delphos. This I gather from the Greek reports of the serpent Python of an immense bulk, bred of the slime left on the earth, by the general deluge, which Apollo here overcame...."

26. Bryant, I. pl. VIII. See Kathleen Raine, *Blake and Tradition* (Princeton: Princeton Univ. Press, 1968), II.261.

27. See Erwin Panofsky, *The Life and Art of Albrecht Dürer* (Princeton: Princeton Univ. Press, 1955), pl. 80. The classical sources for the belief in the destruction of the world by fire and water are given in Richard Payne Knight, *An Inquiry into the Symbolic Language of Ancient Art and Mythology* (1818; rpt. London: Society of Dilettanti, 1835), p. 52.

28. Peter F. Fisher, "Blake's Attacks on the Classical Tradition." *PQ*, 40 (1961), p. 13. This remains the most searching study of Blake's complex relationship to Classical Antiquity, but Blake's archetypes have less in common with Plato's than Fisher believed, and Tannenbaum, pp. 86-123 should be read as a corrective.

29. Joseph Burke, "The Eidetic and the Borrowed Image: An Interpretation of Blake's Theory and Practice of Art," in Robert N. Essick, ed., *The Visionary Hand* (Los Angeles: Hennessey & Ingalls, 1973), p. 284.

30. Virgil, *The Eclogues*, ed. and trans. Guy Lee (Harmondsworth: Penguin, 1980), p. 57.

31. See Edward Miller, *That Noble Cabinet: A History of the British Museum* (London: André Deutsch, 1973), pp. 97-107; and William St. Clair, *Lord Elgin and the Marbles* (London: Oxford Univ. Press, 1967), pp. 166f.

32. See Haskell and Penny, pp. 231, 148.

33. A copy of Johann Winckelmann, *Reflections on the Painting and Sculpture of the Greeks*, trans. Henry Fuseli (London, 1765) was owned by Blake.

34. See Paley in Essick and Pearce, p. 190.

35. The mythographers would have provided Blake with ample evidence of the ubiquity of sun worship. See for example Bryant, I.13f.; Bernard de Montfaucon, *Antiquity Explained*, trans. David Humphreys (London, 1721-22), I.72, IV.255; Antoine Banier, *The Mythology and Fables of the Ancients explain'd from History* (London, 1740), II.378f., III.270, 308; Stukeley, *Abury*, pp. 9, 67; Mallet, pp. 87f., 110; William Jones, *On the Gods of Greece, Italy and India*, in *Works* (London, 1799), I.268; Edward Moor, *Hindu Pantheon* (London, 1810), pp. 6-21, 121-2, 192, 277f., and pls. 87-9; Davies, *Mythology*, pp. 30f., 291f.; and Knight, pp. 18, 22, 38f.

36. See Schiller, I. pls. 529f.

37. In his *Observations on the Antiquities of Cornwall* (Oxford, 1754), pp. 121-3, William Borlase gives an indignant circumstantial account of the different methods of human sacrifice among the Druids noted by classical historians, including what Blake termed the "Wicker Man of Scandinavia" (J 47.7, E196). He explains that "the more dear and beloved was the person, the more acceptable they thought their offering would be accounted. Hence, not only beautiful captives and strangers, but children, and Princes were, upon great occasions, offer'd upon their Altars." His concluding remarks provided a fairly precise gloss on this aspect of Blake's Moloch design. "Whilst they were performing these horrid rites," he observes, "the drums and trumpets sounded without intermission, that the cries of the miserable victims might not be heard, or distinguish'd by their friends, it being accounted very ominous, if the lamentations of either children or parents were distinctly to be heard, whilst the victim was burning."

38. Banier, II.48; see Bryant, I.70.

39. Banier, II.48-51.

40. Stukeley, *Stonehenge*, pp. 23-4; Mallet, p. 107; Davies, *Mythology*, pp. 291f., 305; Borlase, pp. 107f., 116; Bryant, I.235f.; Abraham Rees, *Cyclopaedia* (London, 1819), XII, under "Druids."

"Defending the Bible": Blake, Paine, and the Bishop on the Atonement

Florence Sandler

"It is an easy matter," says Blake, as the enraged Annotator of Watson's *Apology for the Bible*, "for a Bishop to triumph over Paines attack but it is not so easy, for one who loves the Bible.

"The Perversions of Christs words & acts are attackd by Paine & also the perversions of the Bible; Who dare defend either the Acts of Christ or the Bible Unperverted?"[1]

Blake who loved the Bible as the Gospel of Liberty was necessarily in 1798 a supporter of Tom Paine, the voice of liberty now in France as previously in America, and was bound to defend Paine's *Age of Reason* against the storm of official opposition—no matter how strenuously it attacked not only the traditions of the Church but the authenticity of the Bible itself.[2] As Paine explained in the Preface to the Second Part of *The Age of Reason*, he had undertaken the work as a victim of the Terror under Robespierre. Expelled as a foreigner from the National Convention in 1793, seeing his friends carried off to prison and the guillotine, he expected to be imprisoned at any time and realized that he must put on paper straightway the thoughts on religion that had long occupied him. He was arrested within six hours of finishing the manuscript. In prison for nearly a year he suffered near starvation and illness, and presumably only on this account escaped the execution of the order for his death. Released, but still dangerously ill, he completed the Second Part.

Then came the scandal in England in 1796 of the book's suppression—but the suppression only of the cheap edition, lest it disaffect the lower classes. The new Society for the Suppression of Vice and Immorality had launched a notorious campaign to prosecute the poor bookseller

Thomas Williams for selling one copy of Paine's book. Even Erskine, originally the chief prosecutor, had changed his position and pleaded in vain with his erstwhile colleagues to withdraw the case and prevent Williams' trial and imprisonment along with the ruin of his family.

Any publicist like Watson who attempted in these circumstances to refute Paine and his book was necessarily for Blake and other lovers of Liberty the object of detestation. The author of *An Apology for the Bible*[3] was not merely a publicist, but a bishop, and indeed the bishop of a minor see, clearly exploiting the opportunity to gain the favor of the Ministry in the hopes of nomination to a better one. From the outset Blake has the Bishop typed as a "state trickster" and one of the species of Caiaphas who is prepared to murder Jesus or Paine ("one man for the sake of the many") in the interest of public order. When the Bishop purports to be unimpressed with the circumstances of the book's composition and suggests (he hopes with "no want of charity") that it would have been more fortunate for the Christian world if Paine had died before fulfiling his intention, Blake pounces on him furiously. Here is Caiaphas revealed. Here is the cloven hoof. "Presumptuous Murderer dost thou O Priest wish thy brothers death when God has preserved him" (E612). After that, the Bishop's mildest remonstrations will be read by Blake as the slyness and insinuation of the Serpent.

Thereafter, there is a "Well done Paine" (E619) and the memorable verdict at the end: "It appears to me Now that Tom Paine is a better Christian than the Bishop" (E620). And the issue would appear to be closed.

Yet not so. For Paine was not a Christian at all, but a Deist pure and simple. Faced with the "total abolition" in France "of the whole national order of priesthood, and of everything appertaining to compulsive systems of religion, and compulsive articles of faith," he desired to preserve, as he explained, nothing other than Natural Theology and the God who proceeded by rational, indeed mathematical, demonstration, "lest, in the general wreck of superstition, of false systems of government, and false theology, we lose sight of morality, of humanity, and of the theology that is true."[4] He would hardly have appreciated being told he was a "better Christian" than Watson or even that he had "not attacked Christianity" (E612), when he considered it exactly his achievement to have attacked and vanquished Christianity altogether—or, to use his own figure, to have cut down the trees once and for all, so that, though they might subsequently be propped up in the soil, they would never grow again.[5] The iconoclastic author of *The Marriage of Heaven and Hell* and the Books of the Infernal Bible could find many points at which his own critique and Paine's concurred. Yet Paine's standpoint is one where Blake must ultimately find himself uncomfortable, and Paine is another Analytical Angel who would impose his phantasy.

At the same time, though he gets no credit from Blake for his part in the controversy, Bishop Watson himself stood consistently for the reconciling role of religion within the polis, and raised questions that Blake's Los, building Jerusalem, would eventually have to attend to.

What follows is a reconstruction of the argument between Paine and the Bishop for the sake of the light that it throws upon the difficulties involved in Blake's development of his own apologetic position and his role as "Christian poet" in the decade of the Terror and the onset of war with France. Paine's anti-Christian book, precipitated by events in France, was still governed by the theological structure that had obtained in the official Lockean theology of the English Church throughout the century—the structure on which Deism, or Natural Religion, also rested. When Paine's anti-Christian Deism found its rebuttal in Watson's Christian Deism, it was the latter which, exactly because it purported to be Christian, seemed to Blake more invidious.

Blake had set himself to the task of separating true religion from its perversions in his own age and in the Bible itself from his first engraved works announcing that "There is no Natural Religion" and that "All Religions are One." He must disentangle the activity of the Poetic Genius from the religion of the Ratio that he saw as the idolatry of his age, the result of a shrunken Lockean epistemology applied to the mathematically described Newtonian universe. As the satirical seer of *The Marriage of Heaven and Hell*, he had identified true religion and the voice of the Poetic Genius in Isaiah and Ezekiel—and the perversion of religion in the very same biblical text (presumably in the priestly authors and the Deuteronomic historians) wherever the Poetic Genius was appropriated as an exclusive national possession, and wherever prophecy was institutionalized into priesthood or abstracted into philosophy.[6] In *The Marriage of Heaven and Hell* Blake first uses his design of man rising from the earth and the Place of the Skull, which is Golgotha, into Life and Light (*IB* 21). Already the design implies that the Awakening of the human spirit to its full potential in Eternity beyond the limits set by the natural cycle of birth and death is the Christian experience of the resurrection, and that the Poetic Genius speaks most clearly in Jesus himself, the resurrected one.

While in the *Marriage* the task of distinguishing vision from illusion is briskly performed, the illuminations of Young's *Night Thoughts*, as

John E. Grant demonstrates, involve Blake as artist and commentator in closer and finer distinctions between the manifestations of God and Jesus in the interwoven systems of Life and Death.[7] But the last years of the 1790s apparently constitute for Blake a crisis of faith and interpretation. Partly the crisis is precipitated by personal circumstances, when his hopes for the recognition of his art are constantly disappointed, and he and his truth are "hid." Partly the crisis is caused by the tide of conservative reaction and the relentless persecution of the lovers of Liberty by a Government at war with republican France. The result for Blake was that the task of disentangling truth and falsity in the prevailing ideology became more onerous and urgent as it became more dangerous. "The Beast & the Whore rule without control"; "To defend the Bible in this year 1798 would cost a man his life," he protests in the Annotations (E611)—when he must nevertheless undertake the task in some form. By that year he had already embarked upon *The Four Zoas* and his own reconstruction of the Pauline myth of the alienation of man and cosmos, and their restoration in Jesus. The headnote taken from the Greek of the Letter to the Ephesians sets that enterprise in opposition to the political power and ideology of the Age:

> For we wrestle not against flesh and blood, but against principalities, against powers, against the rulers of the darkness of this world, against spiritual wickedness in high places. (Eph. 6.12; KJV text)

The rulers of the darkness of this world in 1798 were well practiced in their task of obscuring vision and prophecy and of depressing art and religion in favor of something more useful to the state. They had always had the art of subtlety and disguise; in Blake's own age they were likely to wear the mask of bland civility and present their ideology as benevolence. They might even believe themselves to be benevolent and their Age of Opacity to be Enlightenment, like Satan in the Bard's Tale in *Milton*, whose demonic nature is not perspicuous even to himself. To wrestle with the rulers of the darkness of this world is to wrestle also with their texts, discerning their true motives and allegiances, as Blake does with Watson's *Apology*, with Bacon's *Essays*,[8] and with Reynolds' *Discourses*.[9] "Read patiently," Blake admonishes himself as Watson's Annotator; "take not up this book in an idle hour the consideration of these things is the whole duty of man, ... the business of Eternity" (E611).

It is true that Blake's Annotations to Watson's *Apology* are fragmentary; that he tires of systematic annotation fairly soon into the

Third Letter and contents himself thereafter with squibs in the margin. The very text he annotates is fragmentary in that Watson had attempted to rebut the Second Part of Paine's book without apparently having read the First. It is true also that, while the Annotator finds both Paine's and Watson's comments on the authority of the Pentateuch for the most part beside the point, his own comments on the authority of the biblical text are hardly consistent one with another. Yet, precisely in their fragmentary and extemporaneous character, Blake's Annotations indicate with some precision the problems that beset his efforts in 1798 to clarify the Divine Vision and "defend the Bible." In particular, he joins issue on the matter which had become central to the "proof" of Christian truth in the Age of Enlightenment, namely, the nature of the authority of the Bible in relation to the authority of Natural Law. Along the way, he addresses the character of inspiration, of prophecy, and of miracles, combatting at each point the Lockean consensus.

Behind these issues stood another, namely the nature of the interpretation of the central Christian doctrine of the Atonement. Already problematical for the *philosophes*, the doctrine of the Atonement was denounced by Paine with a new urgency that came from his experience of the Terror and War that accompanied the birth in France of the modern secular state. For Paine, a doctrine that appeared to sanctify the taking of life as a sacrifice could only be an anomalous vestige of the older dispensation; for Blake, the Christian, it would become increasingly apparent that the very ideology of the State, in the new form as much as in the old, rested on the mystery of Sacrifice which Christianity had erected into the doctrine of the Atonement.

Paine's exposé of the God of the Bible in *The Age of Reason* is sustained by a tone of moral outrage that has its origin in the crisis of the times. Watching the emergence of ideological warfare in Europe with the new political phenomenon of an entire nation under arms and of the state's execution of whole categories of its citizens for the sake of its own ideological purity, he has given some thought to the influence that had contaminated "the just and humane principles of the Revolution, which Philosophy had first diffused." With his roots in the community of Quakers, he found it not difficult to identify the contamination as the continuing influence of the Church which had maintained its own system of Terror and its doctrine of the priestly absolution of sin.

The Idea, always dangerous to Society as it is derogatory to the Almighty,—that priests could forgive sins,—though it seemed to exist no longer, had blunted the feelings of humanity, and callously prepared men for the commission of all crimes. The intolerant spirit of church persecution had transferred itself into politics; the tribunals, stiled Revolutionary, supplied the place of an Inquisition; and the Guillotine of the Stake.[10]

The Atheism of the Revolution was also, to Paine's mind, the legacy of Catholicism, since the Church had obscured a pure philosophic faith in God by the proliferation of Miracles and traditions. Paine's recourse would be to strip away all inessentials so as to show the necessity of faith in "one God, and no more," that being the God of Nature who was to be apprehended in a manner "pure, unmixed, and unadulterated" even by epistemological, let alone by cultural and ecclesiastical elements. He would enjoin faith in the presumably natural creed of "the equality of man," and the natural religious duties of "doing justice, loving mercy, and endeavouring to make our fellow-creatures happy"—and in nothing more.[11] Each man should be accountable only to himself for his beliefs, and none could creditably claim a special privilege or revelation from God that gave him the right to coerce, let alone murder, another for his faith. As he wrote to his friend Samuel Adams, in writing *The Age of Reason* he risked his life "by opposing Atheism." If some priests wanted to call him an infidel and a wicked man, "they might as well add, for he believes in God and is against shedding blood."[12]

Once armed with the perception of the Church's origination of the Terror, Paine could draw upon the *philosophes'* vigorous critique of the theological notions that had sustained "church persecution" in its manifold forms, from the Inquisition to the religious wars of early modern Europe. Moreover, the *philosophes* claimed, the church as the New Israel remained in her persecuting spirit all too faithful to her origins in the Old Israel. The Hebrews had claimed to be a people "chosen" by their God in order to wage a Holy War of extermination against the Canaanites. Like Voltaire, Paine is revolted by the accounts in Judges of the Israelites' wholesale massacre of Canaanite cities—men, women, and children offered up as a "devotion" and "sacrifice." He is appalled by the story in the Books of Kings of the two baskets of children's heads, seventy in number, exposed at the entrance of an Israelite city (2 Kings 10), and the story of the Israelite king, Menahem, who rips up all the women with child, in his capture of the city of Tiphsah (2 Kings 15). Half of Israel's kings, Paine notes, died violent deaths, a number of them murdered at the direct instigation of Jehovah's prophets. In all, the historical books present

> little more than a history of assassinations, treachery and wars. The cruelties that the Jews had accustomed themselves to practise on the Canaanites, whose country they had savagely invaded, under a pretended gift from God, they afterwards practised as furiously on each other.[13]

The Hebrews' cruelty was the reverse side of their own fear of an avenging God, and within the nation itself the fear was manipulated by priests and kings who demanded homage and sacrifice in the name of their God.

True that the Hebrew Bible is a mixed bag. Some of the "compositions" Paine finds there, particularly Psalm 19 and the Book of Job, appear to express not the vindictive tribal God of the Hebrews but a benevolent Ruler of the Universe. These compositions, he suspected, were simply appropriated by the Hebrews from their more enlightened Gentile neighbors.[14] His guess that Psalm 19 is Egyptian in origin is a shrewd one long before the recovery of the texts from the New Kingdom. Nevertheless, since the Hebrew Bible (a phrase that grows increasingly pejorative through Paine's work) reflects the murderous character of that nation and is designed to justify a cult that is the sanctification of cruelty, it is of bad omen for the Christian New Testament that it builds upon such a foundation.

Here indeed was the ultimate target. For Paine and the *philosophes*, the exposé of the cruelty of the religion of the ancient Hebrews was only incidentally an exercise hostile to the Jews (though Voltaire was charged in his time—and justifiably so—with anti-Semitism). More directly it was intended against the Christians, since it was they who, purporting to worship a God of Love, had nevertheless filled Europe for a thousand years with wars, persecutions, and martyrdoms. Let them look to their roots. For all their claim to differentiate a Christian God of Love from a Jewish God of Law and Justice, they admitted the continuity of their own revelation with that of the Hebrew Bible, and to a perspicacious reader of the New Testament the continuity was clear enough. From an Old Testament religion that taught the fear of Jehovah and transferred this fear into aggressive cruelty against an enemy who must be offered up as a sacrifice, Holbach and Boulanger saw the emergence of the New Testament doctrine of a God whose wrath could be assuaged only by the sacrifice of another being designated as a god.

Paine was presumably familiar with the work of the Holbach group, since he quotes Boulanger at one point.[15] But the ideas he encountered in Paris appear to have confirmed a personal abhorrence of the notion of Propitiation that he confesses had stayed with him from childhood:

> I well remember, when about seven or eight years of age, hearing a sermon read by a relation of mine, who was a great devotee of the church, upon the subject of what is called *Redemption by the death of the Son of God.* After the sermon was ended, I went into the garden, and as I was going down the garden steps (for I perfectly recollect the spot) I revolted at the recollection of what I had heard, and thought to myself that it was making God Almighty act like a passionate man, that killed his son when he could not revenge himself any other way; and ... I was sure a man would be hanged that did such a thing.... This was not one of those kind of thoughts that had any thing in it of childish levity; but it was to me a serious reflection, arising from the idea I had that God was too good to do such an action, and also too almighty to be under any necessity of doing it. I believe in the same manner to this moment; and I moreover believe, that any system of religion that has any thing in it that shocks the mind of a child, cannot be a true system.[16]

How, he wonders, have the priests become so callous as not to shudder at the doctrines of Propitiation and Sacrifice that they preach? The only answer that makes sense to him is that they are inured by political interest, and that their minds are corrupted by the traditional education in dead languages and in mythologies that present their own analogous and revolting stories.

The *philosophes* indeed got some of their best effects by drawing comparisons between the heathen stories and rites that Christians purported to despise, on the one hand, and on the other, the Christian versions of those same stories and rites rendered palatable by a rhetoric of mystification. Boulanger, for instance, employs his brilliant irony to commend the horror of all good Christians at the heathen deities' demand for human sacrifices—while they remain complacent about the central mystery of their own religion wherein, "the blood of all mankind, being insufficient to appease the irritated Deity, nothing less than an effusion of divine blood was judged adequate."

> Let not any profane wretch dare to assert, that this was a refining of fanaticism, and the horrours above delineated: no, this is a mystery, if not conceivable by our weak senses, as the fathers of the church

say, to be trembled at and believed by all the faithful, saying with them *O profunditas! O altitudo! O impenetrabilitas consiliorum Dei!*[17]

For the *philosophes* it was axiomatic that all such mystification and miracle-mongering was the fraudulent recourse of priesthoods anxious for psychological and political power. Paine saw the motive of fraud revealed in the very language in which the central Christian doctrine of *redemption* was asserted, its business being indeed the *buying* and selling of salvation. A doctrine of Atonement by way of penal substitution of the god-figure for mankind made no sense, he thought, as it stood, since a person guilty of a *crime* could not justly have his punishment transferred to the shoulders of someone innocent. But substitution would work in another context where one man might pay a financial debt for another. The confusion came from using the language of the penal law to disguise the degradingly commercial nature of the transaction.[18]

Likewise discreditable he finds the gospel miracles designed to make something supernatural out of Jesus' arrival into and departure from the world. If Jesus ascended into the clouds from a hill outside Jerusalem (somewhat as a balloonist might make his ascent from Paris), then surely all the city would be aware of the matter. As it is, we have only a few of his friends vouching for the story; the Jews as a whole knew nothing of it. As for the story of Jesus' conception by Mary, impregnated by a divine Spirit, the tale is obscene, like similar tales in Greek mythology of Zeus' impregnation of Leda and Semele. The more such myths and miracles, the more incredible and discreditable the story.

The God of Nature, says Paine, is wise; above time and space in his universality and unchangingness; and munificent to all. The other God, the God of the Hebrew Bible, is irrational, partial, changeable, and vindictive, altogether a creature of time and space, and easily recognizable as the anthropomorphic projection of a people of a character similar to his own. But, if the Jews had defamed God's moral nature, they had nevertheless held strictly to a monotheistic faith and had always rejected heathen mythologies as unworthy. In the "miracles" of the New Testament and the theological style of the Christian Church, with its trinity of gods, its deification of Mary as mothergoddess, its canonization of saints, Paine detects the direct incorporation of the corrupt mythological style of the heathens: "The Christian theory is little else than the idolatry of the ancient mythologies, accommodated to the purpose of power and revenue; and it yet remains to reason and philosophy to abolish the ambitious fraud."[19]

In *The Age of Reason* itself Paine appears to dismiss as contemptible not merely Jewish and Christian mythology but the very effort to describe in myth a God of Nature for whom mathematics and expository prose are the appropriate descriptive modes. It is of interest then to follow Paine's speculations through his later notes on religious subjects where his determination to expose the corruptness of the Hebrew materials leads him on a quest, like another Jacob Bryant, to reconstruct the pristine universal mythology of the Gentile nations (no longer to be called "heathen"!)—the wise Egyptians and Persians, but also the Phoenicians, the Canaanites, the Greeks, and, inevitably, the Druids.

Paine's Antient Mythology, however, is an ancient Deism, a religion based on Reason and Natural Philosophy. Along the way he identifies Job and Genesis, the two biblical texts most concerned with the divine order of Nature, as borrowings from the Gentiles, presumably Persian magi. (Job he thinks responsibly translated; the Creation Story in Genesis, however, distorts the original wisdom, substituting a "moral *fall of man*" for the natural "*fall of the year*, the approach and *evil* of winter, announced by the ascension of the autumnal constellation of the *serpent* of the Zodiac."[20]) He surmises that the ancient Gentile religion, received into Britain "about 1030 years before Christ," is preserved still, though under judicious disguise, in the rituals and iconography of Freemasonry. He is even prepared to concede for the ancient religion a pantheon and a mythology: a Male/Female pair of gods, Osiris and Isis in Egypt or Baal and Ashtoreth in Canaan, who represented "theologically ... the Supreme Being and universal nature, and physically, the two great celestial luminaries, the sun and the moon, by whose influence all nature was actuated."[21]

For the reader of *Milton* and *Jerusalem*, the additional interest of Paine's mythological speculation is that it presents the contrary of Blake's own. Both Paine and Blake project onto the ancient world what they see as the conflict in their own culture between "prophetic" and "natural" religion. They use similar allusions and mythical materials to build up the same dichotomy in the ancient world between Hebrew prophecy on the one hand and the universal "Natural" philosophy of the Gentile nations on the other. Both read the Bible (and the mythographers) day and night; but Paine reads black where Blake reads white.

Paine's dismissal of miracles as revelation in *The Age of Reason* puts him at the end of the line of Empirical religious discourse that Locke had introduced a century before with *The Reasonableness of Christianity*. In Locke's own account, miracles had occupied a large place, as marking the point at which religion and reason had finally concurred in history. Hitherto, Locke explained, reason had been the property of the philosophic few who had certainly perceived in principle the existence of one supreme God and had some sense of the moral law. Religion, however, in the pagan world, had been vitiated by idolatry and superstition: lust and fear had given the multitude up "into the hands of their priests, to fill their heads with false notions of the deity, and their worship with foolish rites; ... the priests every where, to secure their empire, having excluded reason from having anything to do in religion" (238).[22] Only Israel, "off in a corner," had practiced a monotheistic and moral religion.

But when Jesus came as the Messiah, his miracles (plain, clear, and incontrovertible, Locke thought, even to unbelievers) commanded the attention of the whole world for the new dispensation. Jesus' kingship was manifest in a new world community transcending nationhood; and the moral law which the few had partially apprehended by reason was now available to all as his command. "As it suits the lowest capacities of reasonable creatures, so it reaches and satisfies, nay, enlightens the highest" (243). The miracles of Jesus and the apostles were appropriate as a different order of sign from those in nature, evidencing and confirming the truth which in nature was merely implicit. Their function required exactly that they be the unusual expression of God's arbitrary power, imposing (as Blake would say) upon the "patient":

> Though it be as easy to an omnipotent power to do all things by an intermediate over-ruling will, and so to make any instruments work, even contrary to their natures, in subserviency to his ends yet his wisdom is not usually at the expense of miracles.... He does constantly (unless where the confirmation of some truth requires it otherwise) bring about his purposes by means operating according to their natures. (143)

But Locke had little doubt that the miracles, the extraordinary means of "the confirmation of some truth," were creditable to reason, at least upon the "credit of the Proposer," who was no less than God Himself. Human reason recognized its limitations in the face of God, the author of both nature and history, and was prepared—always on reasonable grounds—to give assent to mysteries beyond its own devising.

Toland and Tindal had strained Locke's position further by flattening out his distinction between those things above reason, and those things contrary to it. For them, an entirely reasonable Christianity, a Christianity not mysterious, would include propositions from neither category; as far as possible, Christianity would not be merely congruent with but identical to Natural Religion, and would eschew precisely the "miracles" which flew in the face of Nature's order. By the end of the century Paine at every point could pit the God of ordered Nature and Reason against the miracle-mongering irrational God of the Hebrew and Christian scriptures.[23]

Needless to say, Paine is no more impressed with the fulfillment of Prophecy as the proof of Christianity than with the claims of miracles. For Locke himself the two had still been interdependent signs of revelation: God had performed his miracles to announce in Jesus the fulfillment of the Messianic prophecies. Paine finds the exegetical structure clumsy in itself; only by distortions of sense can words about the serpent bruising the man's heel, for example, be construed as having any relevance to the kind of life the gospels themselves present Jesus as leading. Indeed, Hebrew prophecy, for Paine, comes down to nothing more than "poetry," that is, verses that differ from prose in their word order and in the use of images to embody "flights and fancies" rather than the description of reality.[24] So much for Blake's Poetic Genius or for Lowth's exposition of the sublime nature of the Hebrew poetry!

More radically, Paine discerns throughout the process of the compilation and transmission of the biblical materials the taint of political interest. The Hebrew prophets, he notes, were usually working for one king or another, while the gospel writers, pursuing sectarian designs, imposed upon people with their claims to report miracles and special revelations. Locke himself had dismissed the possibility of "any thing tending to their own self-interest" or any "tang of prepossession or fancy" in the apostles' teaching, in the light of "the credit and authority Our Saviour and his apostles had over the minds of men, by the miracles they did" (243). Once Paine had dismissed the miracles themselves as impositions, the whole credibility of the apostolic teaching and any special revelation from God falls to the ground. It is still true for Paine in theory that God, being Almighty, could propose some special revelation to a person or group, and that he might be Locke's Creditable Proposer, but

> the thing so revealed (if anything ever was revealed, and which, by the bye, it is impossible to prove) is revelation to the person *only to whom it is made*. His account of it to another is not revelation; and whoever puts faith in that account, puts it in the man from

whom the account comes; and that man may have been deceived, or may have dreamed it; or he may be an imposter and may lie.[25]

When revelation is presented directly by God to Tom Paine, then he will believe it, but not until then. Meanwhile, it would be unworthy of his own dignity to allow himself to be imposed upon, and unworthy of God's dignity if one were to "take the word of man as the word of God, and put man in the place of God,"[26] that is, the God whose revelation in nature is universally available, sufficient, and complete.

Paine's predisposition to admire Nature as the perfect revelation of God and his adherence to a scientific criterion of Truth were congenial enough to Bishop Watson, a man of the Newtonian age who had originally been Professor of Chemistry at Cambridge and was the internationally renowned author of four volumes of Chemical Essays. He was prepared to compliment the author of *The Age of Reason* upon the "philosophical sublimity of some of your Ideas when speaking of the Creator of the Universe," and invite him to extend his appreciation of God's munificence in his work of Creation to his yet greater munificence in the work of Redemption.[27]

Nor were the points Paine made against the Bible new to Watson, who was Regius Professor of Divinity, the champion of Lockean orthodoxy, and an authority on the literature of religious controversy over the previous century in which the Deist critique had reached its height among English theologians and been effectively rebutted or accommodated by the latitudinarian Church.

Watson was likewise a man of peace, alarmed by the murderousness and absolutism of the revolutionary ideology, and his answer, like Paine's, was to insist on the perspicaciousness of the text, though the text this time included the Moral Law of the Bible as well as the Natural Law of the Newtonian universe. This law under either aspect he believed to be universally reasonable, comprehensible, and benevolent, sanctioning the natural order, which was for him not the equality of man but the inequality of rich and poor in society. He too was aware of how much blood had been shed in times past for the sake of the imposition of one version of the Bible over another, but for him, the representative of the Church resettled in 1660 after the Great Rebellion, wars and martyrdoms were the product of the sectarian and usurping spirit (whether within the Church or without) that, not content with God's plain truth in the Bible, wants to give to doctrine an exclusive and partial interpretation. Firmly established in a traditional Church and society, Watson could attribute the murderousness of the Revolution to its having cast off the traditional sanctions: the perpetrators of the guillotine-massacres, he assured Paine, had inherited too little from the practice of absolution in the Church of Rome rather than too much.[28]

It is all too easy to dismiss the Bishop of Llandaff as a lightweight. One recalls the anecdote of how he decided when he was already Professor of Chemistry that the newly vacant post of the Professor of Divinity would be more advantageous, and so qualified for the post by spending a month of two "getting up" Divinity. His post-Lockean theological style is usually characterized by his remark that he determined "to study nothing but his Bible in order to compass the study of divinity within as narrow a compass as he could, seeing no point in attending to the doctrines of a Council promulgated by men no more inspired than himself." "Articles of the Church are not of divine authority," he announced in words that might have come from Tom Paine; "have done with them."[29] For Sir Leslie Stephen, tracing the history of secular thought in the eighteenth century, Watson's gentlemanly demurrers to Gibbon and Paine indicate at best the bankruptcy of the official Lockean position in the last decades of the century, when even the best theological work, Paley's *Natural Philosophy* and *Evidence of Christianity*, was still a summary and clarification of familiar notions.[30]

Nevertheless, a modern church historian like Gerald Cragg can appreciate Watson's stance as teacher and moralist, and even more as ecclesiastical politician.[31] He was the political champion of the latitudinarian Church in the decades when that position was increasingly jeopardized by the polarization of opinion in reaction to the events in France. Organizing in his old age the *Anecdotes* of his life,[32] Watson presented a record that was consistently liberal: he had spoken against the War with America; had supported Wilberforce in the abolition of the slave trade; and in 1795 was the only bishop in the House of Lords to speak for the negotiation of a Peace with France, though by 1798, the year of Blake's Annotations, Watson too, in his *Address to the People of Great Britain*, was urging vigorous prosecution of the War. He stood consistently for the widening of the franchise: as long as the cause was feasible he spoke for the repeal of the Test and Corporation Acts to relieve the disabilities of Dissenters, and later, from the 1790s, advocated Roman Catholic Emancipation.

A protégé of the Duke of Grafton among the Whigs, Watson had risen to the bench as Bishop of Llandaff clearly destined for greater honors. With the fall of his patron's party—more precisely, with its political eclipse as a result of what Watson saw as an opportunistic alliance with the ministry of Lord North in 1783—he was left to pursue his liberal principles alone, and remained for the rest of his life as the absentee bishop of an impoverished see—though not, indeed, for lack of soliciting a better one. The very title of Bishop of Llandaff, which for Paine and Blake indicated that the man was a "state trickster" (any bishop being that by definition) was for Watson himself the badge of his integrity.

Alarmed that in his generation, for the first time, the national Church appeared no longer to include the majority of the nation, he advocated administrative and liturgical reform (financial reform of the dioceses to loosen the hold of political patronage; the abolition of the Athanasian creed) in the interests of removing those features of the Church that were a stumbling block to faith. To the end he maintained the Lockean view of the Church as an institution to be modelled according to the criteria of political utility, and its creed, if not itself accountable to limited human reason, nevertheless not contrary to reason. He was unimpressed by the conservative reaction of the 1790s, by Burke's heavy veneration for prescription and privilege and for the peculiarities of the English Church and Constitution. Prejudice remained for Watson a pejorative word, no more commendable when exercised in favor of the Church than against it.

Watson's chief contribution to theological knowledge was a six-volume anthology of *Theological Tracts* (1785), a collection of the best that he found written on various philosophical and biblical issues. His collection rests, significantly enough, on Locke's *Reasonableness of Christianity*; it includes tracts by Dissenting as well as Anglican and Continental divines; and it is addressed both to the young candidate for orders who finds himself well trained in classics and natural philosophy, but hardly at all in theology, and to the "young man of rank or fortune," who, overwhelmed by fashionable Unbelief, needs to be reassured of the intellectual respectability of Christianity. Voltaire, Helvetius, and Hume notwithstanding, Christianity, Watson is sure, has nothing to fear from investigation, being grounded in reason as well as revelation, as evidenced in the work of illustrious men who were philosophers and scientists as well as Christians—a list that includes (the Blakean notes with interest) Bacon, Locke, Newton, and Hartley. With the confidence of his times, Watson can assert that the principles of truth and hedonism concur: Christianity not only constitutes true doctrine, but it conduces to happiness in that it "regulates, but does not extinguish our affections" as reasonable beings, and is thus "perfective of our nature."[33]

We have the Bishop's official statement of his position in the Charge he delivered in his diocese at Llandaff in 1795, rallying his clergy at a time when the very essentials of the faith had come under attack, openly in France, still covertly in Britain. The challenge, as he saw it, was not to allow the virulence of the attack to drive the Church into bigotry, but to maintain Christian zeal with charity and moderation. Let the clergy concede that unbelievers may still be sincere and upright men—only expecting that unbelievers in turn will give the same credit to the clergy. Let the clergy not censor or fear the force of argument, since ultimately the exercise of reason can lead only to the clarification of Christian truth. Above all, let them be sure that the faith they defend is the simple and clear doctrine of the Gospel, and not manmade doctrines extraneous to the faith and often blasphemous in their implications. Among such doctrines the Bishop includes not only the notion of original sin that insists on the damnation of the unbaptized infant, but also—since he, like Wesley and Blake, is an Arminian—the Calvinist doctrine of personal predestination.[34]

The doctrine of the Atonement itself required more delicate treatment. Biblical it certainly was—and therefore, whatever offense it gave to believer and unbeliever alike, it was to be construed as the work of the merciful God. Certain questions, the Bishop admits, obtrude themselves on even the pious mind:

> Why might not God have restored human kind to the immortality which was lost by the transgression of Adam, without requiring any atonement, satisfaction, or price of redemption? Can the benevolent Author of the universe be induced, by the death of an innocent being, to bestow a blessing on mankind, which, without such a sacrifice, he would have withheld from them? Does God Almighty, like the demons of pagan superstition, delight in blood?[35]

Certainly we know, the Bishop assures his clergy, that God does not delight in blood and has no cruelty in his nature. Yet such questions as he has listed cannot be answered except by falling back on the assertion that God's ways are not our ways, or, in the Lockean formula, that the mysteries of faith are not contrary to reason though certainly above it. We cannot know why God would fix on this death as the satisfaction for sin but, since Christ laid down his life voluntarily to give life to mankind, God's acceptance of that life may be "an *emanation of his infinite mercy*, rather than a *demand of his infinite justice*." Finally, there must be some way, beyond our seeing, in which all this works in the ultimate Felicific Calculus: "We do not know, whether the suffering of an innocent person may not be productive of a degree of good, infinitely surpassing the evil of such sufference; nor whether a *quantum* of good could by any other mean have been produced." Believing that the death of Christ is the fittest ransom for redemption, though not being able, from ignorance, to comprehend its peculiar expediency, the Church is pretty much stuck with the doctrine of Atonement, unless it can "be shewn, which never can be shewn, that more evil than good, either to Christ himself, or to the human race, or to some other part of God's creation, has flowed from the death of Christ."[36]

The Atonement as a doctrine and the Resurrection as a historical and physical event were indeed the linchpin of the system. In his *Theological Tracts*, the Bishop had inserted, in connection with his reprinting of West's treatise on the Resurrection, a note that indicates how close were his assumptions to Paine's own, even as he drew the opposite conclusion:

> The Resurrection of Christ is the very cornerstone on which the hope of the Christian is built; for if Christ be not risen, Christianity is an imposture; and if Christ be risen, Christianity is true; and Deism is a Delusion. Whether Christ be, or be not risen from the dead is a question of fact, and must be decided (not by metaphysical disquisition ... but) by fairly estimating the weight and evidence for and against the fact.[37]

The evidence had been settled and weighed by West, Sherlock, Lardner, and Paley, and decided in the affirmative. The evidence in turn depended, of course, on the authority of the apostles; and it had been part of the judges' task to affirm the basic consistency of the four different gospel accounts, whatever the differences in detail, and at the same time to clear the apostles of any imputation of credulity or fraud. Being reasonable men themselves and properly instructed in the principles of ethical hedonism, the apostles would not have maintained their account of the Resurrection to the point of martyrdom if that account were a lie. It made sense to suffer only as part of the higher happiness of the maintenance of integrity and truth. Moreover, only the power of God in the resurrection could explain the change in the apostles themselves: the contrast between their "selfishness, ambition and cowardice ... shewn during the life, and at the death of Jesus" and "their subsequent disinterestedness, humility, and fortitude."[38]

Not surprisingly, the two particular works that Watson saw as most subversive of Christianity and therefore requiring an answer were Gibbon's *Decline and Fall* (the occasion for his *Apology for Christianity*) and Paine's *Age of Reason* (the occasion for his *Apology for the Bible*). The one, for the first time, had provided an all too plausible account of the motives of the apostles in terms of a psychology of fanaticism and of their need and opportunity to be at least self-deceived in their proclamation of an improbable event. The other had cast doubt yet once more on the "facts" of the Resurrection, along with the rest of the biblical record, in the context of an argument designed to exclude any possibility of rebuttal from within the biblical text itself, as being clearly contaminated from the beginning by political interest.

For the most part Watson is exasperated by Paine's ignorance. How could Paine purport to refute the Mosaic authorship of the Pentateuch on the strength of certain verses in the text which scholarship had already dismissed as mere interpolations? How could he fail to realize that the authenticity of the text was not seriously impugned even by the concession that Moses might not be the primary author? Yet once more Paine brought up the differences between one gospel and another in the account of the Crucifixion and Resurrection as if these were evidence of error or bad faith on the part of the apostolic writers, who had long since been professionally tried and acquitted by Sherlock in *The Trial of the Witnesses*.[39]

Not only was Paine ignorant of the scholarship but he made a virtue of his ignorance. The Regius Professor of Divinity comments on Paine's arguments like a kindly don, commending where he can the student's precocity, gently reproving the raw simplicity of his arguments, indicating from time to time where he would find his own case more competently stated, and pointing out the data to be taken into account on the other side of the issue.

One senses nevertheless the Bishop's discomfort; for, if Paine's arguments were old, yet the animus and stridency of his tirade against the Scriptures was new in England, or seen hitherto only in someone like Peter Annet who could be dismissed as a crank. Paine was no crank, and he had a dangerous appeal as a demagogue. Toland and Woolston, subversive enough in their time, had still been churchmen themselves, and the controversy they aroused had been confined to theologians and gentlemen scholars. Even the influence of the *philosophes* was limited to the élite. But Paine's power lay exactly in his not having pretensions to scholarship, nor any allegiance to the aristocratic order. He posed as the plain

man of common sense talking to other plain men, and announced that
when such a man, having shaken free of the servile habits of mind incul-
cated by the traditional piety and the traditional literary education, took a
good clear look at the Bible, it immediately revealed itself to be a tissue
of contradiction and fraud. Scholars might continue to quibble and parsons
to preach, but from this moment, as far as the plain man was concerned,
the Bible and the Church had lost their credibility.

It is no wonder that Blake noticed certain touches of irritation in the
Bishop's commentary. Besides being the kindly don, he was also one of
the chief pastors of the national church, aware that all too many of the
flock, let alone the stray sheep, were susceptible to Paine's rhetoric. Still,
Watson had put himself on record as being "an enemy to every degree of
persecution for opinion,"[40] even that of the unbeliever, and he had not at
all approved of the suppression of Paine's book. At a time when others
were demonizing Paine and setting the mob on to burn him in effigy,
Watson confined himself to shaking his crook and seriously admonishing
the mischief-maker. He was prepared actually to answer Paine in print and
inform him of his errors, showing—as a controversialist like Warburton
would not have done—some respect for his opponent in the process. At
the same time he invited Paine to appreciate in the biblical revelation and
in Christ's Redemption of mankind the same justice and benevolence of
the universal God manifest in Nature. Watson's mild and undogmatic
style, the style of the "modest enquirer," might appear to Blake to be evidence of the Bishop's hypocrisy; for Watson and for the latitudinarians as
a group, it was the mark of Christian reasonableness and charity in intellectual matters—not murder in disguise, but the offer of brotherly reconciliation.

Yet Blake's criticisms of Watson's argument as an *Apology for the
Bible* are well taken. The Bishop *as bishop* cannot appreciate the force of
Paine's argument that "the Bible is all a State Trick" and the Commentators on it those "who in hopes of a good living adopt the State religion"
(E616). To Paine's objection that the historical veracity of the Pentateuch
falls to the ground if, as the evidence suggested, Moses was not the author, Watson appeals with some complacency to the authenticity of the
Hebrew text as of other public records. "PUBLIC RECORDS!" the Annotator expostulates. "As If Public records were True" (E617).

Moreover, Watson found himself in the position of defending the
Hebrew God's commands for the slaughter of the Canaanites: "Now, I
think, it will be impossible to prove, that it was a *proceeding contrary to
God's moral justice*, to exterminate *so wicked a people*."[41] The destruc-

tion of the Canaanites on the grounds of God's being offended by their sinfulness presumably answers Paine's Deistic critique, since Paine too assumes that any God worth worshipping is chiefly interested in Righteousness according to Moral Virtue; insofar as Paine produces a reply to Watson in his later notes he is intent upon a factual proof to the effect that the Canaanites, though defamed by the Hebrews for their own purposes, possessed the same virtue and wisdom as did the other Gentiles. Blake, however, is unimpressed by the relevance of the argument that the Canaanites did or did not deserve their destruction: "Horrible the Bishop is an Inquisitor God never makes one man murder another nor one nation" (E614).

The implications of the Bishop's being an Inquisitor (or, at least, in the truncated eighteenth-century system of ecclesiastical jurisdiction, a nominal judge in the House of Lords and in the court of his diocese) are borne out for the Annotator when Watson claims for Moses the authority to punish sin in his capacity as God's judge; says Watson, "you may as reasonably attribute cruelty and murder to the judge of the land in condemning criminals to death, as butchery and massacre to Moses in executing the command of God."[42] Cruelty and murder are precisely what the Annotator sees as the business of the penal law and therefore of its need for sanction by such a God through "State Religion." "The laws of the Jews," he protests, "were (both ceremonial & real) the basest & most oppressive of human codes. & being like all other codes given under pretence of divine command were what Christ pronounced them The Abomination that maketh desolate. i.e. State Religion which is the Source of all Cruelty" (E618).

If the Bishop has so far carried Paine and the Deist critic with him in his contention that God rightly commanded the destruction of the wicked, whether by war or by the penal law, it is at the next point of the argument that he exposes what he considers to be the weakness of any Deist position such as Paine's that sets in opposition one to another the God of Nature and the God of the Bible. Paine in his naiveté might declare that the God of the Bible who commanded the destruction of the Canaanites offends the moral justice evinced by the God of Creation; yet the "Word of God is in perfect harmony with his work; crying or smiling infants are subjected to death in both."[43]

The argument is well-poised and decisive. To his own satisfaction Watson has proved the Christian and Lockean position: on the one hand, the consistency of Natural with biblical religion; on the other, the insufficiency of a merely Natural Religion. The indiscriminate destruction evident in the natural world to our admittedly partial view is given moral coherence only in the biblical revelation where a God who proceeds by moral criteria requires the death of the wicked Canaanites to show his abhorrence for Sin, and—presumably his argument would have followed—offers the death of his own Son to release humanity from that same abhorrent power of Sin. But for the Annotator the decisiveness of Watson's argument at this point consists in his clear confession that he, like Tom Paine, is ultimately allied with the God of This World, and that this is the God of Death and not the God of Life: the God who destroys infants, whether smiling or crying, and justifies equally the death of the Canaanites and the death of Jesus according to the Laws of Sacrifice for Sin.

The shrillness of the Annotations at this point conveys Blake's outrage that any God, whether the God of Nature or the Bible, should be invoked to sanction the code of death, and at the same time it betrays the desperation of his own argument which in one paragraph proceeds from the passionate assertion of belief in the Bible to the excoriation of the major part of it. Blake has no doubt of the Canaanites' wickedness. What he must insist upon is the wickedness of the Jews who imported Canaanite abominations into the religion of Israel, conducting slaughter and sacrifice in the name of Jehovah.

> To me who believe the Bible & profess myself a Christian a defence of the Wickedness of the Israelites in murdering so many thousands under pretence of a command from God is altogether Abominable & Blasphemous. Wherefore did Christ come was it not to abolish the Jewish Imposture Was not Christ murderd because he taught that God loved all Men & was their father.... The Jewish Scriptures are only an Example of the wickedness & deceit of the Jews & were written as an Example of the possibility of Human Beastliness in all its branches. (E614)

Jesus may indeed have died as a victim—not of God, but of the High Priest and ultimately of the God of This World and the God of the "Jewish Scriptures" posing as the true God. So far from being a confirmation of the Scriptural claim for divine sanction of slaughter and sacrifice, Jesus' death is the refutation: "Christ died as an unbeliever. & if the Bishops had their will so would Paine" (E614).

Here contradictions abound. Blake believes in Christ, who is himself an unbeliever. He believes in the Bible, something that Christ himself, so he believes, did not believe in. Or rather, he can vindicate Christ only against the God of the "Jewish Scriptures" who is invoked by his persecutors, and if the "Jewish Scriptures" are to be repudiated for their "Imposture" and their "Human Beastliness," what if anything remains of the "Bible?" It is not simply the case here, as presumably with the Gnostic Marcion, that the "Jewish Imposture" can be identified with the Old Testament which is to be repudiated in favor of the New Testament, for the New Testament is informed by the Old and particularly in its recourse to the language of sacrifice. Or how can the Annotator believe in a Christ except on the basis of the text in which he is presented? When Blake protests on the title page of the *Apology* that it is "not so easy, for one who loves the Bible" to triumph over Paine's attack, the difficulties are inherent in the task; they lie not only, and not chiefly, in external and political danger. Paine has attacked the "Perversions of Christs words & also the perversions of the Bible," but who indeed "dare defend either the Acts of Christ or the Bible Unperverted," or even claim to know what the unperverted acts and unperverted text might be?

There are similar difficulties for Blake in the evaluation of Nature which the bishop has all too plausibly invoked as the alternative sanction of the code of death. Blake must repudiate such a Nature, and yet he too must appeal ultimately to Nature if his argument is to have weight. He is prepared to posit an alternative Nature—that is, an original and authentic Nature behind the present fallen one: "The Bible says that God formed Nature perfect but that Man perverted the order of Nature since which time the Elements are filld with the Prince of Evil who has the power of the air" (E614). Ultimately, even "Natural Religion is the voice of God & not the result of reasoning on the Powers of Satan" (E614). But how is the "voice of God" to be differentiated from the voice of Satan when there is no audible difference? How is authentic Nature to be known when it is not apparent? And if Man himself is the perverter of Nature, what actions can Man take that are not further perversions?

For the existence of an authentic Nature Blake himself at this point has evoked (ironically?) the literal authority of the Bible which at the other pole of the argument he is the first to deny. If Paine can appeal from the contradictions of the Bible to the plain manifestation of Truth in Nature; if the Bishop, countering Paine, can appeal to Bible and Nature as mutually supporting texts sufficiently plain for the purpose, Blake's difficulty is that he finds neither Bible nor Nature perspicuous, and neither one reliable. He can gain leverage in the argument only by pitting one against the other, or each against itself, splitting each entity into a dichotomy to open up space between actual and ideal. The very unsatisfactoriness and negativity of the actual Bible and Nature must be employed as the best evidence for the necessity of the projection of the ideal, the projection itself being for Blake the work of vision and the Poetic Genius. Some years before, in his first illuminated plates, Blake had given a confident account of such a projective and generative role for the "Poetic or Prophetic character" and had claimed with equal confidence that the "Jewish & Christian Testaments are An original derivation from the Poetic Genius."[44] Now, so far from being the projection of the Poetic Genius, the Jewish and Christian Scriptures were to be seen as preeminently a distortion and an imposture upon it.

In the meantime Blake as Annotator might dismiss Watson, whose *Apology for the Bible* could be reduced to a defense of State Religion, by aligning himself with Jesus whom State Religion had crucified. Jesus, being an iconoclast and a prophet, an Energetic genius speaking with the voice of Conscience which is the "voice of God" (E614), emerges in this context with remarkable similarities to Tom Paine. Jesus' miracles were indeed genuine miracles—not "an arbitrary command of the agent upon the patient" (E617), as Locke and others had assumed, but genuine exercises of the Spirit, and therefore always on the side of Freedom to the dismay of the established powers. Their quality could be compared with Paine's: "Is it a greater miracle to feed five thousand men with five loaves than to overthrow all the armies of Europe with a small pamphlet" (E617). Such a line of defense would hardly impress Tom Paine himself, despiser of both miracles and the Poetic Genius, yet "How can Paine/ the worker of miracles/ ever doubt Christs" (E617). Both Jesus and Tom Paine in their confrontation with the rulers of the darkness of this world are the vehicles of the Spirit: "let the Bishop prove that he has not spoken against the Holy Ghost who in Paine strives with Christendom as in Christ he strove with the Jews" (E614).

The difficulty remains that if, as Blake concludes impatiently, "the Bishop has not answerd one of Paines grand objections" to the Bible (E620), neither has his Annotator. Paine's indictment had left no doubt that the Bible was indeed in essential features the product of political interest and State Religion, and that it showed a God who ruled by War and Terror, whose miracles were the means of his imposition of his arbitrary power. Even poetry and prophecy were employed in the Bible as the means of mystification. To the most serious objection of all, that deep vein of cruelty that emerged as the rationale of the Holy War and of the Atonement, the Bishop had replied by invoking God's right to destroy life by way of punishment, acting out of his wrath against Sin—a rebuttal that precisely proved Paine's point. Blake's own reply, the repudiation of the "Jewish Scriptures" as an "Example of the possibility of Human Beastliness in all its branches," is hardly more satisfactory. After Paine's grand objections, Blake is left with only shreds of the Bible littered around him—or rather, to use Paine's own figure, with only the treetrunks that Paine had uprooted, boasting that, though propped back into the ground, they could never be made to grow again. The recognition of the extent of the ruin and the attempt to see what might be grown again is, one might say, the whole subject of Blake's major poems of the next decade—*Milton* and *Jerusalem*.

There is no opportunity here to examine one of the poems—*Milton* perhaps—in the way that would be necessary to support such a claim. Suffice it to say that, in an era of renewed wars and martyrdoms, when "the Nations still/ Follow after the detestable Gods of Priam/ Of warlike· selfhood" (*M*, Pl. 14:14-16); (E108), and when the Laws of Sacrifice for Sin have been revived with peculiar urgency, the protagonist of Blake's poem must probe the nature of that idolatry and penetrate the perversion implied in the traditional doctrines of Sacrifice and Propitiation, invoked, however, not in the name of the gods of Priam but the God of the Jews and the Christians. "Tell also of the False Tongue!" the poet of *Milton* commands his muse:

>   vegetated
> Beneath your land of shadows: of its sacrifices, and
> Its offerings; even till Jesus, the image of the Invisible God
> Became its prey; a curse, an offering, and an atonement,
> For Death Eternal ... (Pl. 2:10-14; E96)

Milton is a hero with all of Paine's iconoclasm, all of his impatience with the royal and priestly ideology, and all of his courage in the Mental Wars; more than that, he is a Poet, as Paine is not, and understands the work of visioning and re-visioning as the work of the Poetic Genius. His task is a reconstruction of the essential Pauline experience of atonement. He is to recognize his implication in the body of Sin and to undertake the annihilation of Selfhood and the redemption of the Emanation, becoming at-one with Jesus. But the difficulty is to differentiate this experience at any point from the Atonement, which is a name given by the False Tongue, and to dissociate it from the "Canaanite" Sacrifice of Rahab and Tirzah.

The ghost of Tom Paine still animates Blake's portrayal of the iconoclastic Jesus who is the protagonist of the poem he entitles "The

Everlasting Gospel"—presumably the same "Everlasting Gospel" that Paine in *The Age of Reason* "never saw" (E619). Paine's unbelief has pushed Jesus to a more strenuous nihilistic position: not only does he recognize in the Temptation in the Wilderness the identity of Satan, the source of the sacrificial ideology of kings and priests, as the God of the Natural World, but he is disabused of his faith in a God who exerts Sovereignty by virtue of even the Moral Law. The meaning of the "Religion of Humanity," a phrase Paine had coined in 1778, is spelled out more radically by Blake in the revelation Jesus receives: "Thou art a Man God is no more/ Thy own humanity learn to adore" (*EG* 71-72; E520).

By the time he comes to write the Prefaces to *Jerusalem*, Blake is in a position simply to turn against Paine and the Deists the very charges of cruelty and "Sacrifice" that they have advanced against Christianity itself. The Preface to the Deists does not call on Paine by name, but it charges his fellow Deists, "Voltaire Rousseau Gibbon Hume," with an idolatry that consists in the "Worship of the God of this World by the means of what you call Natural Religion and Natural Philosophy, and of Natural Morality or Self-Righteousness, the Selfish Virtues of the Natural Heart," and hence of "the Religion of the Pharisees who murderd Jesus" (*J* Pl. 52; E201). The same error of placing ultimate reality in the "Mortal" rather than the spiritual Body, and of trusting to "Moral Virtue" and Self-Righteousness rather than the Forgiveness of Sin, is charged specifically to Paine along with Voltaire in the 1810 text to accompany "A Vision of the Last Judgment" (*VLJ* page 92; E564).

With the *Jerusalem* Prefaces, Blake is prepared to defend against Deism not only Jesus himself but even Christianity, defined as "the Religion of Jesus, Forgiveness of Sin," which "can never be the cause of War nor of a single Martyrdom." He can even purport to defend "Christian Europe," which is not to be blamed after all for the wars and martyrdoms of the past, since it was subverted (like the civilization of the Bible which preceded it) by its Satanic negation: "All the Destruction therefore, in Christian Europe has arisen from Deism, which is Natural Religion" (Preface to the Deists). At this point Voltaire, the Deist, with his "wracking wheel," has assumed Satanic proportions, while the type of Jesus is not Paine the iconoclast, but the Grey Monk with his sigh, his bitter groan, and his Intellectual Tear. Likewise, the Preface to the Jews risks much by issuing a summons to "Mental Sacrifice & War" as the opposite of the "compulsory cruel Sacrifices," Hebrew and Druidical, which have withered up the Human Form, and by invoking Jesus by the sacrificial name of Lamb of God.

Even more than the Annotations to Watson, it is the body of Blake's work that demonstrates his commitment to defending the Bible as the task of utmost seriousness, the "business of Eternity." But the situation of 1798 had clarified the nature of the task. He who defended the Bible must be a better Christian than the Bishop and a better iconoclast and prophet than Paine. He must defend Jesus and the Poetic Genius in the Age of Reason not only from State Religion and the Religion of Nature and Moral Virtue, but from the very Bible itself. Responding with all of Paine's horror and outrage to the murders committed in the name of ideology, and to the theological appropriation of merit from the murder of Jesus, he must still, as a Christian, wrestle with the death of Jesus as the access to life. Nor did the obvious deficiencies of Watson's Apology for the Bible allow him to underestimate the difficulty of making his own.

Notes

1. I am grateful to the Newberry Library and the National Endowment for the Humanities for the opportunity to study the sources for the present article. "Annotations to *An Apology for the Bible* by R. Watson, Bishop of Landaff, London, 1797" (E611).

2. *The Age of Reason* [Part One] was published in Paris in 1794, first in English and then in French translation. Two American editions date from 1794; three London editions from 1795 and 1796. "Part the Second, Being an Investigation of True and Fabulous Theology," was first published in London by H.D. Symonds in 1795; D.I. Eaton's shilling edition of 1796 was virtually suppressed. "Part the Third, Being an Examination of the passages in the New Testament quoted from the old and called prophecies concerning Jesus Christ" appeared posthumously (London: D.I. Eaton, 1811).

There are frequent nineteenth-century editions of *The Age of Reason*: the book is published by itself, and also as the main component in a volume of Paine's *Theological Works* set beside a volume of his *Political Works*, according to a tradition established by the printer Carlile in 1817 and 1818, and maintained by Conway's editions of *The Rights of Man* (1895) and *The Age of Reason* (1896) (New York and London: G.P. Putnam's Sons). Paine's *Theological Works* were published in German translation in 1848.

3. R[ichard] Watson, Lord Bishop of Landaff, *An Apology for the Bible, in a Series of Letters, addressed to Thomas Paine, Author of a Book entitled, The Age of Reason, Part the Second, being an Investigation of True and Fabulous Theology*. The book was first published in London in 1796 and ran through a number of editions within the next three years, mostly in London, but also in Ireland, Massachusetts, and Virginia. The copy with Blake's

annotations presents itself as from the eighth edition (London: Printed for T. Evans, in Paternoster Row, 1797), though the British Museum Catalogue lists more eighth editions in 1799 and 1808! There are at least nine editions in the nineteenth century (the last in 1857), along with translations into French (1892) and Greek (1844).

The British Library lists thirty-six replies to Paine's *Age of Reason*, Watson's being the best known and the most official in character. The format was already set by Watson's earlier Reply to Gibbon: *An Apology for Christianity, in a Series of Letters addressed to Edward Gibbon, Author of "The Decline and Fall of the Roman Empire."* First published in Cambridge in 1776, it had run through five editions in England by 1798, the year of Blake's Annotations to the *Apology for the Bible*, with other editions in Ireland and America. From 1806, the *Two Apologies* were published together; I have consulted the edition of 1816.

4. Thomas Paine, *The Age of Reason, Being an Investigation of True and Fabulous Theology*, ed. Moncure Daniel Conway (New York and London: Putnam's, 1896), p. 20.

5. *Ibid.*, p. 151.

6. *The Marriage of Heaven and Hell*, Plate 12, "A Memorable Fancy" (E38-39).

7. John E. Grant in the present volume, pp. 71-115.

8. See Blake's "Annotations to Bacon's *Essays Moral, Economical and Political*, London, 1798" (E635-62).

9. See "Annotations to *The Works of Sir Joshua Reynolds*, ed. by Edmond Malone, London, 1798" (E635-62).

10. *Age of Reason*, p. 85.

11. *Ibid.*, pp. 21-22.

12. See Paine's Letter to Adams, dated Jan. 1st, 1803, in Conway's edition of *The Age of Reason*, p. 205.

13. *Age of Reason*, p. 114.

14. *Ibid.*, pp. 50-51, 123-25. Paine says that he has seen the opinions of Ibn Ezra and Spinoza that Job carries no internal evidence of Hebrew authorship.

15. *Ibid.*, p. 172. He quotes two short passages from Boulanger's Life of Paul.

16. *Ibid.*, pp. 64-65.

17. [Nicholas-Antoine Boulanger], *The Origin and Progress of Despotism*, trans. [John Wilkes] (Amsterdam [*scilicet* London], 1764), p. 123.

18. *Age of Reason*, p. 43.

19. *Ibid.*, p. 25.

20. Thomas Paine, "Extract of a Reply to the Bishop of Llandaff," published posthumously in a collection of his *Theological Works* (London: R. Carlile, 1822), p. 58.

21. "On the Origin of Free-Masonry," in *Theological Works (supra)*, p. 48.

22. Locke's text with the standard section numbers is reproduced here from John Locke, *The Reasonableness of Christianity*, etc., ed. I.T. Ramsey (Stanford: Stanford Univ. Press, 1958). The work was originally published in 1695.

23. Sir Leslie Stephen's *History of English Thought in the Eighteenth Century*, 2 vols. (London: Smith, Elder, 1876) is still authoritative on the controversies of the period, though it is by no means impartial. (See for present purposes particularly Chap. IV, section v, "The Argument from Miracles.") The eighteenth-century Church has found a more sympathetic historian in Norman Sykes, especially in *Church and State in England in the Eighteenth Century* (London: G. Bell & Sons, 1930). A fairly balanced account is to be found in Gerald R. Cragg in *Reason and Authority in the Eighteenth Century* (Cambridge: Cambridge Univ. Press, 1964) and in the chapters on the English Church in his *The Church in the Age of Reason, 1648-1789*, Vol. 4 of the Pelican History of the Church (Harmondsworth, Middlesex: Penguin, 1960). Frank E. Manuel surveys the development in eighteenth-century European religious thought with attention to literary as well as theological figures in *The Changing of the Gods* (Hanover, N.H.: Univ. of New England Press, [1983]). For more detailed accounts of the works of the Deists, especially with reference to the debate on miracles, see Norman Lewis Torrey, *Voltaire and the English Deists* (New Haven: Yale Univ. Press; London: Oxford Univ. Press, 1930).

In the first period of the Deist controversy the pace was set particularly by John Toland's *Christianity Not Mysterious* (1696) and Matthew Tindal's *Christianity as Old as the Creation* (1730). Thomas Woolston's enigmatic defense of the Christian miracles in his *Six Discourses on the Miracles of our Saviour* (1727-9) along the lines that, being too preposterous to be credible as historical events, they were true only in an allegorical and spiritual sense was read, and probably intended, as subversive rather than apologetic. The standard defense of the central Christian miracle, i.e., the Resurrection, remained throughout the century the work published by Thomas Sherlock, then Bishop of Bangor, in 1729: *The Trial of the Witnesses of the Resurrection of Jesus*, a work with a format as forensic as the title suggests.

24. *Age of Reason*, p. 36.

25. *Ibid.*, pp. 183-4.

26. *Ibid.*, p. 184.

27. Paine was sufficiently proud of the compliment to quote it in his Letter to Samuel Adams to assure him that he, Paine, had certainly not become the infidel he was reputed to be (*Ibid.*, p. 203).

28. *Apology*, Letter I, p. 2 (E613).

29. *Anecdotes of the Life of Richard Watson, Bishop of Llandaff*, written by himself at different intervals, revised in 1814, Pub. by his son, Richard Watson, 2 vols., 2nd ed., 1818, I.62 and 38-9.

30. *The History of English Thought in the Eighteenth Century (supra)*, especially Chap. VIII, sections 89-98, for Stephen's treatment of Watson's encounters with Gibbon and Paine.

31. Gerald R. Cragg, *Reason and Authority in the Eighteenth Century (supra)*, Chap. IX and Conclusion.

32. For most of the information on Watson, I rely on the DNB and his own *Anecdotes* (see note 29) which are self-serving but for that reason all the more informative as to Watson's public persona. The *Anecdotes* are well documented; they reprint in full his speech in the Lords in 1795 for a Peace with France, and even the letters of congratulation (one of them written on behalf of the Prince Regent) that he received on what he always considered to be his triumph over Paine.

33. Richard Watson, Lord Bishop of Llandaff, ed., *A Collection of Theological Tracts*, 6 vols. (Cambridge: J. Archdeacon, 1785), I.ix-x.

34. "A Charge delivered to the Clergy of the diocese of Llandaff in June 1795" in Richard Watson, Lord Bishop of Llandaff, *Two Apologies*, etc. (London, 1816), pp. 444-70. For his disapproval of the doctrine of personal predestination as injurious and unscriptural, see pp. 460-62.

35. *Ibid.*, p. 465.

36. *Ibid.*, pp. 467-68.

37. *Theological Tracts*, V.vii.

38. Richard Watson, "The Christian Religion No Imposture," in *Two Apologies*, etc., p. 443.

39. See note 23.

40. "A Charge ... to the Clergy" (*supra*), p. 454.

41. I follow the text and page numbers of *An Apology for the Bible* as given by Erdman from the edition annotated by Blake. The present comment occurs in Letter I, p. 6; quoted in Annotations (E614).

42. *Ibid.*, Letter III, p. 25 (E618).

43. *Ibid.*, Letter I, p. 4 (E614).

44. "There is No Natural Religion," Conclusion (E3), and "All Religions are One," Principle 6 (E1).

Jesus and the Powers That Be
in Blake's Designs for
Young's *Night Thoughts*

John E. Grant

Despite Blake's own professions that he was a Christian, a number of modern scholars, both those who write as Christians and those who do not, have categorically declared that Blake was not a Christian. There have also been many representations of Blake as a sometime Christian, particularly later in life after he had disaffiliated himself from the non-Christian materialism or revolutionism that he had been drawn into during the early days of the French Revolution. Solid evidence of a biographical kind on this question hardly exists before Blake's surviving letters, which begin just before his Felpham years, 1800-1804, during the time that Blake was away from London and thus had a need to communicate thoughts discursively unnecessary either earlier or later. The plain senses of Blake's letters during these troubled years (e.g., E720) do seem to indicate that Blake had recently experienced a major religious crisis, as the result of which he had emerged either as a Christian or as a better Christian than he had been before. The conversion (if there was one) must have taken place during or shortly after the period in which he worked on the *Night Thoughts* project—1795 to about 1797. Blake's treatment of this series of 537 watercolors, however, hardly makes sense as the artistic performance of a non-Christian.

In *The Marriage of Heaven and Hell* (c. 1790) the final debate is to liberate the conception of Jesus from the cult of the Father; in Blake's private annotations (1798) to Watson's *Apology for the Bible*, "the Everlasting Gospel" is first enunciated; in *The Everlasting Gospel* (c. 1818) the good news concerns Jesus the man, rather than some neo-Platonic or post-Christian "spirit." It may be that Blake's concentration on the figure of Jesus, together with his distaste for the Chruch as an institution, ought to be called "Jesus-ism" rather than Christianity. Whatever name is used, we need not suppose that Blake's faith seemed even to himself exactly the same throughout his life; as, for example, before and after his encounters with Swedenborg about 1789, or, for that matter, with Young about 1795. Considering the styles of thinking and feeling of Blake's contemporaries, particularly those whose ideas most resembled his own during the 1790s, such as Coleridge, Blake does not seem to have had an egregious case of divided consciousness. But neither was Blake a hedgehog, preoccupied with idiosyncratic visions, incapable of doubt, and obsessed by one big thing.

Whatever we conclude about the quality of Blake's faith, he certainly possessed a quality of mind and of imagination that marked the character of his literary and artistic life: his responsiveness to the work of his predecessors. I believe that Anthony Blunt and Harold Bloom, as two of the best-informed scholars who have attempted to grapple with aspects of this question, largely failed because they were unable to see things as Blake did: the former was too mechanistic, the latter too psychologistic. And both were convinced by their own belief-systems that Blake must have been wrong; thus they would not permit themselves to encounter many of the ideas and qualities in Blake's work in media for which they had no special scholarly competence. Yet each pursued a richer vein than others who tried to conceive of Blake in English isolation: Eliot's tribe of Robinson Crusoe.

Blake had an unusual capacity to respond to anything he read, as well as to any art he saw (and he saw a large amount), and to react powerfully, even violently, to whatever seemed to him to be wrong. He was also capable of great enthusiasms; they often stimulated him to alter or improve, rather than to praise. His references to Milton or to Dürer exemplify this. These capacities make Blake one of the best of English annotators, as well as undoubtedly the best of English book illustrators. Blake's kind of readiness in formulating a penetrating, ringing response to somebody else's work could only occur in a person whose thoughts were in order. Sometimes I feel oppressed in trying to read Young's *The Complaint and The Consolation, or, Night Thoughts on Life, Death and Immortality* in something like the inquiring and critical spirit Blake would have brought to the task. For a short-tempered genius such as Blake the shilly-shally quality of Young's mind must often have produced exasperation. Even if Blake was troubled with his own spiritual doubts he might well have found himself thinking: "If what Rev. Young stands for is Christianity, I must be a better Christian than he was." Such a Blake might have been provoked into being a Christian. But there are no verbal records that indicate how Blake felt about Young: only hundreds of pictures that show that the artist was willing to express a wide range of sympathies and dissympathies to Young's text—including its opinions and its silences—and to Young as a personality. Indeed, some image of Young appears in well over a hundred of Blake's *Night Thoughts* pictures; usually these images are more distinctly imagined than the self-image(s) that Young the poet built into his famous poem.

At times Blake was very hard on Young and his ideas, but one must bear in mind that Blake as critical artist was always a severe judge of the texts of the authors he illustrated at any length. Whenever Blake studied an esteemed book with the thought of illustrating it—even one he certainly admired, such as the works of Shakespeare or the Bible—he seemed to find something lacking in it (or in common acceptations of it) which, perhaps, the original author ought to have seen and provided, but didn't. Blake's capacity as illustrator enabled him to supply what was missing in the venerated words. Often it is difficult to decide exactly how much in Blake's pictorial presentation of literary ideas is supposed to be perceived as an addition to or correction or criticism of what the author had said. Obviously those who have decided whether or not Blake was a Christian and if so, what kind, will find such interpretive determinations less problematic.

Even late in his life, when Blake seems most clearly to have been a Christian, he insisted in *The Everlasting Gospel* that he expected his vision of Jesus Christ to be unlike any other:

> The Vision of Christ that thou dost see
> Is my Visions Greatest Enemy[.] (E524)

At least with respect to the alleged "Humility" of Christ,

> I am sure This Jesus will not do
> Either for Englishman or Jew. (E524)

The antitheticalism of Blake's vision of Jesus had been announced, under infernal auspices, thirty years earlier in the last "Memorable Fancy" of *The Marriage of Heaven and Hell* (pls. 22-24) in which a "Devil" converts "an Angel" to the view that Jesus Christ had proved his greatness as a man by breaking all the ten commandments. The reader in any age is left to wonder whether the special pleading, as well as the humor, in this exchange is not supposed to be recognized and in some measure dis-

counted, but there can be no doubt that the Angel was converted to the
infernal view. He embraced the devil's "flame of fire & he was consumed
and arose as Elijah" (E43)—who was later declared to comprehend "all the
Prophetic Characters" (E560) and, still later, to be the ultimate identity of
Lord Byron (E270). Blake set the same standard for any author he read:
what is the author's capacity for becoming identified as Elijah?

It is true, however, that except in *The Marriage of Heaven and Hell*,
Blake's earlier writings say little about Jesus and that up until the mid-
nineties Blake's pictorial representations of Jesus are rare and rather
inconclusive. Blake began his canon of illuminated books with a tractate,
All Religions Are One—not, indeed, a particularly Christian motto. In
the frontispiece, however, John the Baptist appears, addressing the reader
with words not written down—words no doubt so well known as not to
need reiteration—and pointing to something not quite distinguishable;
that is, we cannot see enough of the tiny figure in the background to
make a positive identification (*ARO* 1:*IB* 24): possibly it is somebody
new. Only in the last two plates of *All Religions Are One* (*ARO* 9 and
10:*IB* 26) is the viewer shown figures almost distinct enough to represent
Blake's Jesus, but we can hardly be certain until later when practically the
same figures reappear, much magnified and in more distinct settings, in
Blake's designs for Young's *Night Thoughts*. Plate 9 (below) is modified
as Jesus amid the fire of Hell, *Night Thoughts* 121 (IV.2)—engraved as
34E (p. 73) in the 1797 engraved edition. Plate 10 (above) is also modified as the frontispiece to the second volume of the *Night Thoughts* watercolors, *Night Thoughts* 264, where Jesus appears as the Awakener
above the stretched-out figures of the soldiers stationed to keep his body
in the tomb. In the companion tractate, *There is No Natural Religion*
(series bl, *IB* 30), the frontispiece was similarly modified in another design in *Night Thoughts*: 148 (IV.39)-40E, p. 90, in which Jesus also re-
vives a supine man; they recall both miracles of healing and the raising of
Lazarus.

For a writer and artist who has proved to be perplexing to so many in
his potential audience, Blake seems to have been remarkably at pains to
provide guidance as to his intentions. But because Blake believed that art
is a better vehicle than discursive writing for expounding truth, the reader
finds Blake's best evidence is not unequivocal: Sidney's principle that "the
poet never asserteth" applies in some measure even to Blake in his down-
right moods. Moreover, partly because Blake was a restless innovator who
kept modifying or refining his implications, often the result may be that
things turn out, in subsequent versions of the same design, to be

somewhat different from what is promised in the original version. The idea that such alterations need imply a major change of religious ideas on Blake's part seems to me naive, though I cannot here argue the problem. Major changes do, however, certainly occur in *Vala, or The Four Zoas*, Blake's remarkable illuminated manuscript of an illustrated epic poem, which was formally begun in 1797, at the time of the publication of the engraved *Night Thoughts*, and was largely written out of proofsheets of the *Night Thoughts* engravings. While the makeup of the manuscript of *The Four Zoas* was undoubtedly influenced by expedient factors, such as the availability of a proper-size paper, it is suggestive that for this poem in which Blake first casts Jesus in a major role, he incorporates all five of the engravings for the *Night Thoughts* that show Jesus in action—two of these more than once. I say "suggestive," merely, because the manuscript mingles much-revised texts with original sketch drawings and the proof engravings for *Night Thoughts* in so complicated a manner that greater certainty would be unwarranted.

As an epigraph for *Vala* Blake offered, on the half-title page, an (anglicized) Greek text of St. Paul's Epistle to the Ephesians 6.12. The following transcription of the Revised Standard Version (1952) is likely to give a better idea of the meaning Blake wished to convey than the customary King James translation, which Blake deliberately eschewed; that is, he must have felt that the Authorized Version did not accurately render some crucial matters contained in the original language (I shall retain Blake's spacing because it may further enable us to appreciate Blake's point):

> For we are not contending against flesh and blood, but against princi-
> palities,
> against the powers, against the world rulers of this present darkness,
> against
> the spiritual hosts of wickedness in the heavenly places.

Clearly Blake was not satisfied to locate the adversary (as did the Authorized Version) "in high places," which one naturally imagines to be in *this* world. That home of the adversary had been covered in the previous clause. The ultimate "superhuman forces of evil" (New English Bible, 1970) are to be fought "in the heavens."

Blake's motives for presenting his revolutionary epigraph in Greek, rather than his own English, may have included the purpose of escaping the vigilance of the authorities who might, at least hypothetically, have found the work Blake set out to write to be objectionable. In the event, the work he actually produced, or might have produced if he had arranged his often splendid material in publishable form, is certainly too complicated to have aroused the interest of the authorities in censuring the author. For viewing Blake's state of mind on public and religious issues during the last years of the eighteenth century, when he was completing his *Night Thoughts* and starting his *Vala, or The Four Zoas*, there is no better window than Blake's annotations to Watson's *Apology for the Bible ... addressed to Thomas Paine, the Author of ... the Age of Reason.* Here are the first mentions in Blake's writings of "the Everlasting Gospel" and the "God of this World"; the first of which neither the Bishop nor Paine had ever seen, the second of which the Bishop "Worshiped" (E619, 618), but which Paine, to his credit, never would: "Paine has not Attacked Christianity. Watson has defended Antichrist" (E612). How bad things were Blake declared in two initial aphorisms, prompted more by what he saw in society as a whole than by what the hireling Watson had to say: "To defend the Bible in this year 1798 would cost a man his life. The Beast & the Whore rule without controls."[1]

This is Blake's first mention of the Beast-Dragon and Whore, though they were proverbial demons for Protestants, and Blake had recently made one of his best sublime pictures of this pair as the title page for Night the Eighth of *Night Thoughts* (345).[2] We shall study in detail this infernal team as an exemplification of the powers that be against whom Blake vowed at the outset of *The Four Zoas* to contend. As for the reality of this prodigious apparition, we may enlist a verse of explanation St. John in Revelation 17.8 used to describe the Beast, even though Blake does not closely echo it:

> The beast that thou sawest was, and is not; and shall ascend out of the bottomless pit, and go into perdition: and they that dwell on the earth shall wonder, whose names were not written in the book of life from the foundation of the world, when they behold the beast that was, and is not, and yet is.

Had Blake chosen to quote this passage, he probably would not have had recourse to Greek, which may authorize the RSV, because the latter translation dismally substitutes for the three last words the prediction "is to come" for the conclusive "yet is" in the King James. In his annotations to Watson, Blake also made his greatest attempt to say in plain English what a prophet really is: prediction has nothing essential to do with it (see E617).

There is much reason to think that Paul's formulation of the adversarial principle, which Blake took as his epigraph for *The Four Zoas* and which animates his annotations to Watson, is also the motive underlying many aspects of Blake's encounter with Young's highly esteemed *Night Thoughts*, though it would have seemed to most of Blake's potential audience the outstanding long Christian work in English, after, of course, *Paradise Lost* and *Pilgrim's Progress* and, perhaps, *Paradise Regained*.

Blake's most notorious piece of antithetical criticism, that concerning the personages of the Trinity in *Paradise Lost*, can be applied, with less sense of paradox, to Young's vision of divinity in *Night Thoughts*. In the exposition of the second "chapter" of *The Marriage of Heaven and Hell* the polemical transvaluator offers this summary of radical error in Milton's theology: "the Father is Destiny, the Son, a Ratio of the five senses & the Holy-ghost, Vacuum!" (E35). Blake must have found all aspects of the godhead to be underrepresented because distantly imagined, in Young's poem, and therefore set out to provide personifications that would overcome the disadvantages of Young's tendency to employ dimly imagined abstractions. (Young's habit in his human characterizations is no less dim.) Thus the role of the Father, conventionally a bewhiskered but powerful old man, was by Blake given over to the figure of Death. Jesus, who is usually vacuous in Young's poetry, is ingeniously conceived by Blake in some thirty-five designs, most of which eschew standard themes in the life of Christ, such as the Nativity or the crucificion, but some of which are presented to invite comparison with earlier representations of them.[3]

The viewer of the *Night Thoughts* series is perhaps not surprised to find that the first indubitable depiction of Jesus (after the frontispiece to Volume One, which does not purport to illustrate a text) occurs in Night the Second, where he is shown as the Good Samaritan, for traditional interpretation had allowed for that acceptance of Luke 10.30-37. What is peculiar in this, the only depiction of the story in Blake's work, 68 (II.35, cf. 21E) (fig. 1), is that it contains disturbing details which lead the viewer to doubt whether the scene can represent an unmixed blessing: the egg-shaped cup offered by Jesus to the victim bears the image of a writhing snake upon it. Moreover, the mount on which this Samaritan arrived is a horse exactly derived from a donkey included among the ominous familiars of the subterranean goddess "Hecate" in a color print (Butlin #316, 317, 318, Pls. 396, 416, 417) that was probably completed just before the designs for Young.[4] Young's innocuous words: "Love, and

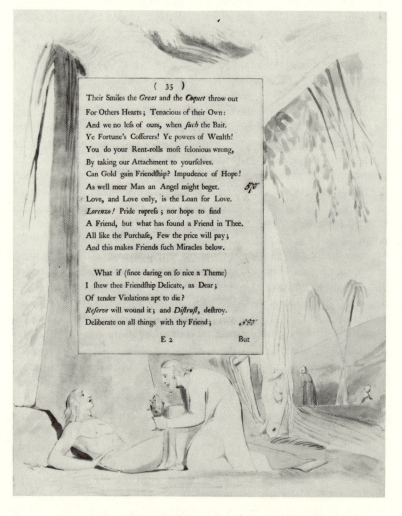

(35)

Their Smiles the *Great* and the *Coquet* throw out
For Others Hearts ; Tenacious of their Own :
And we no lefs of ours, when *fuch* the Bait.
Ye Fortune's Cofferers! Ye powers of Wealth!
You do your Rent-rolls moft felonious wrong,
By taking our Attachment to yourfelves.
Can Gold gain Friendfhip? Impudence of Hope!
As well meer Man an Angel might beget.
Love, and Love only, is the Loan for Love.
Lorenzo! Pride reprefs ; nor hope to find
A Friend, but what has found a Friend in Thee.
All like the Purchafe, Few the price will pay ;
And this makes Friends fuch Miracles below.

What if (fince daring on fo nice a Theme)
I fhew thee Friendfhip Delicate, as Dear ;
Of tender Violations apt to die ?
Referve will wound it ; and *Diftruft*, deftroy.
Deliberate on all things with thy Friend ;

E 2   But

Figure 1. The Good Samaritan, with a dubious potion.
Night Thoughts 68 (II.35)—*British Museum*

love only, is the loan for love" do not contradict the scene as Blake represents it, but hardly authorize the presentation of this biblical episode and certainly do not require it. The startled appearance of Jesus in the watercolor version constitutes a clear sign that he had been unprepared for rejection by the Jewish victim who had been passed by without succor by both the priest and the Levite. Such details indicate that Blake wished to introduce doubts as to whether this Good Samaritan could have succeeded as a benefactor or "Friend of All Mankind" (E524). But when Blake engraved *Night Thoughts* 68 as 21E he altered the features of Jesus (and, to a lesser extent, those of the Jewish victim) so as to remove the strong indication of consternation at the rejection; now Jesus is represented as being masterfully composed and earnest as he proffers his cure. One must look harder to recognize the ominous but still perfectly apparent presence depicted on the cup and to infer what the vessel so marked is supposed to signify. In either version, however, it is evident that Blake wishes to go beyond Young to tell something about the founder of Christianity and the character of his unexpected ministrations.

What it can be is gradually revealed as the pictures of Jesus unfold in subsequent designs. As though to prolong the question there are no representations at all of Jesus in Night the Third and the next stages of his revelation are differently managed in the watercolor and engraved versions of Night the Fourth, which is the final Night of the engraved edition. In the engraved sequence *Night Thoughts* 1, the frontispiece for the first volume of watercolors, is adapted as 31E for the titlepage of Night the Fourth to show "The Christian Triumph." In the watercolor sequence the next appearance of Jesus is further delayed to 121 (34E), which presents Jesus wearing a hideous crown of thorns, displaying his spike-pierced hands and feet, and traversing a fiery furnace. As with 68 (21E) the face of Jesus in the engraved version is altered to remove the indications of anguish and to present him as serene though in torment. The four subsequent Jesus-designs: 127, 142, 143 (38E), and 144, are all relevant to the vision of the Good Samaritan presented in 68, but none as closely as the last of Night the Fourth, 148 (40E) in which Jesus bends down and extends "That Touch, [that] with charm celestial, heals the Soul," here represented as a nude man aspiring to arise from a draped slope of earth. In this picture Jesus appears wholly composed in both watercolor and engraved versions, but in the latter the implication of resurrection is strengthened by the addition of a butterfly that emerges from its chrysalis located above the text panel.

In the watercolor series the pictorial motif of the victim and Jesus is further continued until almost the end of Young's long poem after the poet had made a final attempt to imagine the Trinity (*Night IX*, 225 ff.), not surprisingly concentrating on God as Father. In Blake's designs the creator of humanity is presented as Jesus: 529 (fig. 2) both because Blake believed the successful creator must be Jesus and also because the paternal figure of Death had been presented as dead and therefore unavailable almost a hundred designs earlier (435). Blake had shown Jesus gathering little children of paradise to him, 527, or leading a group of adults in prayer, 528 (both designs reworking materials from the second plate of "The Little Black Boy" of *Innocence*: *Songs* 10:*IB* 51). In the last of this sequence Blake seems to be contradicting his own representation of the creator in the color print *The Elohim Creating Adam* (Butlin #289, Pl. 388) where he appears as a bewhiskered Michelangelesque father who flies above his supine creation; he also contradicts the apparent sense of Oothoon in *Visions of the Daughters of Albion* 5:3-4 (E48), who attempts to address Urizen as "Creator of men!" The rectified point in *Night Thoughts* 529 is anticipated in a distinction Blake had made earlier: "God is a man not because he is so percievd [sic] by man but because he is the creator of man" (E603). Jesus is also the creator of man because he (visibly) breathes the Holy Spirit into whatever potentiality is contained in the red clay that he holds ready in his right hand to add to the top of the head of Adam who is coming into being just above the sea. It is remarkable that, when represented as creating his masterwork, Jesus is depicted as striding upward on the earth while reaching down to potential Adam. This posture strikingly contrasts with the flying position of the paternal Elohim in the first design of the great color print series, *Elohim Creating Adam*, which may well have been completed about the time Blake began work on the *Night Thoughts* designs—though the problems of dating the only known version of this color print before 1805, when it was sold, are considerable. The unusual, perhaps unprecedented, position of Jesus, together with the mostly pink morning sky are details that indicate a fundamental distinction between this optimistic scene in 529 and the pessimistic scene in the *Elohim Creating Adam*, where both Adam and his paternal creator are stretched out horizontally parallel to one another in otherwise similar circumstances except that there the sun is undoubtedly setting. The pessimism of the relationship between Elohim and Adam was further intensified in the eleventh illustration to the Book of Job, "Job's Evil Dreams" (Butlin #550:11, Pl. 707), which was probably also first conceived in 1805 when Blake apparently made the only copy of the color

[111]

" To Laws they know not; Beings lodg'd in Seats
" Of well-adapted Joys; in different Domes
" Of this Imperial Palace for thy Sons;
" Of this proud, populous, well-policy'd,
" Tho' boundlefs, Habitation, plan'd by THEE!
" Whofe feveral Clans their feveral Climates fuit;
" And Tranfpofition, doubtlefs, would deftroy.
" Or, Oh! indulge, Immortal KING! indulge
" A Title, lefs auguft indeed, but more
" Endearing; ah! how fweet in human Ears?
" Sweet in our Ears! and Triumph in our Hearts!
" Father of IMMORTALITY to Man!
" A Theme that * lately fet my Soul on Fire.---
" And THOU the NEXT! yet Equal! THOU, by whom
" *That* Bleffing was convey'd; far more! was Bought;
" Ineffable the Price! By whom all Worlds
" Were made; and One, redeem'd! Illuftrious Light
" From Light Illuftrious! THOU, whofe *Regal* Power,
" Finite in *Time*, but Infinite in *Space*,
" On more than adamantine Bafis fix'd,
" O'er more, far more, than Diadems, and Thrones,

    * Night the Sixth, and Seventh.
                                        " Invio-

Figure 2. Jesus, the Creator of Man. *Night Thoughts* 529
(IX.111)—*British Museum*

print now known. In *Job* 11 the patriarchal Job is supine in the darkness of Hell, while being hovered over by a paternal Devil with cloven hoof, accompanied by a serpent, and tormented by devils as this deity points to the tables of the law which emit thunderbolts. This systematic declension of related motifs in the basic God-Man relationship assures the viewer that it is a distinction rather than a relationship that Blake intends one to recognize in *Night Thoughts* 529. Furthermore, since this picture of Jesus the Son as creator of Man is in a sequence of concluding designs 527-529 and 531-534, practically all of which present Jesus in a favorable unironic light, the viewer is *not* given a context that would encourage the kind of ironic reflections of creation-fall that occur in other Blake pictures of human Genesis.

In the final sequences in *Night Thoughts*, which depict Jesus in a variety of relationships, he is usually shown as a solitary figure even when attended by many other human figures. Even in 527, where Jesus is surrounded by numberless people, the blessed come as a host of little children into the presence of their father; the design is, as it were, a supernalization of the pastoral relationship of children and the Good Shepherd that is depicted in 378 (VIII.30). In 528, however, where Jesus is seated amidst a group of eight bowing disciples, he looms above them as he leads them in prayer, not because he is grander but because they demean themselves. His face appears troubled, probably because of the paternal role their deference causes him to enact. Young's text, with its insistence on the paternity of God, tends to thrust upon Jesus the kind of paternal authority that consorts awkwardly with Blake's vision of Christ. This picture is recognizably a variant of the last of the color print series: *Christ Appearing to the Disciples after the Resurrection*, which is known in three versions (Butlin #325, 326, 327, Pls. 401, 417, 418), all of which show Jesus standing amidst seven of his disciples. The scene (a version of John 20.19-30) depicts all but one of the disciples prostrating themselves before Jesus; the exception is Doubting Thomas (John 20.24ff.), who seems in the gospel to have been rebuked, but is entirely vindicated in Blake's color print depictions. Thomas retains enough of his own humanity to look up at Jesus, though he arose from the dead, while the rest are groveling. The dissatisfaction of Jesus in encountering too much deference is variously expressed in all versions of the color print and also in 528, where the salutary presence of Thomas is lacking.

Blake had already detached the exemplary doubting Thomas and featured him on the title-page design for the second volume of *Night Thoughts*, 265, where (without any prompting from Young's text) we are shown Thomas exclaiming as he examines the wound in the side of Jesus. And in this picture the benign expression of Jesus, as well as his (unheard) words, assure Thomas that his amazement is that of a friend, rather than a slave. It is at bottom an exemplary relationship that we are shown, like that with the little children in 378 and 527, and unlike that of the pagan or Christian idolaters shown in 460, 507, and 528.

In the account in John 20 of the appearance of Jesus to the disciples there is no text to explain their excessive deference; this does occur in Luke 24.37-38, where, however, Thomas is not mentioned at all. In John 20.24 it is explained that Thomas had been absent during the first visit. What Jesus had said and done on his first appearance is, however, of even more interest than the wounds he displayed:

> Peace be unto you: as my Father hath sent me, even so send I you. And when he had said this, he breathed on them, and saith unto them, Receive ye the Holy Ghost: whosesoever sins ye remit, they are remitted unto them; and whosesoever sins ye retain, they are retained. (20.21-23)

In *The Everlasting Gospel* Blake repeatedly declares, "Thy sins are all forgiven thee" (e.g., sec. b, 1. 22, E876) without the original reservation concerning "unforgiven sin," which is the preoccupation of "The God of this World." But Blake did recall the breathing of the Holy Spirit in constructing in 529 an image of the kind of humanity that ought to have been created by the Son.

The remarkable Manneristic stride of the creating Jesus in 529 recalls (as has been noted by A.S. Gourlay) the extraordinary extensions of the suppliant bodies of Doubting Thomas in 265 and of the Woman Clothed in the Sun, 78, the title page for Night the Third. Each of these, in turn, recalls the posture of Christ in the frontispiece for the first volume of *Night Thoughts*, which was more prominently entitled "The Christian Triumph" when it was employed as 31E, the title page for Night the Fourth in the engraved series for the 1797 edition. Jesus in 529, like Thomas and the Woman, rests his weight on the bent left leg and trails the elongated right, whereas the relation of the legs is reversed and otherwise altered in 1, the frontispiece of Volume I, as part of a frontal rather than a profile rendition of the figure. As in theatrical mime, repetitions of distinctively stylized postures take on the aspects of a language. When we look back from the initial creative encounter of Jesus and man in 529 we can see more in the Good Samaritan episode as shown in 68 (fig. 1). There the posture of Jesus crouched beneath the text panel, holding unopened the sinister decorated cup, repelled by the victim he wishes to help, marks (at this stage) his inability to accomplish his mission. In contrast, his springing stride above Adam in 529 expresses the fulfillment of the power latent in 68.

II

In designs such as these Blake's purpose was to refocus the divine vision, which has a paternalistic center in Young, amounting at times to a deification of death, to a fraternal center in Jesus. Young's vast themes of "Life, Death, and Immortality" could hardly remain immune to this great transposition. Blake assumed the prerogative, as creative illustrator, to reshape and adapt Young's vision and even Young's conception of himself as poet. A decade or more after Blake finished the *Night Thoughts* project, Blake's Milton, who had returned to mortal life in order to rectify his own imaginative life, experiences a climactic confrontation with Satan, identified as "my Spectre." Much of what he says to the Adversary is applicable to Blake's conception of Young, who was often characterized as a "graveyard poet" and was certainly a writer famous for his bereavements; to the author of *Night Thoughts* who later became the author of "Resignation," a poem "In Two Parts," Blake would have responded with words such as these:

> Thy purpose & the purpose of thy Priests & of thy Churches
> Is to impress on men the fear of death; to teach
> Trembling & fear, terror, constriction, abject selfishness[.]
> Mine is to teach Men to despise death & to go on
> In fearless majesty annihilating Self, laughing to scorn
> Thy laws & terrors, shaking down thy Synagogues as webs....
> (*M* 38.37-42, E139)

Passages in *Night Thoughts* urging a less abject attitude toward death than Young's norm might be evinced, but mostly Young produces evasions of the issue of Death by extolling the prospects of immortality. Moreover, Blake must have observed how Young's ruminations and confessions often tend to contradict the long passages of advice, usually conventional advice, that he deals out to Lorenzo and the other shadowy characters who seem to need it. Often, indeed, through the deployment of subjunctives and ironies the poem avoids making it clear which side of an issue the author is on.

Two of the most important designs in Blake's whole *Night Thoughts* series, 261 (VI.40) and 305 (VII.33), cast Young himself in Satanic roles for reasons authorized by the words of Young's poem, though Young would certainly have been appalled to see what his creative interpreter was to charge him with. Toward the end of Night the Sixth, Young challenges his materialistic and ambitious friend Lorenzo to mount with him to an elevated place to look down at the vanities of the rise and fall of human enterprise, which are then elaborately surveyed. In Blake's picture (fig. 3) this is translated as the Second (or Third) Temptation of Jesus by the Devil, with Young taking the place of the Devil and Lorenzo the place of Jesus. The angry Satan is stretched out in flames on a dark cloud and shouts at Jesus as he points down into the mostly indefinite lower regions. Jesus stands composedly on a cliff-edge and points with both hands diagonally either toward the text panel or, more probably, in the direction of a tiny object sketched in the lower-right corner of the page: when we look closely at the original (the photograph used for fig. 3 unfortunately omitted this detail) we see that it is an outline drawing of St. Paul's cathedral. It must be acknowledged that the character of this rendering of this tiny object is stylistically quite unlike anything else comparable to it in the entire series and that there is little wash in this area of the drawing; consequently, it could be argued that someone else has added this detail. This does not seem at all likely, however; so I shall discuss this tiny detail as though it were intended to be as momentous as Blake's other depictions of St. Paul's in the illuminated books: *Jerusalem* 46, 57 (where the engraved sketch is much like the one in *Night Thoughts*), and 84.[5]

A glance at Blake's other treatments of the Temptation theme will help to keep the issues in focus, though the discrepancy in the sequence of the Second and Third Temptations in the two detailed Gospel accounts, Matthew 4.1-12 and Luke 4.1-13, tends to produce some confusion. About 1805 Blake painted a watercolor, with an inscription citing Matthew 4.11, thus correctly entitled *The Third Temptation* (Butlin #476, Pl. 557). Christ stands on a promontory, with two angels nearby, and watches as Satan goes down in flames. But about 1818, when Blake illustrated *Paradise Regained*, he followed Milton—and the order of Luke— in painting *The Second Temptation* (Butlin #544.7, Pl. 690) with Jesus standing on a cliff-edge and contending with Satan in an exchange of pointing anent the focal composite scene of the kingdoms of the world as represented by three scenes in semi-circle of temples and enthroned monarchs. *The Third Temptation* in this series (Butlin #544.10, Pl. 693) again follows Milton and Luke in showing Jesus standing on the Temple,

Figure 3. The Second (or Third) Temptation of Jesus by the
Devil: in the roles of Lorenzo and Young.
Night Thoughts 261 (VI.40)—*British Museum*

accompanied by three angels, as Satan falls. Since Satan shows no sign of falling in *Night Thoughts* 261, we can be confident that the reference text is St. Luke's. The fall of Satan (not implied per se by *any* Gospel account of the Temptations) is depicted several times in the *Night Thoughts* series, most immediately thereafter in 305 (VII.33), where the text also applies to Young himself.

The conduct of Jesus in 261 in pointing with both hands diagonally into the abyss only makes sense if he is recognizably pointing toward the tiny image of St. Paul's. Satan is already furious and perhaps distraught as he shouts at Jesus and points with his left hand toward his own dark cloud, perhaps the ominous future, and with his right down the cliff face; presumably he is warning Jesus more than tempting him. In *The Second Temptation* for *Paradise Regained*, Satan appears much more composed (despite the evident agitation of his body, in contrast to the monumental composure of Jesus) as he conjures up an imposing vision of the powers and glory that be.

In the *Night Thoughts* series as a whole, design 261, which occurs almost at the end of Night the Sixth and Volume I, is particularly important in that it marks the first distinct appearance in the series of Satan, who thereafter maintains an important presence as the ultimate Adversary until he is finally disposed of in 508. But Blake's representation of Satan as the guide, in response to a passage in which Young invites Lorenzo to learn a moral lesson about the ultimate vanity of human enterprise, is an astonishing transposition of Young's intended sense. One can imagine Young protesting that there was nothing intentionally Satanic in his appeal to Lorenzo, the man of the world. What Young had in mind to produce was a detachment that is Christlike, not satanic. Blake's response would be that, whatever Young's stratagem, he appears to have been magnifying the glory of human enterprise and thus following a satanic strategy of flattering the all-too-human ambitions of Lorenzo. The example of Christ standing up to such blandishments is ultimately the only model for principled behavior. There need be, of course, no implication that Lorenzo's recalcitrance in the poem is in any sense Christlike.

Young's having been assigned a prime satanic identity in 261 is not significantly developed in the next forty-four designs, which include the end of Volume I, the beginning of Volume II, and almost the first half of Night the Seventh. Figures of an infant in 268 and a wayfaring youth in 373 (VII.[i]) fall into a developmental sequence, and the latter has a textual reference, "I," which certainly indicates that this is supposed to be an image of Young. But the prompt sequels in 276-77 (VII.4-5), of wayfar-

ing maturity and age, dilute the particular applications to Young in most
of the symbolic identities Blake assigns to him. Not so in 305 (VII.33)
(fig. 4) where Young's poetry speaks at length of the Fall of "*Grief*":
"Fall, how profound! Like Lucifer's, the Fall!" immediately after referring
to "my *Despair* [and] Abhor'd Annihilation! [which] blasts the Soul."
Blake provides for these passages a simple design showing a satanic
falling figure who drops from heaven into the dark abyss, being driven by
a single thunderbolt. The likelihood that 305 is supposed to have a particular application to Young is increased when we consider that the same
theme is repeated on a larger scale and in a more conclusive position in
508. The satanic per se can hardly be driven out at such an early point in
the series. On the other hand, it can also be argued that in designs immediately following, 306-309 and 311, figures more or less identifiable as
Young are still unregenerate, still by no means purged of their weaknesses
for evil. This is undeniable. One must, however, recognize that the pat-
terns Blake is imposing on the eddying Youngian narratives, in which
Young is alternately cast down and authoritative, do not always occur in
an orderly sequence. When Blake found a text which provided an occasion
to illustrate a key idea, he often took advantage of it, undeterred by the
pictorial narrative disruption. But such disruptions do not reduce the sense
of overall design to randomness. As in the illuminated books, the reader
of Blake's designs for *Night Thoughts* is required to bring ideas of order to
the series in order to perceive the ideas of order in the series.

One of the most decisive departures from an easily recognizable sequence occurs in the case of 416 (VIII.70) (fig. 5), the last design of the
penultimate Night in which, according to the title page, the following
subjects are to be "Considered, The Love of this Life; The Ambition *and*
Pleasure, *with the* Wit and Wisdom of the World" (*NT* 345). This final
design presents the First Temptation, which in all Gospel accounts is the
Satanic temptation to make bread of stones, and occurs prior to the two
later temptations which are suggested in the design that comes earlier in
the sequence, 261. This version of the First Temptation is quite simple:
an aging, bare-torsoed, and mostly bald, sharp-featured Satan kneels low
before Jesus and, with open mouth, offers two stones that look remarkably like oyster shells. In this forest scene Jesus stands with his right
hand rigidly at his side and his left hand raised in a deprecating gesture; he
does not speak nor even look at Satan but casts his eyes in the direction
of the last two lines of text, which are addressed to the unregenerate
Lorenzo: "Nor think this Censure is severe on Thee;/ Thy Master, *Satan*,
I dare call a Dunce."

[33]

Abhor'd Annihilation! blasts the Soul,
And wide-extends the Bounds of Human Woe?
In *this* black Channel would my Ravings run:

" *Grief*, from the *Future* borrow'd Peace, ere-while.
" The Future vanish! and the Present pain'd!
" Strange Import of unprecedented Ill!
" Fall, how profound! Like *Lucifer's*, the Fall!
" Unequal Fate! His Fall, without his Guilt!
" From where fond *Hope* built her Pavilion high
" The Gods among, hurl'd headlong, hurl'd at once
" To Night! To Nothing! Darker still than Night.
" If 'twas a Dream, why wake me, my worst Foe!
" O for Delusion! O for Error still!
" Could Vengeance strike much stronger, than to plant
" A Thinking Being in a World like This,
" Not over-rich before, now beggar'd quite;
" More curst than at the *Fall?* The Sun goes out!
" The Thorns shoot up! What Thorns in ev'ry Thought?
" Why Sense of Better? It imbitters Worse.
" Why Sense? Why Life? If but to sigh, then sink
" To what I was? Twice Nothing! and much Woe!
F   " Woe,

Figure 4. From "*Grief*" a Fall, "Like Lucifer's."
Night Thoughts 305 (VII.33)—*British Museum*

Figure 5. The First Temptation of Jesus by the Devil.
Night Thoughts 416 (VIII.70)—*British Museum*

Here there is no textual or pictorial indication that Young has again entered the state of Satan; no dwelling upon the implications that Lorenzo is the dupe of a "Dunce." A clarification of the issues by reference to Blake's later depictions of the scene in his *Paradise Lost* series (Butlin #544.2, Pl. 685) or in a still later watercolor (Butlin #546, Pl. 732) also seems unlikely to occur since the differences in the conceptions perhaps require more study. The (previously unnoticed) probable relationship to 416 of a detailed pencil drawing called by Butlin *A Squatted Devil with Young Horns* (Butlin #596, Pl. 829) likewise does not help to interpret this version of the encounter. Indeed, if we disregard the resemblance of what Satan holds in his hands to oyster shells, and assume that they are simply supposed to represent a (split) stone, there seems to be little to explain, save why, with so little textual prompting, Blake chose the end of Night the Eighth as a place to present the First Temptation.

If it be simply a stone that Jesus is called to work a miracle upon, the point at issue may be nothing greater, or less, than synecdoche for all the Temptations, which Jesus first resisted and then exploded into a counterattack which eventuated in his triumph over "The God of this World"—vide "The Everlasting Gospel" section [i] (N 90-91; E523): "John for disobedience bled/ But you can turn stones to bread" if you "be/ Obedient" and "fall down and worship me" (11.17-18, 24), a phrase taken from the Temptation of Earthly kingdoms, the penultimate (Luke 4.7) or final (Matt. 4.9) Temptation.

Whatever the sequence, the solitary Jesus would not be performing a miracle of social relief by turning the stones into bread (like multiplying the loaves in the feeding of the five thousand, Mark 6.37-44) but accepting subordination to Satanic authority. If the depicted "stones" should be further taken to be oyster shells, the point would be somewhat complicated without being basically changed. In 174 (V.19) Young enacts the role of a pearl diver who extracts two pearls from oysters at the bottom of "*Sorrow's* stream," a questionable harvest. In 416 it would appear that what Satan has to offer are empty shells, lacking no doubt the pearl of great price (Matt. 13-45-46). We might then infer that what Satan really wants to get from Jesus is something more material than bread: baubles fit to decorate his minion, the Whore of Babylon, who has appeared so memorably in the title page for Night the Eighth (345).

III
The Powers That Be

In 345 (Night VIII.title page) Blake confronts the viewer with one of his most effective sublime paintings (fig. 6). This revelation of the "hidden Harlot which John in Patmos saw," in company with the "Dragon red" (*M* 40.22:E142), fills a vacuum in Young's poem. In Blake's later prophecies this pair is textually pervasive because they represent the Powers that Be, but Blake reserved a depiction of them, in *Jerusalem* 75 (fig. 9) until their power was about to come to an end. In *Night Thoughts* this apparition of the power of Church and State occurs immediately after 344 (VII.72), which shows the prophetic artist working on his scroll as his lips are touched with a burning coal by a seraph (vide Isaiah 6.6). The reader is to infer that the artist here received the power enabling him to display the adversaries of vision as a single multiplex system. In Dürer's great series of woodcuts for the Apocalypse the scenes were definitively envisioned without, however, being established by Dürer in an invariable sequence; I shall refer to these designs in the order proposed by Strauss, 1979. In Dürer's plate 9 John turns from writing his own book to devour another presented by an angel; then, in plate 10, the Beast with Seven Heads and Ten Horns makes its appearance to the Woman Clothed in the Sun. Blake's visions are in no sense derivative from Dürer's but they appear to their best advantage as conscious and deliberate variations on the language of biblical symbolism as Dürer had established it for artists who aimed at depicting the Escaton. Similarly, Blake's own subsequent presentations of these major themes help the viewer to see what he was getting at in each realization. The Beast and the Whore appear transformed in the 1809 *The Whore of Babylon* (Butlin #523, Pl. 584) (fig. 7) and, again (c. 1824) in the Dante series, *The Harlot and the Giant* (Butlin #812.89) (fig. 8) and also in *Jerusalem*, plate 75 (*IB* 354 (fig. 9) at the end of the third chapter. *Night Thoughts* 345 appears at a similar pivotal position on the title page for Night the Eighth and the issues posed ramify throughout the last third of the *Night Thoughts* series as though to answer the questions that any "Man of the World" might wonder about concerning the nature of Power.

Blake alters the pictorial strategy of Dürer (and also that of Duvet, perhaps Dürer's ablest follower in graphic apocalypse)[6] by making the heads of the Beast significant, rather than mere satirical grotesques, as they appear in Dürer's fourteenth plate (the first appearance of the Whore with the Beast) (fig. 10) where the heads constitute a prodigy, not an in-

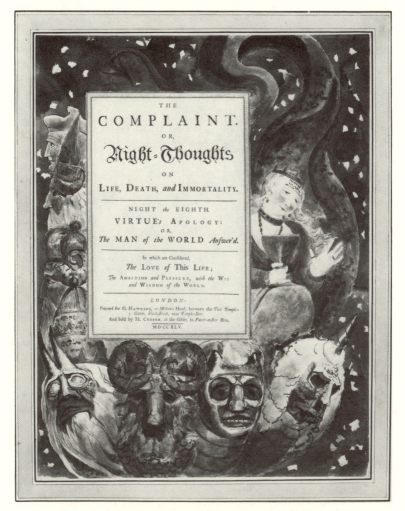

Figure 6. The Whore and the Beast. *Night Thoughts* 345
(VIII.tp)—*British Museum*

Figure 7. The Beast and the Whore transformed: the 1809
The Whore of Babylon (watercolor, 26.6 x 22.3 cm)
—*British Museum*

Figure 8. The Harlot and the Giant, c. 1824 (watercolor, 37.3 x 52.8 cm) —Felton Bequest, 1920, *National Gallery of Victoria,* Melbourne, Australia

Figure 9. The beast and whores; another variation.
Jerusalem, plate 75, copy A—British Museum

Figure 10. Albrecht Dürer's *The Whore of Babylon*, c. 1497–
98 (woodcut, 38.6 x 28.2 cm.)—Felton Bequest, 1956,
National Gallery of Victoria, Melbourne, Australia

telligible form, to bewilder the populace attracted to view it. Blake elimi-
nates almost all the apparatus of spectators, hosts, angels, and destruction
from this depiction of Dürer's but adds from Dürer's plate 11 the long tail
of the Dragon, which draws down an immense number of stars. He had
already selected other material from Dürer's eleventh plate for use elsewhere in the *Night Thoughts* series, notably in 78 (III.title page), the vision of the Woman clothed with the Sun. In *NT* 345 Blake has eliminated
the machinery of attendant figures in order to confront the viewer with an
essentialized vision of an evil system.

The front four heads of Blake's Dragon in *Night Thoughts* 345 represent the Judge, the Warrior, the King, and the Pope, all of whom face the
viewer, though those on the ends direct their attention either down or up
and only the middle pair (both of whom may be suspected of being sight-
less) seem to look at the viewer. The extreme and minutely specific,
though meaningful, grotesquerie of each of the front figures is somewhat
mitigated in the three heads of the Dragon that are arrayed at the left edge
of the design. They are, in ascending order: another king, another high
ecclesiastic, and a priest who wears a biretta. All peer intently to the left.
The priest-head seems different from the others for several reasons: because he is at the top of the column above the other heads of great rank,
because he is clean-shaven and (though he has a furrowed brow and perhaps an excessively pointed nose) is represented as having no caricature-
features, and, most notably, because he lacks visible horns such as are
prominent on all the other heads.

Several considerations, however, must be urged against a tendency
either to exculpate the priest or to declare his status to be indeterminate. A
representation of the Beast is, in principle, a "consolidation of error" (to
employ Frye's useful term) and therefore such charitable ambiguity as
might be appropriate in a less apocalyptic, more existential vision would
be quite out of keeping: here, if ever, the artist must be able to show what
is wrong. In this case the very lack of marks of the Beast on one of the
heads of the Beast reveals this priest-head to be fraudulent. The previous
representation of a (clean-cut) priest wearing a biretta, in *Night Thoughts*
92 (IV.17) (fig. 11), is of a treacherous figure, who stabs in the back a
man he embraces. This treacherous priest is long-haired, whereas in 345
the priest appears to be shaven-headed; in 396 (VIII.50) another priest
appears, hatless and tonsured (fig. 12). This priest's gesture of abasement
in kissing the cloven hoof displayed by a fat Pope indicates that he is a
"man of the world," one who would stoop to anything. Whether covered
or uncovered, therefore, all these priests exhibit behavior no less twisted

(17)

By Fate reforb'd, and funk in endlefs Night.
Man hard of Heart to man! Of horrid things
Moft horrid! Mid ftupendous, highly ftrange!
Yet oft his Courtefies are fmoother Wrongs;
Pride brandifhes the favours He confers,
And contumelious his Humanity:
What then his Vengeance? Hear it not, ye Stars!
And thou, pale Moon! turn paler at the Sound;
Man is to Man the foreft, fureft Ill.
A previous Blaft foretells the rifing Storm;
O'erwhelming Turrets threaten ere they fall;
Volcano's bellow ere they difembogue;
Earth trembles ere her yawning Jaws devour;
And Smoak betrays the wide-confuming Fire:
Ruin from Man is moft conceal'd when near,
And fends the dreadful Tidings in the Blow.
Is this the Flight of Fancy? Would it were!
Heaven's Sovereign faves all Beings but Himfelf,
That hideous Sight, a naked human Heart.
                C   Fir'd

Figure 11. A clerical stab in the back.
Night Thoughts 92 (IV.17)—*British Museum*

Figure 12. Obeisance to the Papal hoof.
Night Thoughts 396 (VIII.50)—*British Museum*

than the other heads who display their horns to show what they are capable of. When a humble-seeming man is elevated to the topmost rank of the heads of the Beast, we cannot suppose he is just following orders. He must be a prime case of the banality of *evil.*

The next lower figure at the left in *NT* 345 represents some kind of ecclesiastic, perhaps, I have suggested, a Muslim (though possibly a Druid), who wears a tall bent-back pointed crown circled by two pointed crowns, and shows only a single horn, thus implying that the priest above him must be concealing at least one horn in order for the Beast to show that it has the canonical ten. Beneath the ecclesiastic is another king who wears a crown made of bent-bars with a knob on top.[7] Apart from his bent horn, his only developed feature that attracts suspicion is the hue of his florid choleric face; he is not bizarre-looking like the king in the front row, but his positioning just above the Pope indicates that he is subject to the same influence.

The Pope is the central head in this infernal apparatus, gazing up piously with horrible cataract-clouded, visionless eyes and uttering a prayer with huge red just-parted lips that are made egregious by his contrasting long stringy white beard. It may be that these extraordinarily repellent characteristics lead the viewer not to take notice of the key feature that marks the figure: atop his typical papal triple-crowned tiara is the formée cross-and-orb of authority. This symbol (sometimes referred to as a "*Reichapfel*") has been widely employed as an affirmation of papal authority, both by the Pope himself and (often without irony) by other artists such as Rubens and even Dürer. Blake had already presented his first Pope wearing a (straight) cross-and-ball atop his triple crown in *Europe* plate 11 (*IB* 169) where the (beardless) bat-winged Pope supervises two angels who abase their sceptres of secular authority. In *Night Thoughts* 345 the Pope-head of the Beast is especially noteworthy because it displays the first cross in the entire series: the previous Popes in 91 and 233 wear no such symbol. And in the rest of the series the cross is also not displayed in the headgear of the Neptune-Pope in 349; only in 396, surmounting the crown of the cloven-hoofed Pope, does the cross per se appear again.

A glance at Blake's subsequent usage of the cross and orb will show that he selected it to represent the ultimate symbolic device of the abomination that makes desolate: in *Satan in his Original Glory*: "*Thou wast perfect till Iniquity Was Found in Thee*" (Butlin #469, Pl. 554) the Covering Cherub displays a large formée cross-and-ball in his right hand and wields the sceptre of authority in his left. As for the Crucifixion per se, which is notably absent from the *Night Thoughts* series (though its consequences are frequently displayed), Blake shows its inception with the application of the "INRI" label by the Jewish High Priest in Butlin #496, Pl. 599), its accompaniment by the Two Thieves and mob in Butlin #494 Pl. 598, and its climax in the Lamentation in Butlin #497, Pl. 600. In the rear view of the Three Crosses in Butlin #495, Pl. 571, the inscription was, of course, not visible, but it appears again in the penultimate design for the first set of watercolors for *Paradise Lost* (Butlin #529.*11*, Pl. 642) in which Michael shows Adam what the Crucifixion is to be. But (unobserved by most of the commentators on the designs for Milton's poems) Blake carefully deletes the "INRI" from the second and third versions of this design (Butlin #536.*11*, 537.*3*, Pls. 655 and 659). Probably Blake felt that the display of the INRI in the *Paradise Lost* designs was all-too-patent a confirmation that "all nations believe the jews code and worship the jews god" and that there could be no "greater subjection" (*MHH* 12, E39) than that. Ultimately the whole apparatus of Cross and Satan had to be cast out: "From the Cloud on which Eve stands Satan is seen falling headlong wound round by the tail of the serpent whose bulk naild to the Cross round which he wreathes is falling into the Abyss" (*VLJ* N. 76, E556) accompanied thence by Sin, Death, and Time, down to where the Whore and Beast are represented as still holding sway (Butlin #645, Pl. 871, etc.).

Let us return to the Beast and Whore in *Night Thoughts* 345. The three heads of the Beast at the viewer's left are troubled by whatever it is they are looking at, a prospect that falls outside the picture. Blake several times employed the motif of a threatened, anxious Establishment, often represented by three figures, as in the print known as *The Accusers of Theft Adultery Murder* (Essick VIII: Pls. 2, 3; Figs. 17-18; Butlin #262.2, Pl. 333; #285, Pl. 383)[8] where the figures of authority stand terrified by some spectacle offstage left. In the third state of this print (c. 1805-10) Blake added the inscription: "Satan's holy Trinity The Accuser The Judge & The Executioner." This is curious in view of the fact that the central figure in all versions wears a pointed crown, that is, a king's hat rather than a judge's. In another print, *Lucifer and the Pope in Hell* (Essick X, pp. 41-43, figs. 20, etc.; Butlin #287, Pl. 349), of c. 1794, the captive pope, who wears a very conventional triple crown (unlike the varied crowns of the popes in *Night Thoughts* ; cf. 91, 345, 396), looks resolutely backward, rather as does the other pope in *NT* 349, though for a different reason, to avoid being viewed by the three damned kings who, buried up to their chests, regard the newcomer pope with contempt or wonder. The evidence of changed identities in these and other related pictures, such as the watercolor *The King of Babylon in Hell* (Butlin #467, Pl. 548) of a decade later, caution us against taking the indubitable signs of office too restrictively. When the system requires it, a king may function as a judge, or vice versa, as we are shown also in the case of the front line judge in *NT* 345: as noted, he wears a judge's wig, but also, on the back of his head, a thin crown with three visible knobs.

The figure of the Harlot who rides the Beast bears on her forehead the inscription "Mystery" together with a further inscription in two illegible lines that do not need to be transcribed for those familiar with the text of Revelation 17. The heavily rouged, plump, and attractive, sly-eyed Whore is gorgeously bejeweled and wears a crown (to show her identity as the queen of Babylon) as she holds in her right hand the goblet containing the blood of saints and martyrs, which makes her drunk;[9] with her left hand she gestures in a way that might be an infernal benediction but is more likely a sign of alarm at something she foresees. This can only be her overthrow (Rev. 18), which, according to St. John, was accomplished by a mighty angel who cast a great millstone into the sea. In Dürer's Apocalypse 15 the city Babylon is already burning and one of two angels prepares to drop the millstone, which will bring on out of the sky an armed host that will overcome the still-triumphant Whore. She still holds high her intricately formed chalice and appears as a wonder to the king, merchants, priest, warriors, and multitude who have assembled to gaze at one who "hath glorified herself and lived deliciously" (Rev. 18.7). The lead horseman of Dürer's host, which, like a whirlwind, is about to sweep over the Whore and her multitude, is "Faithful and True" (Rev. 19), though only the crowns on the head of his white horse distinguish the appearance of this knight from that of ordinary warriors. At this moment the avenging army has already begun to emerge from behind the clouds and has just been sighted by one of the fatuous heads of the Beast.

In Blake's *NT* 345 the freckled red dragon-body on which the Harlot is seated (chiefly above the Judge-head) twists as a tail to the top of the page and then writhes across it before bending back sharply in a barbed arrow-head that points in the direction of the Harlot: this threat of self-destruction (a variation on Rev. 17.16) is, however, as yet poised on the other side of the text panel where it is outside the ken of the Powers that Be. At this time depicted, the whole tail of the Dragon is engaged in collecting a third part of the stars of heaven (Rev. 12.4: Dürer 10 and Duvet 15) which are represented as myriad snowflakes in all corners of the dark nether sky. In Revelation (17.1ff.) it is said, before any mention of

Babylon's beast-mount, that she "sitteth upon many waters"; in Dürer this is represented by a stream that flows beneath the legs of the Beast. Perhaps the snowflakes are intended partially to indicate her watery mount at the same time they represent the hosts being recruited and falling into the cause of the Beast, the counterparts of the gathering storm of the forces of Faithful and True in Dürer's picture. In any case, the Dragon assimilates to the symbol of the sea serpent called Leviathan in Job and depicted by Blake (following Young's text) in 349 (VIII.3), where it is the mount for a scaly Neptune who wears a papistical crown and carries a crozier as he directs the attack of the sea beast against what are called, in the text, "bubbles," but may well represent planets "floating" in the Sea of Time and Space: such planets are to be seen elsewhere in the *Night Thoughts* series (esp. 231, VI.10).

Each of Blake's later depictions of the Beast and Harlot is significantly different from *Night Thoughts* 345. In *The Whore of Babylon* (Butlin #523, Pl. 584) (fig. 7) the Scarlet Woman, though unveiled, wears Rhea's triple crown of fenestrated walls and displays an elaborate serpent-entwined golden cup of which, as fumes, female spirits flow, and debauch among fighting armies. The warriors are being devoured by at least one of the heads of this incarnation of the Beast—who lacks a tail since he has a human body, and thus is not recruiting amid the stars. This pair are yet more triumphant than their predecessors in Blake's picture of c. 1795. (After all, the Peninsular War was raging during the carefully explicit date of 1809.) The sidelong glance of this Whore probably indicates that she is fascinating, rather than apprehensive. But at least one head of this Beast has sighted something ominous offstage that distracts him from the carnage. In the last version, the final illustration to Dante's *Purgatory*, entitled *The Harlot and the Giant* (Butlin #812.89) (fig. 8), the Beast again appears with a serpentine body and tail raised but only up into the fruit of the Tree of the Knowledge of Good and Evil. All seven heads of the Beast are crowned and equipped with horns, but, as Klonsky points out, the viewer must assume there are two horns (largely) concealed beneath the papal crown worn by the first head in order to account for the requisite ten horns.[10] This recalls that the priest in *Night Thoughts* 345, who appears without horns, probably bears one beneath the oddly shaped crown of his biretta. In the Dante design the Harlot wears a triple bristling-pointed crown as she spills wine from her cup while kissing her companion the Giant, who leads the Beast-chariot, and points the way for its progress. Presumably this Whore is pointing and glancing toward Dante himself, whom Blake, rather oddly, chooses to leave offstage, but in the poem the Whore is attracted to him, thus provoking a sequence of events in which the Giant beats her and drags away the chariot, concluding this pageant of the Powers that Be who have taken over the Garden of Eden, now located at the top of the mountain of Purgatory. Probably a still closer view of Blake's picture would indicate an even more mordant understanding of the proceedings: Beatrice wears a crown (like the heads of the Beast) as she kneels, veiled, before the huge Tree of the Knowledge of Good and Evil; the tail of the Beast waves among the fruit of the Tree, one of which drips its essence into the Whore's cup, etc.

At this point there is a hiatus of many cantos in the sequence of pictures Blake is known to have executed. It is difficult to be certain whether this absence is to be filled with implication derived from the previous pictures and from the poet itself—whether, in short, the viewer is to imagine that the hiatus implies more of the same—or whether it is to be attributed merely to the exigencies of Blake's fading health, which may not have allowed the artist to execute a scene in which the sentiment could be articulated: "In his will is our peace." In any case, the sequence of the existing Dante designs is problematic, but in the order adopted by Roe and Butlin, *The Harlot and the Giant* is immediately followed by *Dante Adoring Christ* (Butlin #812.90) in which Christ appears in cruciform position but also as wholly alive and wielding the celestial luminaries, as Dante kneels before him, with outspread arms, adorant. That this may represent the intended sequence is suggested by the fact that these designs exactly repeat the invariable order of plates at the end of the third chapter in *Jerusalem*, where in 75 there is a vision of a (dual) Whore and Beast, followed in 76, the frontispiece to the last chapter, by a vision of Albion standing in "Glad Day" posture before the image of Jesus crucified on a huge forked tree (fig. 13). Lesnick and Erdman have argued that the image of Christ crucified on a tree in *Jerusalem* 76 indicates that he was there transformed into "Satanic Selfhood" or even the "God of this World." Mitchell and Paley have presented good arguments for vindicating the figure from this imputation.[11]

Paley in particular declares that Satanism as triumphant evil is not suggested here but is instead to be found in the image of "Hand" in *Jerusalem* 26, who strides along with outspread arms surrounded by snaky flames. The figure of "Hand" does indeed practically duplicate the monstrous personification of Plague in *Pestilence: The Death of the First Born* (Butlin #442, Pl. 518). But it must be acknowledged that Christ himself was, in a major design in *Vala, or The Four Zoas*, p. 108 [116], drawn in a posture that closely resembles those of Pestilence and Hand.

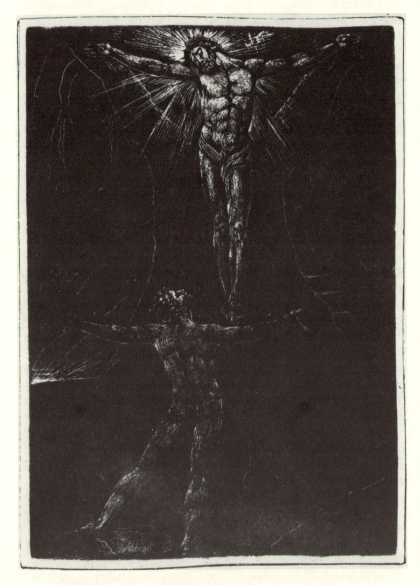

Figure 13. Albion's "Glad Day" posture before Jesus
crucified on a tree. *Jerusalem*, plate 76, copy A
—British Museum

And textually this picture is enmeshed in an exceedingly tangled dialectic involving Satan, Rahab, the Crucifixion of the Lamb, etc., which constitutes a mighty maze not easily negotiated even by a patient exegete. But even if it is conceded that the first form of this drawing depicted Christ taking a major stride (like Pestilence and Hand), before his stride was much shortened, the figure of Christ should not be confused with the postures of such Antichrists: instead the reader is led to understand that their resemblances to Christ are deliberate or structural deceptions: their way of prevailing in the world is to imitate Christ in order to produce bondage rather than to work at liberating mankind from Mystery, Power, and something that is called Reason.

In *Jerusalem* 76, as Paley wisely observes, there is no piece of evidence or argument that can refute an antithetical interpretation determined to see Antichrist in Jesus crucified upon the darkened mysterious tree and in Albion adorant before him. There are indeed grounds elsewhere in Blake's work for entertaining such suspicions. However, the large differences between the uncolored and colored versions of this design, which have never been recognized or discussed, have a bearing on how positive a scene is supposed to be presented. On the whole, the single colored version is much more positive than the four uncolored versions; indeed, the plausibility of an antitheticalist case must rest on the uncolored copies, which were evidently done both before and after it. The spirit of the colored version of the design is eloquent and, for most viewers (even those who have no personal attraction to Christianity), positive. Among other considerations is the fact that the image of Christ crucified upon a tree is not the image under which, for a time, the cult of Christianity effectively conquered the world. It was understood, of course, that the Cross was made from the wood of the Tree of the Knowledge of Good and Evil: "Man stole the fruit, but I must climb the Tree;/ The Tree of Life to all but only me" as paradoxically rendered in the familiar imagery of George Herbert's "The Sacrifice."[12]

To explain Blake's purposes in representing the Cross as a tree in *Jerusalem* 76, in contrast to the dressed-wood Cross he employs elsewhere, would take us far afield from the *Night Thoughts* context and the Powers that Be as they are represented in this vast series. It is clear, however, that Blake always distrusted the Cross since its corollary is passivity and Blake usually sought to present energetic images of Jesus. We see this in the frontispiece for the *Night Thoughts* series, *NT* 1, as relocated as the title page for Night the Fourth in the engraved version: Jesus' arms are in cruciform position as he rises, parting the clouds, above the guardian angels who remain attentive only to "the linen clothes folded up" (E45) rather than to the Resurrection. This quoted phrase, from the first exposition of *The Marriage of Heaven and Hell*, is there metaphorically applied to the writings of Swedenbourg; in the frontispiece to *Night Thoughts* it implicitly applies to the kind of limited perception of Jesus attained by the poet Edward Young and his cohort of angelic disposition. In *Night Thoughts* 512 (IX.94) Jesus represents the Vine of Life but his arms are lowered to beneath cruciform position in order to dispense blessings. Jesus assumes a cruciform position again in 532 (IX.114) (fig. 14) attending the burial of old Young and dispersing two devils who had gathered to see whether they could salvage some part of the Young legacy. They are dismissed by the outspread arms of Jesus so that the four angels burying Young will be undistracted. Blake probably thought of these angels as representing the Four Zoas. But nothing in the picture or text could so inform the reader who was unaware of Blake's own writings, particularly those done after 1796. It is, however, necessary to consider the evidence that makes it certain that the figure being buried is indeed Young—till then the longest lived of English poets of stature—who is elsewhere in the series almost never represented as being older than a vigorous middle age and who is often represented as a youth. The best reason is the marked lines, in which he prays God: "at *Thy* good Hour/ Gently, ah gently, lay me in my Bed,/ My *Clay-cold Bed!*" (IX.2346-8). There is an additional reason, though it is more inferential since there is no text to prove it. In the general title page, *Night Thoughts* 2, Young is represented as reading a large tome in bed; probably, as Erdman has suggested, Young is reading his own *Night Thoughts* as transformed by Blake's designs. There are two vignettes, with figures on a smaller scale representing adventures contained in the narrative of the book. The one at the right depicts the aspirations of a young man; the one at the left depicts an old man sleeping in the grave while being watched over by a youthful gravedigger who stands in a posture of reservation looking down. This old man bears the closest possible resemblance to the one being buried in 532. This closure of the series cannot have been unintentional; it must be indicative of identity.

Blake about 1805 recycled the bottom half of the design almost exactly and worked a variation on the top half in the watercolor *The Devil Rebuked: The Burial of Moses* (Butlin #449, Pl. 536). This has misled some viewers (e.g., Butlin #330.532) into supposing that the old man in *Night Thoughts* 532 is likewise supposed to be Moses. Although Moses does put in an appearance much earlier in the *Night Thoughts* series,

[114]

" Or, lower,---an *Immortal* in his Crimes :

" His Crimes forgive! Forgive his Virtues, too!

" Thofe Smaller Faults; Half-Converts to the Right :   25

" Nor let me clofe Thefe Eyes, which never more

" May fee the Sun (tho' Night's defcending Scale

" Now weighs up Morn), Unpity'd, and Unbleft!

" In *Thy* Difpleafure dwells *eternal* Pain ;

" Pain, our Averfion; Pain, which ftrikes me *now* ;

" And, fince all Pain is terrible to Man,

" Tho' tranfient, Terrible; at *Thy* good Hour,

" Gently, ah gently, lay me in my Bed,

" My *Clay-cold Bed !* by Nature, now, fo near;

" By Nature, near ; ftill nearer by Difeafe!   2

" Till Then, be *This*, an Emblem of my Grave ;

" Let it out-preach the Preacher ; Every Night

" Let it out-cry the Boy at *Philip's* Ear ;

" That Tongue of Death ! That Herald of the Tomb !

" And when (the Shelter of Thy Wing implor'd)

" My *Senfes*, footh'd, fhall fink in foft Repofe ;

" O fink *this* Truth ftill deeper in my Soul,

" Suggefted by my Pillow, fign'd by *Fate*,

      " Firft,

Figure 14. Jesus, in cruciform position, superintends the
burial of old Young. *Night Thoughts* 532 (IX.114)
—*British Museum*

where his identity is clearly proven by a marked text, the only reason for imagining Moses in 532 would be the watercolor executed in the next decade for another purpose. The pictures are, however, remarkably comparable. What may be at first surprising is that the sometimes-Satanic Young should have become so conclusively reconciled with Jesus that he should appear in person to supervise Young's burial. Surely this is something that Young did not dare hope for or ask for in his *Night Thoughts*. In the case of the great Moses, the Devil himself appeared, in his capacity as anointer of princes of this world, to claim his part of the bargain. But, as the verses in the Bible marked on the mount of the picture indicate (Deut. 34.6, Jude 9), he encountered Michael, an adversary sufficient to rebuke the Devil. Michael does so by pointing on high and the Devil looks up in malicious frustration at being robbed of his prey. The viewer of *Night Thoughts* 532 has already been shown who is ultimately responsible for the Devil's ineffectuality at the death of Moses. Blake himself probably recalled that this Devil was much the same figure, further degraded, as the Devil with clenched teeth and fist who crouches in defiance in a flame of fire in *Night Thoughts* 338 (VII.66). When he reappears in the *Burial of Moses* he is outfitted with imposing dragon or bat wings and emits ten lightning bolts. But his much more furrowed face shows clearly that his growth in eminence, in authority, is taking its toll. His creatures, the Powers that Be, are almost always shown to suffer for their accession to power. But Blake doesn't waste time in feeling sorry for them. As he showed, they have had their hour and their reward.

Notes

1. The problems of this text and its exact implications are discussed in my article "A Re-View of Some Problems in Understanding Blake's *Night Thoughts*," *BIQ*, 18 (1984-85), pp. 170 and 180 n. 4.

2. All references to Blake's pictures for Young will be to John E. Grant, Edward J. Rose, Michael J. Tolley, eds.; coordinating editor David V. Erdman, *William Blake's Designs for Edward Young's Night Thoughts: A Complete Edition* (Oxford: The Clarendon Press, 1980), 2 vols.: The Plates, with an introduction. Often a complete citation of a picture will consist of a single number, from 1 to 537, to indicate its place in the whole sequence; it will then be followed by a roman numeral and an arabic number to indicate the "Night," I-IX, and the page in the printed text of *Night Thoughts* that was mounted in windows cut in all but two of the 16-x-12-inch drawing sheets used by Blake for his designs. For many years this team of editors has been engaged in developing a detailed commentary on all 537 watercolor designs, 43

engravings, and related proofs and drawings. My understanding of the designs has been much enhanced by discussing and reading draft comments by all members of the team, particularly those of Michael Tolley, who is also the best informed discussant imaginable of Blake's understanding of the Bible. In those cases about which we still have disagreements I have been made aware that there are powerful reasons for seeing the pictures differently. Recently I have also consulted with William L. Pressly, whose knowledge of British art of the later eighteenth century much exceeds my own.

The labor of Mary Lynn Johnson, Alexander Gourlay, and Carolyn Brown in condensing a thousand pages of third-draft descriptions, written while looking at the *Night Thoughts* designs, to a compendious computer analysis intended to accompany the Iowa Blake Videodisc, has been invaluable in enabling us to comprehend the designs in the mind's eye without forgetting the connections. Thanks also to Karen A. Mulhallen for letting me read her formidable 1975 University of Toronto thesis, *William Blake's Illustrations to Edward Young's Night Thoughts: Context, Christology and Composite Work*, and for extensive subsequent correspondence. In 1968-69 I spent nine months in the British Museum Department of Prints and Drawings studying the *Night Thoughts* watercolors in company with the late Thomas H. Helmstadter; comparing notes with Tom was always worthwhile because he didn't jump to conclusions. Three of the great Blake scholars, who have mastered major aspects of Blake's art, have been very helpful both in their published writings and in conversation: Martin Butlin, Robert N. Essick, and the late Sir Geoffrey Keynes. The books, essays, and conversations of Northrop Frye and Jean H. Hagstrum concerning Blake's religion have seemed to me most often in the spirit. I am most grateful to my wife, Mary Lynn Johnson, whose sense of what Blake is about is invariably sound and who has striven to reduce my speculations to some kind of form even when she had many better things to do.

3. Thirty-five designs certainly represent Jesus, and two others present figures who bear some resemblances to the Jesus figure; another, not of Jesus, illustrates a passage of Young's poem that deals with the Crucifixion. The distribution of these designs throughout the series probably gives an indication of their intended weight and significance. This seems more likely because Blake often represented Jesus where there is little or no textual call to do so, most notably in prefatory designs for the entire series. One might well refer to Blake's transposition of Young as a "Christianized *Night Thoughts*" — even if the Christ Blake presented does not agree with everybody's vision.

The number of each design in the watercolor series is followed (in parenthesis) by a roman and an arabic number which indicate the position of the design within a particular Night. Each of the designs that was engraved is additionally designated by a number according to its position in that sequence and also by the printed page number in Edwards' 1797 edition of Nights One through Four.

To list: 1 (frontispiece, Volume I of the bound watercolor series), 31E (as a title page for Night the Fourth in the 1797 edition), p. [65]; 68 (II.35), 21E, p. 37; 121 (IV.12), 34E, p. 73; 127 (IV.18); 142 (IV.33), 143 (IV.34), 38E, p. 87; 144 (IV.35); 148 (IV.39), 40E, p. 90; 261 (VI.40); 263 (VI.42); 264 (frontispiece, Volume II of the bound watercolor series); 265 (title page for Volume II of the watercolor series); 324 (VII.52); 325 (VII.53); 378 (VIII.32); 416 (VIII.70); 417 (Night IX, title page); 421 (IX.3); 431 (IX.13); 482 (IX.64); 483 (IX.65); 485 (IX.67); 488 (IX.70); 511 (IX.93); 512 (IX.94); 513 (IX.95); 518 (IX.100); 527 (IX.109); 528 (IX.110); 529 (IX.111); 531 (IX.113); 532 (IX.114); 533 (IX.115); 534 (IX.116); 535 (IX.117). To these may be added *NT* 44 (II.11), 13E, p. 23; 62 (II.29); and 125 (IV.16), 35E, p. 75—the last not of Jesus but depicting the reaction of the witness-sun *to* the Crucifixion.

In summary, there are ten certain designs of Jesus in Volume I; one, the frontispiece of Volume I, serving as the title page for Night the Fourth in the engraved version; one in Night the Second (engraved); six in Night the Fourth (2 engraved); two in Night the Sixth. There are twenty-five certain designs in Volume II: one the frontispiece of Volume II, one the title page of Volume II; two in Night the Seventh; two in Night the Eighth; and nineteen in Night the Ninth. The disproportionate number in the last Night may be a consequence of the fact that this Night is a third longer than the next longest Night. Even, however, if the three other possible designs are considered (two in Night the Second, one in Night the Fourth) there are still almost twice as many designs of Jesus in Volume II as in Volume I, despite the fact that the second volume is only eleven pages longer than the first. Such a weighting of representations of Jesus indicates that, in Night the Ninth, Blake felt the urgency to complete his essential vision.

4. Whenever possible, except for *Night Thoughts* designs, I shall refer to pictures by catalogue and plate numbers in Butlin. The actual chronology of Blake's color prints is a more complicated question than was suspected before this decade; the latest investigations of the matter are reported in Martin Butlin, "The Physicality of William Blake: The Large Color Prints of '1795'." *The Huntington Library Quarterly* 52, 1989, 1-17.

5. A splendid version of the Third Temptation (as indicated by the inscription, which quotes Matthew 4), but recalling the earlier temptations as well, was designed by M. deVos and engraved by Joannes Sadler in 1582. Satan, bat-winged, *stands* beside Jesus, and the great cliff is not barren, in contrast to *NT* 261, but the kingdoms of the earth are represented by tiny

buildings far below the enormous cliff. One of these is a sketched domed cathedral, much like Blake's miniscule St. Paul's. This Vos-Sadler engraving must have been known to Blake; it is reproduced as illustration 42 in Ernst and Johanna Lehner, *Devils, Demons, Death and Damnation*, New York: Dover, 1971. Another engraving in this series, of the Good Samaritan, combines elements Blake used in his own Good Samaritan, *NT* 68, with others he employed in the creation of Adam, *NT* 529.

  6. I have described this picture (*NT* 345) in considerable detail in "A Re-View of Some Problems in Understanding Blake's *Night Thoughts*" in *BIQ*, 18 (Winter 1984-85), pp. 171-72 and 174, chiefly with respect to the adequacy of the reproductions of the picture in various books. This account also contains observations on some significant details that are not repeated here. The recent comments on this picture by Morton D. Paley, *The Apocalyptic Sublime* (New Haven: Yale Univ. Press, 1986), esp. pp. 78-80, do not engage the problematic details. Paley is simply wrong, for example, to assert that the middle head at the left of the Beast is a "bishop," who wears a "mitre." The distinctive feature of a bishop's mitre is that it has a slice removed, resulting in pointed horns fore and aft. Blake does depict exactly this sort of bishop's hat in *NT* 233 (VI.12), but the peculiar headgear of the figure in 345 is as different as can be: its odd, bent-back, towering peak (ringed with two spike-crowns) must signify a totally different kind of regal cleric, probably non-Christian. A similar canonical hat (though less sharply pointed and adorned with a scarf in the back) is worn by the standard-bearer and his follower who appear in an Islamic ceremonial parade in an illustration attributed to Hogarth, entitled "A Procession Through the Hippodrome, Constantinople," in Aubrey de la Motraye, *Travels: Europe, Asia and Part of Africa* (London, 1723/24) (reproduced in Joseph Burke and Colin Caldwell, *Hogarth: The Complete Engravings* [London: Thames & Hudson, 1968], plate 31). This hat lacks the regal crowns that encircle the hat of Blake's figure, but perhaps Blake wished to suggest that this "Turk" has adopted an affectation modeled on that of the papal tiara. A comparable emulation is exhibited by the judge, at the right, who has added a crown to the back of his wig; such an appendage could hardly be affected with impunity in any governmental system in which judges dress with wigs! But the apparently Muslim hat reminds the viewer that Blake would not depend exclusively on Western symbolism to convey a sense of the powers that be.

  Dürer's famous series can be studied most easily in *Albrecht Dürer: Woodcuts and Wood Blocks*, ed. Walter F. Strauss (New York: Abaris, 1980), pls. 40-55. Duvet's series "L'Apocalypse Figurée," is quite clearly reproduced in Jean-E. Bershier, *Jean Duvet: Le maître à la Licorne* (Paris: Berger-Levrault, 1977), pp. 71-119. Colin Eisler's *The Master of the Unicorn: The Life and*

Work of Jean Duvet (New York: Abaris, 1977), pp. 246-93 also contains good reproductions in a smaller format. The facsimile edition of *L'Apocalypse Figurée* issued by the Eugrammia Press, London, in 1962 is almost as satisfying to look at as the original prints.

7. Lines, both vertical and horizontal, above the knob on the crown of the king positioned just above the pope suggest that Blake may have considered providing this ruler as well with the cross and ball of authority. But these pentimenti were not confirmed, probably because it would only have produced incoherence in the symbol.

8. All references, where appropriate, are to Robert N. Essick, *William Blake: A Catalogue* (Princeton: Princeton Univ. Press, 1983) and are included in the text.

Conceptually the other prints and watercolors in this group are related to the scene finally depicted in "The Simoniac Pope" (Butlin #812.*35*) of the Dante series in which an occupant of Hell reacts to a new arrival: "What, Boniface, are you here already?" (*Inferno* 19, 1. 53). Blake's annotations to Boyd's Dante (pub. 1785) were probably written down after the turn of the century, but Blake was familiar enough with the *Comedy* to write confidently about it in *The Marriage of Heaven and Hell.*

9. According to Paley, *Apocalyptic Sublime*, p. 78: "Blake's whore is vapidly ugly rather than seductive-looking, as is Dürer's." The interpretive issue is whether Blake's viewer is supposed to think that the kings of the earth are getting their money's worth; I believe that Blake wants us to think that at least the kings have reason to think they are. The taste of princes, such as, in Blake's time, the Prince of Wales, need not be supposed impeccable: Prinny might have found Dürer's Whore meagre, but Blake's adequate to his requirements.

As regards the Whore's cup, Paley clearly misunderstands Blake's purposes. Though the cup may signify "debauchery all through the *Night Thoughts* series" (80), in this picture it is "filled with the blood of the saints and with the blood of the martyrs of Jesus" (Rev. 17.6). The intoxication is cannibalism, rather than mere dissipation.

10. Milton Klonsky, *Blake's Dante: The Complete Illustrations to the Divine Comedy* (New York: Harmony Books, 1980), p. 159. This detail was overlooked by Albert S. Roe, *Blake's Illustrations to the Divine Comedy* (Princeton: Princeton Univ. Press, 1952), p. 172.

11. Henry Lesnick, "Narrative Structure and the Antithetical Vision of *Jerusalem*," in *Blake's Visionary Forms Dramatic*, ed. David V. Erdman and John E. Grant (Princeton: Princeton Univ. Press, 1970), p. 399. Erdman, *IB* 355. W.J.T. Mitchell, *Blake's Composite Art: A Study of the Illuminated*

Poetry (Princeton: Princeton Univ. Press, 1978), pp. 208-11; Morton D. Paley *The Continuing City: William Blake's Jerusalem* (Oxford: Clarendon Press, 1983), pp. 113-18. In other recent books on *Jerusalem* the plates are reproduced but the issues are at most lightly considered. Minna Doskow in *William Blake's Jerusalem: Structure and Meaning in Poetry and Picture* (Madison, N.J.: Fairleigh Dickinson Univ. Press, 1982), p. 138, regards the crowned female in plate 76 as recalling "Rahab's earlier triple crown" of plate 53, and the "phallic seven-headed serpent" as recalling "the seven spectrous ages of history, so their graphically present destructive history within fallen nature, the hermaphroditic combination of Deism...." Joanne Witke, *William Blake's Epic: Imagination Unbound* (New York: St. Martin's Press, 1986), p. 163, reminds us, as regards the Beast with Whores of *Jerusalem* 75, that the heads of the Beast represent "the seven deadly sins and its horns offenses of the ten commandments."

My discussion of the problematics of *Jerusalem* 76 will here indicate only the outlines of what I believe to be an adequate interpretation of this famous picture. Many of the varied details in the five main versions have not received critical attention. And the pictorial context for the theme of the crucifixion upon a living tree, insofar as it has been thought of at all, has been supposed to be medieval, and therefore arcane in Blake's time.

Two pictures in the popular idiom that must have been known to Blake help situate the expected effect of the symbolism of *Jerusalem* 76: Quarles' Emblem 4.14, which shows Cupid crucified upon a forked tree, attended by the patient Psyche, had passed through some twenty-five editions between its first English publication in 1634 and 1815. And the central figure of a Methodist woodcut of c. 1770 is Christ crucified upon the Tree of Life. Since this picture shows the preachers Wesley and Whitefield in action, it also connects closely with Blake's concerns in *Milton* 22, with these preachers as martyrs. I shall discuss these matters in a separate essay, to be entitled "The Vision of the Crucifixion in Blake's *Jerusalem*."

12. George Herbert, *The English Poems*, ed. C.A. Patrides (London: Dent, 1974), p. 54, ll. 202-3.

David's Recognition of the Human Face of God in Blake's Designs for the Book of Psalms

Mary Lynn Johnson

Blake's eighty watercolors on biblical subjects, executed between 1800 and 1806 for his faithful patron Thomas Butts, contain some of the artist's most highly esteemed and most often reproduced visual creations. Partly because the designs, now widely dispersed, could not conveniently be studied as a group until the 1981 publication of Martin Butlin's monumental *catalogue raisonné, The Paintings and Drawings of William Blake*; partly because they are not perfectly consistent in style and format; and partly because there is no evidence that Blake ever formulated a master plan for the series, little has been written about their cumulative effect as a critical response to the Bible.[1] Remaining to be explored in detail are the intricate and extensive interconnections among the designs, their relationship to exegetical and iconographical traditions, and their adumbration of themes developed more fully in *The Four Zoas*, the long poem Blake was struggling to compose at roughly the same time.[2] Even within shorter sequences such as pairs or small groups focusing upon a single book of the Bible or a single character, Blake forged subtle but significant motival links—with the expectation, presumably, that Butts would view the designs in biblical order, perhaps in the form of an extra-illustrated Bible.[3] One such grouping, made up of three illustrations to Psalms executed at different times, is held together by the recurring figure of Christ: *David Delivered out of Many Waters* (fig. 1; B 462, pl. 552; dated by Butlin c. 1805), *Mercy and Truth are Met together, Righteousness and Peace have Kissed each other* (fig. 2; B 463, pl. 553; dated by Butlin c. 1803), *Christ Girding Himself With Strength* (fig. 6; B 464, pl. 551;

delivered to Butts on 12 May 1805).[4] This clustering of images of Christ in Psalms is especially striking since all other depictions of Jesus in the series are based on New Testament texts. The fourth illustration to Psalms, *By the Waters of Babylon* (fig. 7; B 466, pl. 541; dated 1806 in Blake's signature at bottom right), will not be closely examined here; it stands apart as a sort of epilogue, a view of the entire collection of devotional songs from the perspective of exiles who refuse to perform the Psalms for the entertainment of their captors.

Throughout the watercolor series Blake maintains a delicate equilibrium between straightforward illustration and pictorial reinterpretation; he emphasizes meanings compatible with his own ideas while keeping up appearances as a guileless visual translator who refrains from ruffling the tranquil surface of familiar texts. When the whole set of designs is viewed in biblical sequence rather than in order of composition, it tells a story of loss and recovery familiar to readers of Blake's poetry. Beginning with the illustrations to Genesis, humankind begins to lose the divine vision, and man and woman fall into estrangement; in the fullness of time, especially in the illustrations to the Gospels, human beings awaken to a sense of shared identity with the "Divine Humanity," whom they come to recognize as an inward presence; that sense of oneness animates the human-divine community depicted in *The River of Life* (B 653, pl. 587), the concluding illustration of Revelation. At least ten of the biblical watercolors depict a transcendent visionary experience, a vision or a dream in which a human observer forms an image of a divine being. In each human-divine encounter, the manifestation of the deity—whether stern and aloof or loving and redemptive, whether seen from the rear, at a distance, or face to face—depends upon the observer's state of mind and level of imaginative energy. The visionary and the deity envisioned reflect one another, with a degree of dimness or clarity that depends upon, and reveals, the prophetic imagination's capacity to create an image of the "human form divine." Differences among these visions confirm Blake's principles that "As a man is So he Sees" (E702) and that "All deities reside in the human breast" (E38).[5]

In the succession of prophetic visions, the illustrations to Psalms mark a turning point. *David Delivered out of Many Waters* depicts a prophet *in extremis* as he catches sight of the "Divine Humanity" and brings into focus what was blurred, distorted, or left implicit in the visions of his predecessors. Blake emphasizes David's vision of a companionable human face—in contrast, for example, to Moses' terrified glimpse of the "hinder parts" of a colossal lawgiver in *God Writing upon the Ta-*

bles of the Covenant (B 448, pl. 535) and Job's awed head-on encounter with an enigmatic divine force in *Job Confessing his Presumption to God who Answers from the Whirlwind* (B 461, pl. 538). The other two designs in the series from Psalms, *Mercy and Truth are Met together* and *Christ Girding Himself with Strength* further develop the implications of David's perception and explore other aspects of the compassionate deity he envisioned.

Throughout Blake's work, in poetry as well as designs, any mysteriously remote conception of God is to be understood as delusory, dehumanizing, and alienating. To the degree that the imagination of an individual, a nation, or a historical era is enlightened, it conceives of the divine as essentially at one with the human spirit. Blake presents this insight with enormous force in *The Four Zoas*, in his compressed myth of the Seven Eyes of God. Arranging enigmatic biblical names for the divinity in a roughly chronological order, Blake delineates stages in the clarification of humanity's visionary powers.[6] Or, stated reciprocally, the Seven Eyes highlight episodes in the godhead's development as it overcomes selfishness and barbarity and accepts the necessity of self-sacrifice. Over the course of history, humankind outgrows its need to worship such anti-human deities as Lucifer and Moloch and even Jehovah, and, with the maturing of the imagination, comes to recognize true divinity in Jesus' uncorrupted and exuberant humanity.

In the watercolor series, Blake seems to have worked out the concept of a progressive revelation of the divine nature as he went along; the relative tameness of his presentation probably reflects the tentativeness of the concept, as well as a concern for satisfying Butts's expectation that familiar biblical episodes would be recognizably illustrated. Indeed, the execution of this assignment seems not to have been particularly easy for Blake. Although by 1805 he managed to establish enough links among the designs to form a synoptic pictorial commentary on the Bible, he did not make steady progress. Evidence of a hiatus of almost three years, a "painter's block" extending virtually the entire length of his residency in Felpham under the condescending patronage of William Hayley, has only recently come to light.[7] The undemanding arrangement whereby Butts apparently paid in advance for a substantial number of the watercolors to be sent from Felpham probably heightened Blake's anxiety about this unexpectedly long period of inactivity. After many postponements, apologies, and unfulfilled promises, Blake's justification for his delay was that he had spent two years reexamining his fundamental principles of art and reassessing his technical proficiency in order to regain a sense of direction after experimenting with incompatible styles (E718). The interval can of course be accounted for by many other things going on in Blake's life at the time—not least his heavy workload on projects instigated by his new patron, as well as the converging marital, religious, and professional crises that seem to have been precipitated by the strain of catering to Hayley's wishes. But the gap also hints at an untold story, the story of a Blakean christology in formation, and the story of a struggle to present fresh insights in a way that would be compatible with Blake's own views yet inoffensive to Butts.

It should be borne in mind that Butts apparently chose at least some of the subjects for illustration, while leaving their treatment entirely up to Blake.[8] In both tone and content the correspondence between artist and patron suggests that the project was conceived in a context of friendly arguments on biblical passages, with Blake of course reading black where Butts read white. Replying to Blake's first letter to him from Felpham, Butts good-naturedly chided the artist for addressing him as "Friend of My Angels," in light of "the difficulties that have unceasingly arisen to prevent my discerning clearly whether your Angels are black white or grey."[9] Butts took the opportunity of Blake's sabbatical from London to express the hope that his friend would give up "certain opinions imbibed from reading, nourished by indulgence, and rivetted by a confined Conversation"; that he would "become a Member of that Community of which you are at present, in the opinion of the Archbishop of Canterbury, but a Sign to mark the residence of dim incredulity, haggard suspicion, & bloated philosophy"; and that he would eventually become "a more valorous Champion of Revelation & humiliation than any of those who now wield the Sword of the Spirit." The jocularity of Blake's response, in which he corrected his salutation to "Friend of Religion and Order," indicates a comfortable atmosphere of give-and-take in which Blake accepted the necessity of reining in his exuberance and exercising some measure of self-censorship, even for a patron as liberal-minded and open-handed as Butts certainly was. Butts, for his part, more than met Blake half way: when at last the biblical designs were substantially completed in 1805, he began purchasing a newly-printed set of Blake's disturbing 1795 color prints, a group that included such plainly heterodox treatments of biblical subjects as *Elohim Creating Adam*, *Satan Exulting over Eve*, and *God Judging Adam*. At about the same time, Butts also commissioned the watercolor series on the Book of Job, a project that stimulated Blake to work out some of his most profound theological insights in pictorial form.

The Archbishop of Canterbury's hypothetical opinion notwithstanding, Blake approached his commission from a perspective well within the established interpretative framework of Christian expositors. He devotes more than half of the Butts series of biblical watercolors to the Gospels and Revelation, and he follows other Christian interpreters in reading the Hebrew Bible wholly in the light of the New Testament.[10] Blake's introduction of the figure of Christ into the illustrations of Psalms probably owes more to exegetical than to iconographic tradition. Psalms is of course primarily a book of poetry and music, used by both Jews and Christians in public liturgy as well as private devotion. For illustrators, it presents a special challenge because its powerful imagery, unlike the dramatic action of most books of the Bible, is not readily translatable into visual terms. As Bindman observes, without elaborating, Blake's designs for Psalms are "perhaps the most innovatory" of the biblical watercolors that he completed after the Felpham period: they "illustrate the imagery of the Psalms in a way apparently unprecedented since the Middle Ages" (141). Most illustrators of medieval psalters depicted David playing upon his harp, perhaps translated a few poetic metaphors into visual terms, and then concentrated on decorating the prayerbook with those scenes from the life of Christ which could be typologically linked to the Psalms. Few attempted psalm-by-psalm illustration or made Christ a part of David's visionary experience within his own historical period.[11] But Blake, as Bindman points out (142), emphasizes "not just ... the reactions of David, as previous illustrators of the Psalms had done, but ... the actual vision"—that is, he depicts not just a crowned lyrist with eyes turned aloft but an anguished being in the act of experiencing "a vision of Christ's mercy" that is visible also to the viewer.

Whatever Blake may have lacked in the way of visual models was more than made up for in the rich tradition of biblical exegesis available to him.[12] For Christian commentators especially, because of a profound and many-faceted association with Jesus himself, the Psalms offer one of the most fertile fields in all scripture. By Blake's time, according to Thomas Coke's *Commentary on the Holy Bible*, the Psalms had accumulated some 600 commentaries "exclusive of those which have been written on the whole body of the Scriptures, and on particular Psalms."[13] Within the scope of this essay, it would obviously be impossible to provide an accurate layperson's summary of the "precritical" state of biblical hermeneutics in Britain in Blake's time.[14] Suffice it to say that David's authorship of at least most of the Psalms as well as his prophetic authority were generally accepted by Protestants and Catholics alike but rejected by Deists.[15] Robert Lowth's aesthetic evaluation of the book as a work of poetry had been largely assimilated into the mainstream of commentary. Before the impact of the German "higher criticism" was widely felt in England in the middle of the nineteenth century, virtually any Christian expositor whose work Blake is likely to have encountered would have unhesitatingly read the Psalms as David's own collection of prophecies or typological prefigurations of Jesus' life, death, and resurrection.

All books of the Old Testament, read typologically, were of course thought to contain prophecies of Christ's coming. But the Psalms are recognized as holding a special place in Jesus' life and ministry. In the words of the perceptive late-eighteenth-century commentator George Horne, the book "appears to have been the Manual of the Son of God," by which Horne meant primarily that it was Jesus' hymnbook and prayerbook.[16] Even Satan, in tempting Jesus, quoted from Psalms (Matt. 4.6; Ps. 91.11-12). Jesus wove lines from Psalms into the Beatitudes (Ps. 37.11, 24.4-5; cf. Matt. 5.5,8), referred to it in rebuking the Pharisees (Ps. 110.l; cf. Matt. 22.41-46), and quoted from it on the cross (Ps. 22.1, 31.5). As Horne puts it, Jesus "chose to conclude his life, to solace himself in his greatest agony, and at last to breathe out his soul, in the Psalmist's form of words, rather than his own" (vi). After the Resurrection he "opened [the] understanding" of his followers to a christocentric interpretation of Psalms by elucidating what was "written in the law of Moses, and in the prophets, and in the psalms, concerning me" (Luke 24.44-45).

The master's method of exposition was quickly adopted throughout the early church and applied to texts not explicitly mentioned by Jesus. The Gospel writers emphasized the association of Psalms 22 and 69 with the Crucifixion; after Pentecost, Peter converted three thousand by citing Psalm 16 as evidence that David, "being a prophet," "spake of the resurrection of Christ" (Acts 2.25-36); and Paul associated Psalm 18 with his own mission (Romans 15.9). Blake, with his well-thumbed Bible, could scarcely have been unaware of these and countless other Christian readings of the Psalms. The text supporting the prophetic intent of "the sweet singer of Israel" is II Samuel 23.2-3, "the last words of David," in which the psalmist proclaims that "The Spirit of the Lord spake by me, and his word was in my tongue." Opinions differed as to whether David knowingly predicted Jesus' messianic role through the inspiration of the Holy Ghost, unconsciously prefigured Christ, or merely wrote of contemporary events which take on additional meaning for Christians, as Horne states, "from a sense of accommodation, as passages may be quoted from poems or histories merely human, for the illustration of truths of which their authors never thought" (x). But virtually all Christians considered David and Jesus to be intimately and inseparably related—even identified—as type to antitype, prophecy to fulfillment, figurative representation to actual embodiment.

For Blake, however, David stands at an uncertain boundary between history and prophecy. On the one hand, he is a poet and prophet who transcended his own time to express an inkling of a loving and compassionate deity, envisioned by Blake as Jesus. On the other hand, within his own historical period, he is a vengeful warrior-chieftain, ruthless in victory, insatiable in conquest. Blake consistently seeks to liberate the visionary David from the historical David. He invariably emphasizes the side of David that is compatible with the description of the psalmist that Blake placed in the mouth of Ezekiel in *The Marriage of Heaven and Hell*, 12-13:

> The philosophy of the east taught the first principles of human perception   some nations held one principle for the origin & some another[.] we of Israel taught that the Poetic Genius (as you now call it) was the first principle and all the others merely derivative, which was the cause of our despising the Priests & Philosophers of other countries, and prophecying that all Gods would at last be proved to originate in ours & to be the tributaries of the Poetic Genius[.] it was this. that our great poet King David desired so fervently & invokes so patheticly, saying by this he conquers enemies & governs kingdoms.... (E39)

Blake's Ezekiel implies that David's distinction as a conqueror and ruler stems from his ability as a poet to recognize, underneath the militaristic trappings of his tribal deity, the sacredness and universality of the spark of divinity within humankind, through the power of imagination which Blake identified with the Holy Spirit, or the Poetic Genius. In *All Religions are One*, a tractate usually dated 1788, Blake made the same point in his own voice: "The Religions of all Nations are derived from each Nation's different reception of the Poetic Genius which is every where call'd the Spirit of Prophecy" (E1). If David was a man after God's own heart, it was not because of the morality of his actions but because of the power of his imaginative insight.[17] Accordingly, in illustrating the Psalms, Blake emphasizes situations and metaphors that link David with Christ, rather than the deeds and impulses that render some of his lines, in the opinion of John Wesley, unfit for the mouths of Christian congregations. Of

Figure 1. In Blake's watercolor drawing *David Delivered out
of Many Waters*, the prophet attains a "state of human
consciousness that invokes Jesus's presence"; c. 1805, 41.5 x
34.8 cm.—*Tate Gallery*, London

David's public actions, Blake takes up only two, the challenge to Goliath and the forgiveness of Absalom. Both are compatible with Blake's characterization of David as a Christian prophet: in *Goliath Cursing David* (B 457, pl. 525), he is a stripling facing up to a monster in a daring act of faith; in *David Pardoning Absalom* (B 459, pl. 540), he is a loving father reconciling himself with a perfidious and undeserving son. These designs depict a Christlike boldness and strength rather than what Blake would have seen as the earthly military prowess and kingly power celebrated in many of the Psalms and in the historical books of Kings and Chronicles.

Blake's keynote design for the Psalms is the picture known as *David Delivered out of Many Waters*, to which Butlin adds "He Rode upon the Cherubim" as a subtitle (fig. 1; B 462, pl. 552). The vision depicted in this design opens a messianic sequence that is continued in *Mercy and Truth are Met together, Righteousness and Peace have Kissed each other*, and *Christ Girding Himself with Strength*. As Butlin notes, the traditional title for David's vision, *David Delivered out of Many Waters*, is first recorded in Rossetti's 1880 catalogue, unaccompanied by descriptive notes. The alternate title, "He Rode Upon the Cherubim," which comes from the 1853 Foster's catalogue for the sale of part of Butts's collection, makes plural the "cherub" in the presumed text, Psalm 18.10, but it does not really fit the details of the design. Unlike the deity in *Ezekiel's Wheels* (B 468, pl. 542), who is supported by the Living Creatures, Jesus is floating above, not riding upon, the cherubim—somewhat in the manner of the deity in Psalm 104.3-4 "who maketh the clouds his chariot: who walketh upon the wings of the wind: who maketh his angels spirits; his ministers a flaming fire," or Milton's Christ who rides "on the wings of cherubim/ Uplifted" (*PL* VII.218-19).[18] Butlin suggests that this title may reflect a lost inscription of the type that appears on many of the old mats and mounts.[19] If Psalm 18 is indeed the text that Blake had in mind, his illustration is a thoroughly antithetical reconsideration of its implications, for this thanksgiving after battle is one of David's most distressingly warlike acts of worship.

Although allegorizing biblical commentators were of course able to extract edification from any biblical passage before them, nothing in the literal text of Psalm 18 provides any basis whatsoever for Blake's interpretation of David as a proto-Christian. For all its magnificent imagery, and despite the large body of commentary that associates it with messianic prophecy, Psalm 18 revolves around what Blake called "War & Princedom & Victory & Blood" (*FZ* I.311, p. 11, E306; cf. *J* 4.32). It celebrates the special favor a fierce war-god bestows upon his chosen tribal chieftain. It would not be lost upon Blake that the entire psalm appears almost verbatim in II Samuel 22, as part of history, not prophecy.[20] The "floods" and "snares" that encompass David are transparent metaphors for his enemies in Saul's camp. The military situation is even described in the headnote that is a traditional part of the text, and the temporal nature of David's distress is repeatedly emphasized (Ps. 18.3, 17-18, and 37-45). Throughout, the psalmist represents himself as a merciless warrior who seeks divine aid for the primary purpose of grinding his enemies into the dust, and he glories in his own righteousness:

> The Lord rewarded me according to my righteousness; according to the cleanness of my hands hath he recompensed me. (Ps. 18.20; cf. 21-24)

For the David of Psalm 18, the operative sign of divine favor is the enhancement of his military superiority by a God who "teacheth my hands to war" (Ps. 18.34; cf. 39). In victory, David prides himself on giving no quarter: "I have wounded them that they were not able to rise" (Ps. 18:38). In his view, both God and his champion are properly indifferent to the sufferings of the vanquished:

> They cried, but there was none to save them, even unto the Lord,
>   but he answered them not.
> Then did I beat them small as the dust before the wind:
> I did cast them out as the dirt in the streets. (Ps. 18.41-42).

The divinity whom the David of Psalm 18 has created in his own image is closely akin to the imposter that Blake caricatured as "Old Nobodaddy," an idol who loves "hanging & drawing & quartering/ Every bit as well as war & slaughter" (E499). To David as warrior, God's presence is terrifying and mysterious. David's imagery of fire and lightning parallels that of Moses' experience on Sinai:

> There went up a smoke out of his nostrils, and fire out of
>   his mouth devoured: coals were kindled by it.
> He bowed the heavens also, and came down: and darkness
>   was under his feet.
> And he rode upon a cherub, and did fly: yea, he did fly upon
>   the wings of the wind.
> He made darkness his secret place; his pavilion round about
>   him were dark waters and thick clouds of the skies.
> At the brightness that was before him his thick clouds
>   passed, hail stones and coals of fire....

Yea, he sent out his arrows, and scattered them; and he shot
out lightnings, and discomfited them. (Ps. 18.8-14)

An appropriate Blakean commentary on these verses might be drawn from
an inscription on a later design: "God out of Christ is a Consuming Fire"
(E691), an apothegm adapted from Deuteronomy 4.24 and Hebrews 12.18.
Blake addresses through illustration the same problem that Isaac
Watts attempted to address, in his quite different way, in his 1719 book of
translations and imitations:

> I could never persuade myself that the best Way to raise a devout
> Frame in *plain Christians* was to bring *a King* or *a Captain* into
> their Churches, and let him lead and dictate the Worship in his own
> Style of Royalty, or in the Language of a Field of Battel.[21]

Unlike the David of Psalm 18, who according to the headnote is fighting
his battles during the reign of Saul, the David of Blake's design is already
a mature king, bearded and crowned, about the same age as in *David Pardoning Absalom* (B 459, pl. 540). A troubled visionary rather than an
embattled captain, Blake's David concentrates his whole being on his
compelling need for spiritual deliverance; he is a spiritual conqueror
whose nadir of suffering and defeat is also spiritual. We see him at the ultimate point of despair, in a night dark of the soul comparable to Job's, as
he undergoes a redemptive experience that quickens his imagination and
reveals to him the human face of God, the face of Christ, the Poetic Genius.

The metaphors for David's state of desperation are represented visually in a night scene on a storm-tossed ocean. Seen from the rear, he
looks up slightly to his left as he sinks in waves up to his chest. His
outstretched arms are bound with knotted ropes, the "snares of death" in
verse 5.[22] No mighty *deus ex machina* in battle array rides to the rescue,
mounted upon a cherub, to attack David's enemies. Instead, the merciful
figure of Christ appears, open-armed. Although he may appear to be on
the verge of descending physically to David's rescue, his primary role as
savior is to offer him spiritual succor as a comforter and an inspiration;
his pose resembles the one he assumes (seen from the rear) in *Jerusalem*
31 (35). As Albert S. Roe observes, Blake repeated the scene of open-
armed communion with the Savior in Albion's contemplation of the
Crucified Christ in *Jerusalem* 76 and in "Dante Adoring Christ," number
90 of the Dante series.[23] On Jesus' side, this open-armed gesture of course
brings to mind the cross, as well as a calming action and a reaching out,
an invitation; on David's side, it is a floundering gesture of panic that

becomes an expression of supplication and of self-forgetful adoration. The mutuality of the gesture signifies a movement toward an embrace, an act of reconciliation.[24]

The seven angelic figures between David and Christ, as Michael J. Tolley first pointed out, are analogous to the Seven Eyes of God in Blake's later poetry.[25] The Seven appear in differing configurations at intervals throughout Blake's biblical watercolor series—in a mandorla, in *God Blessing the Seventh Day* (B 434, pl. 511); in a vortex, in *Job Confessing his Presumption to God Who Answers from the Whirlwind* (B 461, pl. 538), and again, with two presumed out of sight over the top of the design, in *The Conversion of Saul* (B 506, pl. 575); here, they are aligned in the rank and file of a matrix, or, in Bindman's words, "a continuous rhythmical row" (141). Clyde R. Taylor notes that their "uplifted wings form reminiscences of the arches, vaults, and spires of a Gothic cathedral" (83). With mouths open, the Seven are presumably singing, as the figure of Christ hovering over them apparently regulates their orderly arrangement and floats upon their field of energy.

What Blake depicts in *David Delivered out of Many Waters* is a conception of David, and of David's God, that can be glimpsed only in texts other than Psalm 18. In a letter to Butts of 25 April 1803, for example, Blake mentions that just before he received Butts's letter he was reading Psalm 139 (E729). Although in that psalm David says of his enemies, "I hate them with perfect hatred" (Ps. 139.22), he is speaking of the wicked in general, not specifically of his military enemies; most of the psalm deals with God's omnipresent and compassionate understanding: "If I make my bed in hell, behold, thou art there" (Ps. 139.8). In this same spirit David opens Psalm 130 with "Out of the depths have I cried unto thee." Even more pertinent is Psalm 69, the New Testament's richest source of what the apostles took to be allusions to Christ. Indeed, were it not for "He Rode upon the Cherubim" in the 1853 Butts sale catalogue, we might well take *David Delivered out of Many Waters* to be an illustration of the beginning of Psalm 69. Or rather, Blake blends the imagery of the two psalms, correcting David's errors in Psalm 18 by superimposing upon his worst fantasies his genuinely imagined visions:

> Save me, O God; for the waters are come in unto my soul.
> I sink in deep mire, where there is no standing; I am come
>   into deep waters, where the floods overflow me
>   ....
> O God, thou knowest my foolishness; and my sins are not
>   hid from thee.

....

Deliver me out of the mire, and let me not sink; let me be
delivered from them that hate me, and out of the deep
waters.

Let not the waterflood overflow me, neither let the deep
swallow me up, and let not the pit shut her mouth upon
me.

Hear me, O Lord; for thy lovingkindness is good; turn unto
me according to the multitude of thy tender mercies.

And hide not thy face from thy servant; for I am in trouble:
hear me speedily.

Draw nigh unto my soul, and redeem it: deliver me because
of mine enemies.

Thou hast known my reproach, and my shame, and my dis-
honour: mine adversaries are all before thee.

Reproach hath broken my heart; and I am full of heaviness:
and I looked for some to take pity, but there was none;
and for comforters, but I found none.

(Ps 69.14-20)

The David of Psalm 69 is not self-righteous; he sinks from his own
"heaviness" into "the deep." Rather than showing no mercy for his enemies, as in Psalm 18, he expresses his own need to obtain mercy. With
no sense that he deserves favor, he seeks the face of his savior as a friend
and comforter. Even though in the remainder of Psalm 69 David reverts to
his usual belligerent preoccupations, he has said enough to show that he
is looking for the "Divine Humanity" in the right spirit; he is capable of
seeking the true God where he is likely to be found.

Unlike Moses in *God Writing upon the Tables of the Covenant* (B
448, pl. 535) and Ezekiel in *Ezekiel's Wheels* (B 468, pl. 542), who are
diminutive in comparison with their visions, David is on the same scale
as his deity. Moses has chosen not to continue conversing with God "face
to face, as a man speaketh unto his friend" (Ex. 33.11), and so he must be
hidden in a "clift of the rock" for his own protection while God grants his
request to witness a manifestation of his full glory. But David looks directly into the eyes of his deliverer, as Jesus responds to his plea to "hide
not thy face from thy servant" (Ps. 69.17). This direct, certain vision of
David's is the foundation for Peter's sermon at Pentecost: "For David
speaketh concerning him, I foresaw the Lord always before my face, for he
is on my right hand, that I should not be moved" (Acts 2.25; cf. Ps.
16.8). In short, Blake depicts the merciful and empathic response to the

human situation of a deity conceived within the imagination of a sufferer who, like Albion at the end of *Jerusalem*, has transcended his own self-pity. David's experience marks a breakthrough in the sequence of visionary experiences that for the first time admits the presence of Jesus into the visions of the prophets. David's troubled glimpse from the depths of Jesus' face in the supernal realm—partially mediated by the cherubim or Seven Eyes—opens the way to the more intimate divine-human relationships and the clearer insights explored in Blake's New Testament pictures.

The next design in biblical order is the illustration to Psalm 85, entitled *Mercy and Truth are Met together, Righteousness and Peace have Kissed each other* (fig. 2), in which the prophetic insight of David begins to be fulfilled, and Christ prepares to come into the world.[26] Believed to prophesy the incarnation of Christ, Psalm 85 is in the Church of England one of the traditional readings of the Psalter for Christmas Day.[27] If the meaning of Christ's appearance as savior in *David Delivered out of Many Waters* is immediately understandable on an emotional level, the meaning of his presence as one of the embracing figures dominating the bottom third of *Mercy and Truth are Met together* certainly is not. Without Blake's inscribed reference to the text, Psalm 85.10-11, it would be difficult to identify Jesus and his partner as Peace and Righteousness, who have "kissed each other," or to recognize the angels who meet at the top of the design as Mercy and Truth.

The language and imagery of the psalm raise some intriguing questions that Blake may have taken into account in designing the watercolor illustration. The opening reference to the return from captivity as an event in the past, together with the sudden infusion of the present tense in the allegorical passage beginning with verse 10, challenged some commentators to produce alternate translations in an attempt to make the time period consistent; Blake doubtless would have been on the side of those who believed simply that the psalm transcends time. Another challenge for commentators was the psalmist's paradoxical characterization of God as one who has "turned thyself from the fierceness of thine anger," while at the same time pleading with him to "cause thine anger toward us to cease" (85.3, 4). Blake sets the scene in heaven, with an angelic court adoring a robed and white-bearded deity. In the cold formality of Blake's almost oppressively symmetrical composition, this conventional image of the deity, benign and grandfatherly, occupies the ostensible position of power in the upper two-thirds of the picture, while the kinetic energy of the design is concentrated in the kiss below. With a large book open

Figure 2. In *Mercy and Truth are Met together,*
Righteousness and Peace have Kissed each other, the
downward gaze of God is one of several devices directing
attention to Jesus, who identifies himself here with the human
virtues of Mercy and Peace; c. 1803, 43 x 37.5 cm.
—*Victoria and Albert Museum*, London

across his knees, suggesting a scene of judgment, the deity is elevated on a four-stepped pyramidal dais and framed by a Gothic canopy formed by the heads and wings of twelve hovering angels. The downcast eyes and lowered heads of the deity and his court appear to be aimed in the general direction of the book. But the pensive gaze of the deity himself seems to extend beyond the top of the page, as if taking in the strange embrace at the foot of the stairs.

The viewer passes quickly from the bland, almost vacant face of the deity—far and away the least animated divine face in the entire biblical series—and the virtually undifferentiated mass of sweet-faced angels, to puzzle over the surprising kiss. In addition to the downward focus of almost all the sight-lines in the upper portion of the design, Blake uses several other devices to draw attention to the embrace, the most striking of which—next to the sheer unexpectedness of Christ's participation—is the extreme awkwardness of the couple's pose. Translating a poetic metaphor into visual terms, Blake jolts the viewer's sense of anatomical verisimilitude and violates artistic decorum by introducing Manneristic tensions into a composition as symmetrical and orderly as a scene from Fra Angelico. With Jesus turning to face the viewer and his partner turning in the other direction, they reach with difficulty around a central cross, each to place a hand on the other's back. Both figures twist their upper bodies away from their lower bodies, each leaning at an obtuse angle backward from outwardly thrust hips, with legs bent double to brace their full weight inconveniently upon straining toes—for Jesus, the toes of both feet; for his partner, apparently only one foot, with the other probably outstretched (redrawn from a bent-back position visible as pentimenti). In contrast, the topmost angels in the divine court fly easily toward each other to meet above the head of the deity and gracefully form the peak of the Gothic arch framing him. A triangular array of beams of light radiates from the presence of the deity toward the outstretched bodies of the embracing couple, sharply silhouetted against the narrowing stairs of the dais. Their bodies, separated except for the single point of contact at which their lips meet in the tentative, even gingerly kiss, form a broad-based triangle that shares its longest line with the base of the dais and reaches a flattened apex just under the horizontal line of the top stair. A downward-turned smaller triangle formed by the deity's outspread knees and crossed legs narrows to an imaginary point just above the heads of the embracing couple and serves as an additional reinforcement of the emphasis upon their kiss. The torque of this embrace, as odd in its insistently nonsexual way as the ambiguous embrace of the central couple on the title page of *The Marriage of Heaven and Hell* (*IB* 98) and the couple in *Jerusalem* 28 (*IB* 307), rivets the viewer's attention.[28] The closest analogue elsewhere in Blake's work is the abrupt and problematic appearance of Christ in Book II of the *Night Thoughts* designs, and the strangeness of the poses and situations that Blake contrives in that series for many of the human figures who represent Young's metaphors. Such personifications in designs for a secular author are unsettling enough, but in a biblical illustration, especially when the figures are awkwardly posed and when one of them is represented as Christ, the effect is to break down a familiar interpretative framework and force the viewer to begin anew. Clearly, Jesus is meant to be noticed: what is this familiar figure doing in such an unfamiliar situation?

Psalm 85 is the basis for the myth of the "deliberation of the Trinity," developed in a famous sermon for the feast of the Annunciation by Bernard of Clairvaux; according to Gertrud Schiller, this myth of a divine council inspired Mechthild von Magdeburg's vision of the Son's offer to redeem mankind, and that vision in turn inspired the very few artists who have been drawn to the subject. As Schiller summarizes Bernard's sermon, the four original human virtues of Mercy, Peace, Righteousness, and Truth "could only work in concert," but they came into conflict after the Fall, with Mercy and Peace taking humanity's part against the denunciations of Righteousness and Truth, or Justice:

> They appealed to Christ to settle their differences; he decided that the death of an innocent for the sake of mankind would satisfy all four virtues. Veritas searched on earth for an innocent man and Misericordia in heaven for an angel prepared to undertake the sacrifice. Both returned ... with their mission unfulfilled, whereupon ... [Christ] offered himself for the sacrifice....[29]

Horne's commentary, especially since it is one that Blake might actually have known, is even more to the point. Referring to Bernard and to a sermon by Launcelot Andrewes, Horne summarizes the allegory as follows:

> These four divine attributes parted at the fall of Adam, and met again at the birth of Christ. Mercy was ever inclined to save man, and Peace could not be his enemy; but Truth exacted the performance of God's threat,—"The soul that sinneth, it shall die"; and Righteousness could not but give to every one his due.... Now, there is no religion upon earth, except the Christian, which can satisfy the demands of all these claimants, and restore an union between them.... When Christ appeared in our nature, the promise

was fulfilled, and "Truth sprang out of the earth."... And this could only happen at the birth of Jesus, in whom "the tender Mercy of our God visited us, and who is the Truth; who is made unto us Righteousness, and who is our Peace." (354-55)

In Blake's design, the awkwardness of the cross-centered embrace reflects the tension of the text, the tension of long separation—a tension captured by Milton in several of the italicized additions to the Hebrew text that he made in his poetic translation of the passage:

> Mercy and Truth *that long were miss'd*
> Now *joyfully* are met,
> *Sweet* Peace and Righteousness have kiss'd,
> *And hand in hand are set.*
> Truth from the earth, *like to a flow'r,*
> Shall bud and blossom *then,*
> And Justice from her heav'nly bow'r
> Look down *on mortal men.*

The conceit of a heavenly reconciliation appears also in one of Blake's *Night Thoughts* designs, in which male and female figures illustrate the marked line: "Stern *Justice* and soft-smiling *Love,* embrace" (fig. 3, *NT* 123 [IV.14]).[30] For several pages Young elaborates on the council in heaven, loosely based on Psalm 85, and the sacrifice that reconciles without compromising the virtues of the "consummate, absolute" God. Infidels, in contrast, "set at odds Heaven's jarring Attributes;/ And with one Excellence, another wound;/ Maim Heaven's Perfection, break it's equal Beams./ Bid *Mercy* triumph over—God himself," for "A God *All* Mercy, is a God unjust" (*NT* 124 [IV.15]). Eventually, paraphrasing Psalm 24, Young builds up to a passage that Blake illustrates with a scene of Resurrection in which he depicts Christ from the rear (*NT* 127 [IV.18]), in a pose he later used in *The Ascension* (B 505, pl. 574) for the biblical watercolor series.

This same tension, of course, expressed as a conflict between Mercy and Justice, animates the deliberations between Father and Son in Book III of *Paradise Lost*, and Blake was to return to this subject in his two sets of illustrations to *Paradise Lost*, in the design for Book III known as "Christ Offers to Redeem Man" (B 529:3, pl. 634; B 536:3, pl. 647). In the Milton design, the Father is on the judgment seat, but we cannot know his expression; his head is bowed, his body slumped, his face hidden from view by the exultant, energetic figure of Jesus, who springs up with arms outstretched in a cruciform gesture. As Stephen C. Behrendt notes, this is

(14)

Thou moſt indulgent, moſt tremendous Power!
Still more tremendous, for thy wondrous Love!
That arms, with Awe more awful, thy Commands;
And foul Tranſgreſſion dips in ſevenfold Night.
How our Hearts tremble at thy Love immenſe?
In Love immenſe, inviolably Juſt!
Thou, rather than thy *Juſtice* ſhou'd be ſtain'd,
Didſt ſtain the *Croſs*; and Work of Wonders, far
The greateſt, that thy Deareſt far, might bleed.

Bold Thought! ſhall I dare ſpeak it? or repreſs?
Shou'd Man more *execrate*, or *boaſt* the Guilt,
Which rouz'd ſuch Vengeance? which ſuch Love inflam'd?
O'er Guilt, (how mountainous?) with outſtretcht Arms,
Stern *Juſtice*, and ſoft-ſmiling *Love*, embrace,
Supporting, in full Majeſty, thy Throne,
When ſeem'd its Majeſty to need Support; —
Or *That*, or *Man* inevitably loſt?
What, but the Fathomleſs of Thought divine,
Cou'd labour ſuch Expedient from Deſpair,

And

Figure 3. Like *Mercy and Truth are Met together*, a scene of heavenly reconciliation: *Night Thoughts* 123 (IV.14) —*British Museum*

one of Blake's unmistakably positive representations of self-sacrifice.[31] Instead of alluding to the Crucifixion through the emblem of the cross, as in the illustration to Psalm 85, Blake simply depicts Jesus in a pose that he associated not only with the Crucifixion but also with the Resurrection, in *Night Thoughts* 127, and, as Behrendt points out, with the Ascension; the gesture of outspread arms appears also in Christ's rescue of David in *David Delivered out of Many Waters*. By contrast, as Bette Charlene Werner observes, in depicting the Father, Blake "emphasizes the severity of the figure and perhaps intimates the sterility of Milton's conception of heaven by picturing the Father seated on a massive and block-like throne."[32] To a lesser degree, this same contrast between a cold, sterile Father and a passionate, energetic Son is implied in *Mercy and Truth are Met together, Righteousness and Peace have Kissed each other*, where Christ plays the role of one of the virtues rather than acting as the judge who settles their dispute. Since Jesus and his partner are so much more prominent than the embracing angels at the top of the design, and since the quatrefoil cross suggests a union of four equal members, the viewer is also invited to extend the roles played by the couple at the bottom of the design, to have Jesus represent both Peace and Mercy and his partner both Righteousness and Truth. Through his gesture of reconciliation, as he identifies himself with both Peace and Mercy and embraces Righteousness and Truth, Blake's Jesus "marries" heaven and earth. In this kiss ratifying their union, or reunion, both the Incarnation and the Crucifixion are implicit.

Whether Blake derived his imagery only from Milton or also incorporated suggestions from such biblical commentators as Horne, the allegorical conflict and its resolution surely influenced not only his designs for Young, Milton, and the Bible but also his poetic myths of the Four Zoas and the Council that elects Seven Eyes of God before it finds one who will willingly die for the guilty. Traces of its influence may also be surmised in the four virtues of "Mercy, Pity, Peace, and Love" who form "The Divine Image" of *Songs of Innocence*. As Horne transmits the myth, the reunion of the four virtues reconciles the conflict among the divine attributes but does not fully resolve the deeper tension it betrays between Father and Son. Along with Gnostic doctrine, this version of the myth perhaps helps to account for Blake's often-quoted exclamation in "A Vision of the Last Judgment": "Thinking as I do that the Creator of this World is a very Cruel Being & being a Worshipper of Christ I cannot help saying the Son O how unlike the Father First God Almighty comes with a Thump on the Head Then Jesus Christ comes with a balm to heal it" (E565).

The upraised hair of the figure who embraces Jesus in "Mercy and Truth" suggests, perhaps, an abrupt descent or an ecstatic transport, as of someone barely managing a kiss on the fly, as it were. The hair and face of this celestial being strongly resemble those of the central spirit in *David Delivered out of Many Waters*, the only one of the Seven who is not symmetrically placed opposite a counterpart of the same age and type. But unlike this figure, the being who embraces Jesus cannot be taken to be masculine; although doubtless meant to be seen as transcending gender, she is perceived as feminine in the context of the embrace. Traditionally, when Christ is represented as a lover, the reference is to Christ and his church, or to Christ and the human soul. But in Blake's picture Christ has left the sterner virtues of Truth and Righteousness to be embodied by his more ethereal partner, while he fully identifies himself with the earthly realm, with Mercy and Peace, with the virtues that take the side of humanity. The embrace then suggests an even broader and fuller range of reconciliations than that celebrated in the text of the psalm—a reconciliation not only among the four divine virtues but also, as the early commentators had noted, between God and humanity, heaven and earth, and, in Blake's addition, between male and female, rather than the embracing "sisters" of earlier tradition.

The symbolism of the embrace is complicated by Blake's use of a cross of the type known as a Teutonic cross or, in heraldry, a cross patée or cross formée; that is, a "broad-footed" cross with equal vanes widening at the ends.[33] The four triangles of the Teutonic cross exhibit what J.E. Cirlot calls "a centripetal tendency" in the conjunction of opposites;[34] in relation to major motifs in Blake's later poetry the design of the cross possibly suggests four forces passing into one another through a single vortex. In the context of the passage in Psalms, the equal members suggest Mercy, Truth, Righteousness, and Peace, as they meet in the cross, which stands for the sacrifice necessary to bring them together. But the cross symbolizing this fourfold union is at the same time a rigid gold ceremonial object that stands between those who are reconciled, partially blocking their embrace. The central placement of this stylized form of the cross, made of gold and embellished with raised edges, suggests an altar; the slight mound on which it rests may allude to Calvary—or, negatively, to the curvature of earth, the Mundane Shell, or the cross-surmounted orb which signifies papal authority.

In a New Testament counterpart to this design, the watercolor known as *The Holy Family* (fig. 4; B 471, pl. 556)—not associated with any particular text—most of the tensions of Psalm 85 are resolved. As Anne Kostelanetz Mellor has noted in connection with one level of her interpretation, "the scene signifies the willingness of Christ to assume a human body and to sacrifice himself in order to redeem mankind from the state of Satan."[35] As with the illustration of Psalm 85, the figures in *The Holy Family* are arranged in a formal tableau: wings of three symmetrically placed guardian angels form a Gothic canopy and side-pieces to set off the central figures of Mary and the infant Jesus.[36] This central image of Madonna and Child is flanked by the figures of Joseph and (presumably) Elizabeth; at the bottom of the design, the infant John the Baptist, described by Mellor simply as "a child," reclines among flowers and plays with a lamb, as in Blake's design for the second plate of "Spring" (*IB* 64) as Mellor notes.

The essential elements of the illustration of Psalm 85 are balanced, point for point, in the Gospel scene. Whereas in the Old Testament design the Father holds a book of judgment on his lap, Mary holds Jesus in a cruciform pose, stretching out his arms and resting his feet, crossed at the ankles, on the central point where his mother's legs are crossed at the shins. Rather than the golden cross of Psalm 85, which partially impedes the scene of reconciliation, Mary displays the living cross, her Son offering his Incarnation to the viewer in an act of acceptance and of blessing. The more awkward poses of the figures beside Mary, leaning their upper bodies toward the child but resting most of their weight on their toes, with their knees braced outward, somewhat resemble those of Jesus and Truth in the illustration to Psalm 85, but here the awkwardness is caused by Joseph's and Elizabeth's apparently self-conscious effort to maintain a contrived symmetry in the design. At the bottom, occupying a position analogous to that of Jesus and the allegorical figure in the illustration of Psalm 85, John, kissing the Lamb, embodies and fulfills the final line of Psalm 85, which has traditionally been interpreted as a prophecy of his mission: "Righteousness shall go before him; and shall set us in the way of his steps" (Ps. 85.13). The sacrificial implications of "The Holy Family," emphasized by the Lamb and the cruciform posture of Christ, are reinforced by the thoughtful, otherworldly expression of Mary, the contemplative solemnity of Joseph and Elizabeth, and the sorrowful poses of the praying and protecting angels.

David Bindman has called attention to the "hieratic quality" of many of the watercolor designs, achieved in part by Blake's placement of a

Figure 4. *The Holy Family* is Blake's New Testament
counterpart to *Mercy and Truth are Met together*, but while in
fig. 2 a Teutonic cross impedes reconciliation between the
embracing figures, in this watercolor Mary displays Christ
himself as a living cross; c. 1805, 37.8 x 32.6 cm.
—*The Cleveland Museum of Art*, purchase from the
John L. Severance Fund

"rigidly frontal" figure on "the central axis of the composition" to create a "rigidly centralized symmetry" (38). Both *Mercy and Truth are Met together* and *The Holy Family* exemplify this kind of symmetry, but not nearly so much as the final design in the Messianic sequence from Psalms, *Christ Girding Himself with Strength* (fig. 5; B 464, pl. 551), which is based on Psalm 93. Here Christ, enthroned in austere majesty, is seen securely possessed of his kingdom. For modern scholars, still under the sway of Hermann Gunkel's and S. Mowinckel's epoch-making investigations early in this century of Ugaritic, Babylonian, Assyrian, Canaanite, and other middle eastern textual parallels, the most interesting thing about Psalm 93 is its position as one of the Enthronement or "Ascension-Psalms," interpreted as formulaic remnants of a cultic new year's festival centering on the elevation of the king and renewal of the world at the time of the autumnal equinox.[37] Even in Blake's time, as John Rogerson points out with reference to an anonymous review of a German study of Psalms by J.C.K. Nachtigall, "Full justice was done to this early attempt to place the Psalms in the context of an annual festival of Zion commemorating the bringing of the ark to Jerusalem by David" (160). In *On the Nature and Occasion of Psalm and Prophecy*, published in 1800 by Joseph Johnson, James Hurdis cites imagery from Psalms 85 and 93 to support his thesis that all the psalms were sung and danced during an autumnal festival celebrating the return of the rains. But Horne (395), Coke (206), and mainstream Christian commentators continued to read Psalms 93 through 100 according to Jewish and Christian tradition, as a prophecy of the Messianic age, and it is this reign that Blake depicts.

The scene is one of Christ in majesty, Christ as sovereign and judge. He is seated on a two-stepped foundation raised above the "floods" (thrice mentioned), "the noise of many waters," and the "mighty waves of the sea." Whereas in *David Delivered out of Many Waters* the stormy waves are on the point of overwhelming the psalmist when Jesus arrives to rescue him, in *Christ Girding Himself with Strength* the waves know their master. Modern scholars emphasize Yahweh's assumption of his kingship "after his victory in the battle with the mythical monsters of the primeval deep,"[38] and Blake seems to have intuited this primitive level of meaning in his handling of the roiling ocean.

Blake's Christ the Judge sits calmly reading a large limp book on his lap, which he holds open (and perhaps prevents from slipping) with the outspread fingers of his left hand, while his right hand, also with fingers outspread, touches his sash. Contrary to the traditional title of the picture, but in accordance with the biblical text, this gesture of reassurance

Figure 5. *Christ Girding Himself with Strength* signals the installation of Mercy as humankind's judge; c. 1805, approx. 38 x 32.5 cm.—*City of Bristol Museum and Art Gallery*

indicates that the girdle is already securely in place; he is not in the act of girding himself: "the Lord is clothed with strength, wherewith he hath girded himself: the world also is established, that it cannot be moved. Thy throne is established of old; thou art from everlasting" (Ps. 93.1-2). Yet there is an almost Bronzino-like tension in his hands, as if he may change positions at any moment.

Blake's dry, streaky brushstrokes give rise to what Rossetti called a "slovenly" appearance, as of a pastel sketch. Although the design is dated 1805 on the basis of its delivery date to Butts, it has the stippled appearance of several designs executed in 1803, perhaps in haste. Yet the existence of a preliminary pencil sketch for this design—unusual in the biblical watercolor series—indicates considerable care in preparation. Blake made several changes as he developed the composition, some of which may bear on his interpretation of the biblical text. In the preliminary pencil sketch (fig. 6; B 463, pl. 549) Christ is not touching his sash, which flows from the high-waisted belt area down his lap, across his knee, and down the side of his robe. The water level of the turbulent ocean is higher in the sketch than in the finished design, and some of the circular waves beneath the vertical lines of the throne look almost like scales or balancing pans, emblems of judgment. Also, in the sketch Jesus looks straight out at the viewer rather than down at the scroll; his hands rest on the arms of a massive throne omitted from the finished picture, and his feet rest directly on the globe of the enduring firmament rather than on stone pedestal steps mounted upon the globe just visible at the sides of the steps in the finished picture. In the finished watercolor, two thoughtful angels, seen in profile back to back on either side of Jesus, stand guard with their heads slightly bowed, facing outward, their exceptionally long flaming swords grounded and resting on their points. In the preliminary drawing, the sword of the angel on the right is not visible, and both angels appear to be mourning. In the finished design, the short-haired angel on the left rests his elbow on the hilt of his sword; the long-haired angel on the right rests his left hand on his sword's pommel and his right hand on the crosspiece of its hilt. Contributing to Blake's *tour de force* in contriving an astonishing variety of ways in which angels' wings can be arranged to form Gothic architectural designs, the wings of these angels form a double-arched canopy and a smaller pointed arch framing the figure of Christ; in the pencil drawing a single pointed arch is formed by wings pointed upward.

The purpose of some of these changes was perhaps to make the foundation of the throne more secure while softening the emblems of

Figure 6. Preliminary pencil sketch for *Christ Girding
Himself with Strength* (fig. 5). In changes for the final
illustration, Blake seems to have "made the foundation of the
throne more secure while softening the emblems of might and
justice."—*Tate Gallery*, London

might and justice. Blake's representation of Christ as a merciful judge in *Christ Girding Himself with Strength* is more evident when this picture is compared with the judgment scene in *Mercy and Truth are Met together*. In *Mercy and Truth are Met together*, the expressionless Father, in the very act of judgment, looks above his book to see the Son make a dynamic gesture of reconciliation. In *Christ Girding Himself with Strength*, it is Christ who sits in the judgment seat, and the flaming swords that his flanking angels have grounded reveal the spirit in which the judgment is to be conducted. The conjunction of cherubim and flaming swords is fraught with biblical associations of profound significance to Blake, brought together in this illustration. First, the presence of the cherubim indicates that this seat of judgment is also the Mercy Seat, which is guarded by two cherubim; Blake considered Christ the typological fulfillment of this sacred object in the Hebrew temple, and he cited Exodus 25.20 along with a New Testament text in his inscription on *Christ in the Sepulchre, Guarded by Angels* (B 500, pl. 603). Second, the flaming swords allude to the expulsion from Eden (Gen. 3.24), and the fact that they are grounded indicates that the Mercy Seat has become the no-longer-barred gate of Paradise, fulfilling Blake's own defiant command in *The Marriage of Heaven and Hell*: "For the cherub with his flaming sword is hereby commanded to leave his guard at the tree of life, and when he does, the whole creation will be consumed, and appear infinite and holy whereas it now appears finite & corrupt" (E39). And there are other ameliorating details: Jesus' book, following the curve of his knees and lacking the central gutter of the stiffly bound book that the Father holds in *Mercy and Truth are Met together*, seems on the verge of turning into a scroll, so that it does not appear to be as formidable an emblem of judgment as his Father's imposing tome or the book Blake gave him in "The Day of Judgment" in the designs for Blair's *Grave*.[39]

Finally, the vertical folds of Jesus' robe, intersecting the horizontal lines of his sash, form the outline of a cross of the same Teutonic design as the cross in *Mercy and Truth are Met together*.

Although a full consideration of the final illustration to Psalms, *By the Waters of Babylon* (fig. 7, B 466, pl. 541), would lengthen this essay beyond reasonable limits, I would like to point out that it, too, has its christological parallel and reversal. As the text states, the captive Hebrews refuse to sing the Lord's song in a strange land, and they hang their harps (and other instruments) on a willow tree. The New Testament counterpart to this design, *The Hymn of Christ and His Apostles* (B490, pl. 546), depicts a scene on the Mount of Olives in which Jesus and his male and

Figure 7. *By the Waters of Babylon* completes the Psalm
sequence and finds its typological counterpart in *The Hymn of
Christ and his Apostles*, 1806, 40.4 x 38.1 cm.—Fogg Art
Museum, *Harvard University*, Grenville L. Winthrop bequest

female disciples are singing to the accompaniment of musical instruments. The contrast in the use of instruments is one that Blake made more pointed in his Job designs. As Horne and other commentators note, the hymn Christ would have sung on that occasion is one of the psalms for Passover night, from the Hallel (Ps. 113-118).

In summary, Blake's three christological illustrations of the Psalms, taken together, show, first, the state of human consciousness that invokes Jesus' presence, then its fulfillment in time in Christ's incarnation, and finally its triumph in eternity in the installation of the personification of Mercy as the judge of humankind.

Blake's watercolor biblical designs may appear on first acquaintance to be straightforward, even pious illustrations, without the ironic bite of many of his designs for Young, Gray, and Milton. But Blake's interpolation of Jesus into Psalms 18, 85, and 93, while well within orthodox Christian tradition, nevertheless bears out Frye's suggestion that for the artist the Bible yields its fullest meaning only when it is "shaken upside-down" (*Fearful Symmetry*, p. 120) and made to say something not quite intended by its human authors. Blake's biblical watercolors form a lively, if subdued, critical commentary on the Scriptures, a mild and gentle reading of the Bible in Blake's famous "infernal or diabolical sense." To Butts and other viewers of the biblical watercolors, Blake has revealed some of his most radical theological insights in a luminous and accessible form.

Notes

1. The thematic unity of the series has long been recognized. Anthony Blunt, who first examined the watercolors as a set, states that the group "must have been intended to be 'Blake's Bible,' as the [Vatican] loggia frescoes are 'Raphael's Bible'" (*The Art of William Blake* [New York: Columbia Univ. Press, 1957], p. 69). Darrell Figgis had earlier perceived the illustrations to the Gospels as a complete "poem" on the life of Christ (*The Paintings of William Blake* [London: Ernest Benn, 1925], p. 66). Martin Butlin has long maintained that the watercolors "seem to have been intended as a unified series, perhaps embodying Blake's own commentary on their texts" (*The Paintings and Drawings of William Blake* [New Haven: Yale Univ. Press, 1982], p. 336), despite stylistic changes from "the rather bold watercolours of 1800, often with considerable chiaroscuro, to the bright colours and soft stipple technique, usually with an unusually prominent use of pencil, of 1803, and from there to the more linear, flatly coloured watercolours of 1805" (336). Bo Lindberg remarks that the "Bible designs are interpretative rather than illustrative in the ordinary way" (*William Blake's Illustrations to the Book of*

Job [Abo, Finland: Abo Akademi, 1973], p. 282); indeed, Ronald Paulson's comments on Blake's "deconstruction" of the Bible in his illuminated books might well be applied to his watercolors: Blake is a "great illustrator of the repressed text who brings out its latent meaning which has been covered over by pious and tendentious commentators" ("Blake's Bible," in *Book and Painting: Shakespeare, Milton, and the Bible: Literary Texts and the Emergence of English Painting* [Knoxville: Univ. of Tennessee Press, 1982], pp. 116, 118).

    2. The fullest recent discussions of individual designs are Christopher Heppner's sensitive and well-informed historical-critical analysis, "The Woman Taken in Adultery: An Essay on Blake's 'Style of Designing,'" *BIQ*, 17 (1983), 44-60, and Terence Alan Hoagwood's militantly antithetical interpretation, "'God Blessing the Seventh Day': Blake's Visions of God and His Biblical Watercolors," *Studia Mystica*, 7 (1984), 65-77. My own essay, "Blake's Judgment on the Book of Judges," in *Reconciliations: Studies in Honor of Richard Harter Fogle*, ed. Mary Lynn Johnson and Seraphia D. Leyda (Salzburg: Salzburg Studies in English, 1983), interprets two paired groupings on Jephthah and Samson as a pictorial critique of Judges. See also my article cited in note 18 below.

    3. David Bindman, in *Blake as an Artist* (New York: Dutton, 1977), suggests that the series was "not to be hung on a wall but to be either bound in a volume or interleaved in a large Bible" (144). Bindman speaks slightingly of the "episodic nature" of the watercolor series, which largely for stylistic reasons he finds "quite without the overall coherence of the Butts tempera series," and he condescendingly represents Blake as working "at odd intervals at the dictates of [his] angels, perhaps when he was in need of money or when he was not occupied with engraving or writing" (144). On other grounds, the literary critic and printmaking specialist Robert N. Essick, reviewing Butlin's *Paintings and Drawings* in *BIQ*, 16 (1981), cautions against a naive search for patterns of meaning: "Just as it is virtually impossible to select at random two or more passages in the Bible between which a clever exegete cannot find some relationship, so it is with any grouping of Blake's biblical subjects.... If we pursue the hermeneutics of such studies far enough we may be led to that dangerous borderland between semiotics and the mathematics of finite sets" (40). Essick also warns that the structure of both the tempera and the watercolor series may have been "less affected by an iconographic program than by such practical exigencies as available canvas sizes or the remaining wall or cabinet space in Butts' home." But neither Essick's nor Bindman's caveats rule out the genre of the extra-illustrated Bible, an open-ended pictorial series that allows for a thematic coherence without the necessity of a preordained

organizational scheme. Bindman recognizes a Crucifixion series (131) and a cycle on the life of Moses (143-44).

4. References to pictures catalogued in Butlin, *Paintings and Drawings* (B) give first the catalogue number, then the plate number.

5. For abbreviations used in citing Blake, see the List of Abbreviations at the beginning of this volume.

6. This symbol is first mentioned in *The Four Zoas* VIII, 115.42-43, E381), in one of the latest sections of the poem to be composed. As is well known, Blake derived the myth of the Seven Angels of the Presence from Zechariah 4.10 and Revelation 5.6, and he took their individual names from other scriptural sources. In separate entries in *A Blake Dictionary* (Providence: Brown Univ. Press, 1967; 2nd printing), Damon discusses these figures. The most relevant citations are as follows: Lucifer (Isaiah 14.12), Moloch (Leviticus 18.21), Elohim (Genesis 1), Shaddai, the Almighty (Exodus 6.3), Pachad, Fear (Genesis 31.42), Jehovah (Genesis 2.4), and Jesus. Later, Blake added an obscure Eighth Eye (*M* 13.17-27, E107; *J* 55.31, E205), apparently to represent humanity's capacity to recognize its own divine potential. The fullest discussions of the Seven Eyes symbol, incorporating earlier scholarship, appear in Michael Ferber's excellent Appendix in his *The Social Vision of William Blake* (Princeton: Princeton Univ. Press, 1985), pp. 213-21), and in Rachel V. Billigheimer, "Blake's 'Eyes of God': Cycles of Apocalypse and Redemption," *PQ*, 66 (1987), 231-57.

7. The story of Blake's unhappiness in Felpham has often been retold, but not from an angle that reveals the plot-strand of his inability to get on with the commission for Butts. The gap in Blake's correspondence and transmission of pictures could not be detected until E.B. Murray's redating of a crucial letter which Blake wrote to Butts in January 1803 but carelessly dated 1802; see "A Suggested Redating of a Blake Letter to Thomas Butts," *BIQ*, 13 (1979-80), 143-51. When this letter is placed in its correct chronological position, it becomes obvious that Blake produced no biblical watercolors at all until the summer of 1803, just before he returned to London. Indeed, he sent Butts no illustrations of the Bible in any medium, with the possible exception of a few tentative sketches, until November 1802, when he began filling the three canvases he had brought with him from London for final work on the tempera series. Blake's two-year pause before finishing the tempera series and his delay of almost three years in getting the watercolor series moving is hardly what one would expect from an artist who in 1795 and 1796 could turn out a watercolor per day to illustrate Young's *Night Thoughts*.

8. In working on the related tempera series, Blake wrote Butts to ask "what subject you choose to be painted on the remaining Canvas which I

brought down with me (for there were three)" (E720). But when Blake sent "the Riposo" with an explanation of its symbolism (E729), he also commented that he would "relinquish Any engagement of Designing at all unless altogether left to my own Judgment. As you My dear Friend have always left me for which I shall never cease to honour & respect you" (E731). The most detailed account of Butts's financial and spiritual generosity as a patron appears in G.E. Bentley, Jr., "Thomas Butts, White Collar Maecenas," *PMLA*, 71 (1956), 1052-66.

9. Draft letter of late September 1800, *William Blake's Writings*, ed. G.E. Bentley, Jr. (Oxford: Oxford Univ. Press, 1978), pp. 1543-45. Butts also teased Blake about being "under the protection of the blackguard" and ended his letter with a sly valediction: "I commend you to the protection of your Guard."

10. Probably by chance, Blake's (or Butts's) selection of Psalms 18, 85, 93, and 137 for illustration distributes the designs among four of the five "books" or subdivisions of Psalms recognized in the Hebrew Bible on the basis of formal openings or closings, and on such contrasts as the use of Yahweh in the first "book" and Elohim in the second. According to J.W. Rogerson and J.W. McKay, *The Cambridge Biblical Commentary on the New English Bible, Psalms 51-100* (London: Cambridge Univ. Press, 1977), "The division of the Psalter into five books (Pss. 1-41, 42-72, 73-89, 90-106, 107-150) presumably dates from the time of the completion of the Psalter, probably in the third century, *B.C.*" (5); the division was recognized also by Christian commentators in Blake's time. The second "book" is referred to in Acts 13.33.

11. Most psalters emphasized Christ's infancy and Passion but not his public ministry: see Lucy Freeman Sandler, *The Peterborough Psalter in Brussels and Other Fenland Manuscripts* (London: Harvey Miller; Greenwich: New York Graphic Society, 1974) and her *The Psalter of Robert de Lisle* (London: Harvey Miller; Oxford and New York: Oxford Univ. Press, 1983); Francis Wormald, *The Winchester Psalter* (London: Harvey Miller; Greenwich: New York Graphic Society, 1973); Otto Pacht, C.R. Dodwell, and Francis Wormald, *The St. Albans Psalter* (London: Warburg Institute, 1960). According to E.T. Dewald, *The Illustrations of the Utrecht Psalter* (Princeton: Princeton Univ. Press; London: Oxford Univ. Press; Leipzig: Karl Hiersemann Verlag, [1932]), the Utrecht Psalter is unusual in placing at the head of each Psalm detailed illustrations of several episodes or images, rather than scattering illustrations throughout the text.

12. Although Blake insisted that the meaning of the Bible is clear to all without explanatory notes, he claimed in defending Thomas Paine against

Bishop Watson to have read "an hundred" biblical commentaries that bent the scriptures to the ends of state religion (E616). Hayley's library, to which Blake had daily access from 1800 to 1803, contained more than thirty commentaries, tracts, or sermons published between 1640 and 1800; see A.N.L. Munby, ed., *Sale Catalogues of Libraries of Eminent Persons*, vol. 2, *Poets and Men of Letters* (London: Mansell, with Sotheby Parke-Bernet Publications, 1971), 2.83-171.

13. (London: G. Whitfield, 1802), III.1. Leslie Tannenbaum, *Biblical Tradition in Blake's Early Prophecies: The Great Code of Art* (Princeton: Princeton Univ. Press, 1982), pp. 288-89, n. 17, cautions that this six-volume work by Coke, "Wesley's right-hand man," appropriates without acknowledgment "one of the best biblical commentaries of the period," William Dodd's *A Commentary on the Books of the Old and New Testaments,* 3 vols. (London, 1770).

14. Hans Frei, *The Eclipse of Biblical Narrative* (New Haven and London: Yale Univ. Press, 1974), has excellent chapters on "Precritical Interpretation of Biblical Narrative" and "Change in Interpretation: The Eighteenth Century"; E.S. Shaffer, *'Kubla Khan' and The Fall of Jerusalem* (Cambridge: Cambridge Univ. Press, 1975), *passim*, discusses the reception of German biblical criticism in England; and Thomas R. Preston, "Biblical Criticism, Literature, and the Eighteenth-Century Reader," in *Books and Their Readers in Eighteenth-Century England*, ed. Isabel Rivers (New York: St. Martin's Press, 1982), pp. 97-126, shows that biblical criticism was widely read by a lay audience. For the most pertinent account of exegetical tradition from a Blakean perspective, see Tannenbaum, *Biblical Tradition*, pp. 3-123, and his extensive Bibliography, pp;. 337-62; see also Paul Korshin's discussion of Blake in *Typologies in England, 1650-1820* (Princeton: Princeton Univ. Press, 1982), pp. 348-58, and his helpful chapter "Typology: A Bibliographical Essay," pp. 396-408, as well as John Rogerson's *Old Testament Criticism in the Nineteenth Century: England and Germany* (London: SPCK [Society for the Promotion of Christian Knowledge], 1984), especially his chapters "English Critical Old Testament Scholarship Prior to 1800," pp. 147-57; "German Old Testament Criticism in England 1770-1859," pp. 158-79; and "English Critical Old Testament Scholarship 1800-57," pp. 180-96.

15. David Dickson's *A Commentary on the Psalms* (1653-55; rpt. London: Banner of Truth Trust, 1965) takes the usual line: David is "a type of Christ, and fellow partaker of the sufferings of Christ in his mystical members" (76). Coke states that "as David was a type of Christ," the Psalms "undoubtedly in the spirit refer to him." As Bindman points out, the typological relationship between David and Christ is "implicit also in the

Swedenborgian conception of Christ as the only true God" (142). There were, of course, notable opponents of this view: according to R.G. Barnes, ed., *The First Separate Edition of the Psalms of David and Others as Rendered into English by Arthur Golding; his Translation of Calvin's Later Version Extracted from Commentaries on the Psalms*, 2 vols. (London, 1571; San Francisco: Arian Press, 1977), Calvin was the first scholar since St. Jerome to question what Ambrose and Augustine had assumed, that David was the author of the entire psalter; Calvin also rejected the theory that David might have been inspired to write about events such as the Babylonian captivity that took place after his death. Calvin's skepticism on these points anticipates that of the Scottish Roman Catholic Alexander Geddes, the most advanced British biblical scholar of Blake's time. Less scholarly commentators expended much effort in assigning psalms to specific episodes in David's life. A denial of David's authorship, his prophetic powers, and his typological relationship to Christ is characteristic of Deistic commentary. As pointed out by Bertram Eugene Schwarzbach, *Voltaire's Old Testament Criticism* (Geneva: Librairie Droz, 1971), "Ridicule of the christological figures is one of the most prominent elements of Voltairean Bible criticism" (46); moreover, Voltaire "discussed David's cruelties in most of his anti-biblical sorties, often associating with them several of the more blood-thirsty psalms" (151). In the second volume of *The Age of Reason*, Thomas Paine declares roundly that it is "an error or an imposition to call them the Psalms of David. They are a collection, as song-books are nowadays, from different song-writers who lived at different times" (*The Complete Writings of Thomas Paine*, ed. Philip S. Foner [1945; rpt. New York: The Citadel Press, 1969], I.549). Paine mocks the parallels and contrasts between "the type and the thing typified, the sign and the thing signified" as interpretations "industriously rummaged up and fitted together like old locks and pick-lock keys" (II.589). Consistent with his defense of Paine, Blake in his old age told Henry Crabb Robinson that "all he knew was in the Bible, but then he understands by the Bible the Spiritual Sense; For as to the natural sense, that Voltaire was commissioned by God to expose" (G.E. Bentley, Jr., *Blake Records* [Oxford: Clarendon Press, 1969], p. 322; my punctuation added). As illustrator of the Book of Psalms, Blake adopts the mythic continuity developed by the typological interpreters while sharing with Deists and liberal Christians an abhorrence of David's lapses into barbaric militarism.

16. *A Commentary on the Book of Psalms* (London, 1830), p. vi; Horne's popular commentary, first published in 1771, went through many editions; it provides a synthesis of the "best critics" and steers a middle course between overly ingenious patristic and medieval allegorizations of "spiritual or evangelical applications" of texts, such as Augustine's, and narrowly

prosaic investigations of their "literal scope and meaning." Without denying the value of historical verification, textual criticism, source study, and critical reassessments of the intended purpose of the author in his own time, Horne seeks to elucidate the *"prophetical, evangelical, mystical,* or *spiritual"* sense of the text (viii), i.e., the sense with which Blake was concerned.

17. For well-documented summary accounts of the most influential views of David's character, see the editors' "Introduction: Transformations of the Myth of David," 1-10, 179-81; Jan Wojcik, "Discriminations against David's Tragedy in Ancient Jewish and Christian Literature," pp. 13-35, 181-85; and Edward A. Gosselin, "Two Views of the Evangelical David: Lefevre d'Etaples and Theodore Beza," pp. 57-67, 191-94, in *The David Myth in Western Literature,* ed. Raymond-Jean Frontain and Jan Wojcik (West Lafayette, Ind.: Purdue Univ. Press, 1980).

18. All quotations of Milton are from *Complete Poems and Major Prose,* ed. Merritt Y. Hughes (New York: Odyssey Press, 1957).

My discussion of *David Delivered* draws upon my essay "Human Consciousness and the Divine Image in Blake's Watercolor Designs for the Bible: Genesis through Psalms," pp. 20-43 in *The Cast of Consciousness: Concepts of the Mind in British and American Romanticism,* ed. Beverly Taylor and Robert Bain (New York, Westport, and London: Greenwood Press, 1987).

19. An abbreviated biblical reference in Blake's hand, in ink, appears just outside a framing line at the bottom right of many of the designs. Butlin (p. 335) suggests that all the pictures once bore such inscriptions, "but in some cases the paper has been trimmed and the inscriptions lost." Twenty-nine of the pictures also have penciled inscriptions in a large "copperplate hand," either in the blank area above and below the design (the mount) or on the mat. These interesting inscriptions, which occasionally sound quite "Blakean" and introduce fresh perspectives on both the text and the design, have never been positively attributed to Blake and have sometimes been ascribed to "Butts or members of [his] family" (Bindman, p. 144). They are not, however, in either Butts's clerkly or his normal handwriting, both of which are represented in the draft of his September 1800 letter to Blake that is now in the Westminster Public Library in London. Erdman includes the inscriptions from the watercolor series in his new edition, without discussing the handwriting, which resembles that in a penciled inscription on the verso of *The Fall of Man* (dropped from Erdman's new and complete 1982 edition but included in Bentley, ed., *William Blake's Writings,* p. 1332). In an unpublished paper Michael J. Tolley has questioned the traditional attribution of this verso inscription to Blake, partly on the basis of the atypical spelling "Tiger" (Bentley incor-

rectly gives this word as "Tyger"). Whoever actually penciled in the inscriptions (Butlin describes some of them as "imitations" of the copperplate hand), it seems safe to agree with Essick (pp. 43-44) that they express Blake's ideas.

20. In this setting, the psalm falls between an account of four giants defeated by David and his men and a report of David's "last words" in which he identifies himself as a prophet. One of the giants, a son of Goliath, "had on every hand six fingers, and on every foot six toes, four and twenty in number"—just as Blake depicts Goliath in his watercolor of *Goliath Cursing David* (B 457, pl. 525); an extra digit, which Blake apparently considered characteristic of the race of giants, appears also on the exposed left foot of the overpowering deity in *The Angel of the Divine Presence Clothing Adam and Eve with Coats of Skins* (B 436, pl. 513), sinister evidence of humanity's fallen perspective.

21. *The Psalms of David: Imitated in the Language of the New Testament, And Apply'd to the Christian State and Worship* (London: J. Clark, R. Ford, R. Crittendon, 1719), p. xiii. Watts is defending his decision to imitate rather than translate "the great Number which have something of *Personal Concerns, Prophetical Darknesses, Hebraisms,* or *Jewish Affairs* mingled with them" (v).

22. Clyde R. Taylor, "Iconographical Themes in William Blake," *Blake Studies*, 1 (1968), 39-85, first pointed out that "cords" is an alternate translation of "sorrows of death" in verse 8, and Michael J. Tolley, reviewing Butlin's *William Blake: A Complete Catalogue of the Works in the Tate Gallery* in *Blake Newsletter* #21, 6 (1972), 28-30, calls attention to the translators' original marginal references which are "a standard feature" of the Authorized Version, though omitted from most modern copies (p. 29). Even without access to alternate translations, Blake might have developed the image from the "snares" in the next verse.

23. *Blake's Illustrations to the Divine Comedy* (Princeton: Princeton Univ. Press, 1953), p. 177.

24. In an illuminated letter "S" from a psalter in the Bodleian Library, Oxford (MS Canon Liturg 378, p. f75v.; reproduced as an illustration to Psalm 69 in *The Book of Psalms*, compiled by Shuckburgh Reynolds Limited [New York: Henry Holt and Company, Inc., 1986]), both David and God are white-bearded; David is nude, up to his neck in swirling water, with his hands clasped toward the heavens; in the top portion of the "S," God leans out of a red enclosure, robed in blue and holding an orb. The reproduction does not specify which psalm had the illuminated "S" as an opening letter in the original psalter.

25. Review of Butlin's Tate Gallery catalogue, *Blake Newsletter*, 6 (1972), 29.

26. Although Psalm 85 is attributed in its headnote to the "sons of Korah," most commentators ignored the distinction among Psalms and attributed them all to David, as collector if not author.

27. Although Blake was certainly no churchgoer, if he got within earshot of a church at any time between his baptism and his burial by Anglican clergy, it would probably have been on Christmas Day; in any case, Horne and other biblical commentators note the calendar of readings. It may be worth recalling, however, that the Psalter of the English church, used both for singing and for responsive readings, is not from the King James Version but from Coverdale's translation prepared for the Great Bible; see, for example, Harold R. Wolloughby, *The Coverdale Psalter and the Quatrocentenary of the Printed English Bible: with a Facsimile Reproduction of the Psalter* (Chicago: Caxton Club, 1935), and Stella Brook, *The Language of the Book of Common Prayer* (New York: Oxford Univ. Press, 1965).

28. For an erotic version of this pose, see the flame-encircled vignette of Paolo and Francesca in *The Whirlwind of Lovers*, no. 10 in Roe, *Blake's Illustrations to the Divine Comedy*; see also Teodoro Ghisi's *Venus and Adonis*, engraved by Giorgio Ghisi (Bartsch 42), No. 42 in Michal Lewis and R.E. Lewis, *The Engravings of Giorgio Ghisi* (New York: Metropolitan Museum of Art, 1985), p. 146. A joyous scene of divine-human reconciliation takes place in the foreground of Botticelli's *The Mystic Nativity*, as three angels bearing olive branches embrace three mortal men, and small devils take cover; see Gabriela Mandel, *The Complete Paintings of Botticelli*, introduction by Michael Levey (New York: Harry N. Abrams, 1967), No. 150; repr. in color in Bettina Wadia, *Botticelli* (Feltham: Paul Hamlyn, 1968), pl. 47. Nowhere is the theme of divine-human reconciliation presented with more explicit sexual implications than in designs near the conclusion of Blake's *Jerusalem*, plates 96, 99 (*IB* 375, 378).

29. *Iconography of Christian Art*, i, trans. Janet Seligman (Greenwich: New York Graphic Society, 1971), p. 11; see also Robert F. Gleckner, "Blake and the Four Daughters of God," *ELN*, 15 (1977), 110-15.

30. References to this design series are to *William Blake's Designs for Edward Young's Night Thoughts*, ed. John E. Grant, Edward J. Rose, and Michael J. Tolley, with the assistance of David V. Erdman (Oxford: Clarendon Press, 1980), 2 vols. A few of the designs, and some related items, are to be found in B).

31. *The Moment of Explosion: Blake and the Illustration of Milton* (Lincoln and London: Univ. of Nebraska Press, 1983), p. 138.

32. *Blake's Vision of the Poetry of Milton: Illustrations to Six Poems* (Lewisburg: Bucknell Univ. Press; London and Toronto: Associated University Presses, 1986), p. 68.

33. This cross is often confused with the Maltese cross, in which the vanes are straight-edged rather than slightly curved, and split on the ends to form eight points representing the Beatitudes; the cross patée is depicted and briefly discussed by Arnold Whittick, *Symbols, Signs and Their Meaning* (Newton, Mass.: Charles T. Branford, 1961), pp. 165-66, fig. 40 (f). In the nonscholarly opinion of George Willard Benson, *The Cross: Its History & Symbolism* (1934; rpt. New York: Hacker Art Books, 1976), the cross patée "symbolizes the open wings of a bird, suggestive of the protective power of the cross" (p. 71; depicted on p. 81). In Edward Hulme's *Symbolism in Christian Art* (1891; rpt. Dorset: Blandford Press, 1976) this form of the cross is depicted with nine others as a crusaders' emblem (p. 81, fig. 38).

34. *A Dictionary of Symbols*, trans. Jack Sage (New York: Philosophical Library, 1962), p. 67.

35. *Blake's Human Form Divine* (Berkeley, Los Angeles, London: Univ. of California Press, 1974), p. 334. Mellor identifies the older woman at the right as Jesus' grandmother Anne; at what she calls the anagogical level she identifies Mary with the figure of Truth, on the basis of the alternate title "Christ in the Lap of Truth," given by Rossetti to a tempera painting of similar composition (B 671, pl. 893). Butlin gives the alternate title as a second title but considers it a "rather strange misidentification of the main figures" (485).

36. For distantly comparable compositions, see the discussion of "enthroned Madonnas" in Frederic W. Farrar, *The Life of Christ as Represented in Art* (London: Adam and Charles Black, 1901), pp. 190-209.

37. For a summary account of this line of interpretation and its pervasive influence, see A.R. Johnson, "The Psalms," in *The Old Testament and Modern Study: A Generation of Discovery and Research* (London: Oxford Univ. Press, 1961), pp. 162-209. Lawrence E. Toombs's chapter on the Psalms in *The Interpreter's One-Volume Commentary on the Bible*, ed. Charles M. Laymon (Nashville and New York: Abingdon Press, 1971), pp. 253-303, for example, does not even mention the existence of the tradition of typological exegesis but takes for granted the central importance of agricultural festivals of ancient near eastern kingdoms.

38. *The Interpreter's Bible* (New York: Abingdon Press, 1955), IV.504.

39. Reproduced in Robert N. Essick and Morton D. Paley, *Robert Blair's "The Grave" Illustrated by William Blake: A Study with Facsimile* (London: Scolar Press, 1982), facing facsimile page 28.

Striving with Blake's Systems[1]

Mark Trevor Smith

> "It's equally fatal for the mind to have a
> system and to have none. It will simply
> have to decide to combine the two."[2]

Foster Damon with his dictionary definitions[3] and Northrop Frye with his summarizing symmetries[4] reveal tantalizing glimpses of Blake's promised land. These guides, and others, insist, implicitly if not explicitly, that they will lead us into Blake's "system." However, most readers do not feel so sanguine about crossing over into that world. Denied entrance, they see at most the view from Pisgah. This border restriction does not fall only on beginners and shirkers. No one could exhibit more brilliance and learning than does Leopold Damrosch, Jr., when he sets Blake in philosophical contexts, but even he finally gives up on Blake as incomprehensible.[5] Irene Chayes cleverly takes Damrosch to task for finding the long way round to the beginner's bafflement: Blake is a cult figure for the few.[6]

How is it that Blake's poetry creates such certainty in some of us and such confusion in others? It is almost as if we were reading two different poets, one clear and diagrammatic, prescriptive and static, triumphantly proclaiming his product, the other murky and confused, creative and dynamic, painfully struggling through process.

I would like to explore this problem by means of one of Blake's most famous lines: "I must Create a System." Often this statement is conscripted in defense of Blake's clarity and accessibility (although sometimes of his crankiness and obstinacy). After all, he said he created a system; let us delineate it and be content. In the minority opposition is George Gilpin, who, when I was his student, laughingly insisted that the joke is on Los. Blake's character, said Gilpin, mistakes his task; he does not know as much as his creator does. There is no system; Blake abhors systems. Similarly, according to Thomas Altizer, the joke is on us: "Blake's is a 'system' which is not the product of a rational analysis and it can not be translated into rational terms. Blake profoundly opposed all of the established forms of conceptual coherence."[7]

This tension between Blake's enthusiastic construction of systems, which makes it easy for us to understand him, and his scornful smashing of systems, which makes it impossible for us to understand him, becomes especially evident in *Jerusalem*. I choose *Jerusalem* not only because we find the intention to create system stated there, but also because, even though the issue appears often in Blake's earlier works, he works it through to a triumph in *Jerusalem*. Central to my inquiry are the Reuben episodes and the birth of Jesus, because these two Bible allusions are the longest and most powerful examples (although the poem contains many others) of the paradoxical combination of system-smashing and system-constructing.

The fundamental paradox, pervasive in Blake, is that disaster and blessing are inextricable; the fallen and the visionary, although opposed, cannot be separated. We cannot choose between them on moral grounds because such a discrimination cannot be made. Therefore it is impossible to decide *either* to build systems *or* to destroy them. We must, as Los learns in *Jerusalem*, simply decide to do both. We cannot always clearly distinguish between acts that cause falls and acts that create vision. The fact that man finds himself compelled to create systems provides evidence of the disaster of the Fall but at the same time it also contains a blessing of the imagination, the only way to re-construct what is lost. Whenever a system is constructed, it is a terrible mistake, leading to pain and loss. But any system is also, in the same place and at the same time, a merciful safety net, at worst preventing us from falling further, at best springing us back up where we belong.

Throughout this essay I am indebted to Hazard Adams, who has given us some penetrating insights into this question, couched in different Blakean terminology. What Adams calls myth (the Prolific, creative) and what he calls antimyth (the Devouring, restricting) must not be reduced into reconciliation; they must both be allowed to exist. He thereby advises an unreconciled juxtaposition and thereon bases his theory of the literary symbolic.[8] I would add to his formulation a deepening of the paradox: we must hold in our mind simultaneously an absolute acceptance of the lack of reconciliation—that is, an inability to create system—and an absolute insistence on reconciliation—that is, a need to create system.

Recently Nelson Hilton, in an article that continues his analysis of "polysemous words" in *Literal Imagination*,[9] explores some of the same kinds of paradoxes. For example, in applying Douglas Hofstadter's studies of infinite regress to Blake, Hilton states, "The system has ... an interacting structure of cells coded into levels which in some places are *both same and other*"[10] (Hilton's emphasis). At the beginning of his essay he invokes Steven Shaviro's idea that the phrase "striving with systems" is "an emblem for the contradictory determinations of Blake's poetry."[11] I find the approaches of Hilton and Shaviro compatible with my own, although my conclusions differ from theirs.

I have also learned much from the Jungian approach of Christine Gallant. She points out that in the early Lambeth books (*The Book of Urizen, The Book of Ahania, The Book of Los*) Blake finds himself in a paradox when he tries to fight the rigidities of myth by constructing his own myth, which is in danger of becoming too rigid itself. There is a necessity for clear outlines, according to Blake's aesthetic, political, and religious beliefs, but clarity can become a Urizenic mistake. Putting the matter in its bluntest form, she observes that Urizen's earliest impulses toward fixed form are Blake's own.[12] I believe that Blake worked his way through this paradox and that *Jerusalem* shows his character Los undergoing a similar experience.

The paradoxical task of constructing systems and destroying systems is the work of Los throughout *Jerusalem*, especially when he tries to force Reuben over Jordan. It is the work of Jesus in *Jerusalem* when he creates his own body in the Incarnation. It is the work of Blake in writing *Jerusalem*.

Blake is not to be fully identified with his character Los; Blake in a sense knows more than his character knows. At the same time, Blake is not to be completely separated from his character; the struggles of the character are also the struggles of the poet. Perhaps it can be said that the poem knows more than either Los or Blake knows. Perhaps it can even be said that art itself, which is Blake's Christianity, knows even more.

Only a few plates into *Jerusalem* we hear Los cry: "I must Create a System, or be enslav'd by another Mans" (*J* 10.20, E153).[13] Just before this line we see the system which would enslave him:

And this is the manner of the Sons of Albion in their strength
They take the Two Contraries which are calld Qualities,
    with which
Every Substance is clothed, they name them Good & Evil
From them they make an Abstract, which is a Negation

Not only of the Substance from which it is derived
A murderer of its own Body: but also a murderer
Of every Divine Member: it is the Reasoning Power
An Abstract objecting power, that Negatives every thing
This is the Spectre of Man: the Holy Reasoning Power
And in its Holiness is closed the Abomination of Desolation.

                                                                      (10.7-16)

This last line evokes two Bible contexts which are essential to understanding Los's fury. First, in the Old Testament the Holy of Holies stands in the middle of the Temple, empty, forbidden to any but the High Priest.[14] That central part of the Temple becomes in *Jerusalem* the most important example of an abstract center for a religion. Blake has the Sons of Albion construct an abstract and secret religion in their eagerness to separate good and evil. Second, the "Abomination of Desolation," mentioned three times in the Old Testament (Daniel 9.27, 11.31, 12.11), and once by Jesus in the New (Matthew 2.15, quoting from Daniel), is some undefined violation of the Temple.[15] By combining the void religion of secrecy and the heathen violation of that void, Blake thus gives us a desecration within an abomination.

The Sons fear evil and take strenuous measures to protect against it; at bottom they do not trust any scheme which is not abstractly, coherently moral. They seem to need to protect themselves from the encroachment of the details of life. Blake sees traditional religion enslaving itself to this system of abstraction, and thereby entombing the very life it seeks to love while enshrining the Abomination which desolates humanity's hope. A foolish abstract consistency works against the very goals which a religion thinks it desires: the finding of the eternal in the temporal.

Any abstraction of good and evil, such as that constructed by the Sons of Albion, sets up a standard of morality which can never be attained because its very standards are opposed to life itself. By defining God and religion in terms which are not really definitions at all, but negations of definitions, it makes all definite acts into sins, violations of its coherent code. It claims to be definite because it is rigid, but Blake's religion takes on definite shape without becoming rigid. Abstract religion refuses to give definite shape to good and evil, couching its tyranny in a hidden and capricious God who demands subservience and sacrifice. "Evil" is forbidden, and "good" is invisible, hidden, empty.

Traditional Christianity (not to mention many a Blake critic) makes a distinction between good and evil and assigns the former to the sheep and the latter to the goats at the Last Judgment.[16] The traditional Last Judgment is a form of mass murder, whose purpose is to reassure those who abstract and separate in their exclusive self-righteousness. What is commonly considered the foundation of religion—the distinction between good and evil—is thus for Blake the basic negation perpetrated by religion. Negation murders because it abolishes half of life. Such an idea, in less inclusive form, structures Blake's earlier *Marriage of Heaven and Hell*, in which he juxtaposes the energetic voice of the Devil against the reasoning restrictions of God.

Los specifically tries to counter this system of moral discrimination: "Therefore Los stands in London building Golgonooza" (10.17). The "Therefore" expresses a cause-and-effect relationship. If Los does not build, then he becomes a victim of the system of abstract religion with its mystifications. He does not construct his new System in order to define a new tyranny, a rock-built refuge from which he is unassailable, but in order to prevent something worse from happening. He seems to believe that if he can just take actions exactly opposite to those of the Sons of Albion, then he can solve the problem. It is in this context that he makes the declaration in question:

> I must create a System, or be enslav'd by another Mans
> I will not reason and compare; my business is to Create.
> (10.20-21)

The theology of the Sons of Albion is consistent, coherent, and rational, resolutely avoiding chaos because it is formulated from abstractions around an empty center prescribing good and evil. It is tempting to believe that good and evil are easily distinguishable and that Los can therefore abstract his principles as the Sons of Albion do, make general rules of morality, and build his system against theirs. And indeed, many readers of Blake see him doing just that in plate 10 and throughout his entire *oeuvre*. But that very mode of thinking can lead to a trap, the same trap which the Sons of Albion set and catch themselves with. What is gradually revealed in *Jerusalem*, in precise detail, is that each such system must be constructed along with its contrary, which is the need to smash systems, or it leads to eternal death.

Throughout the poem, Los seems well-intentioned but somewhat ignorant. He never gives up; he keeps hammering until he learns that the distinctions he wants to make are impossible, until he learns to wait and watch as well as to weep and work, to be passive as well as active. Although Blake the poet knows more than Los the character, he implicates himself in the errors. Although Blake has worked his way through the problem before, *Jerusalem* shows him working his way through it again. Having gone through it once, or several times, is no guarantee against having to go through it again. The work and the waiting are always difficult, intricate, necessarily painstaking. Complacency never arrives. From this perspective, Blake does not present us with a *fait accompli.* Such an attitude would be the worst of complacent systematizing. He presents us with a never-ending process. But from another perspective he does not present us with an infinite repetition; there is an absolute end to time at the conclusion of *Jerusalem.* That paradox is the reason that Blake's "system" is impossible to pin down. The poet, and Los, and each one of us, must create precise systems, but there is no foolproof rule book, no consistent and coherent pattern handed down from on high. Each time is new. Success must include its apparent opposite. System and anti-system cannot be cloven in two.

This paradoxical combination of striving process and absolute end invests every action of Los. He is, we are told, "Striving with Systems to deliver Individuals from those Systems" (11.5). On the surface the phrase in 11.5 means that Los strives "against" (the obvious meaning of "with") the destructive systems of others, especially the Sons of Albion, in order to bring innocent victims out from bondage to those systems. Los certainly knows this meaning. But since Los himself is constructing systems, then we must also read the "with" as meaning "by means of." The way that he delivers individuals from systems is by creating his own systems. From this perspective the last words of the line take on additional meaning as well. Los constructs systems not only to bring the innocent away from the systems of others but also to deliver them from his own system. Like Blake, he builds systems in order to free individuals from systems, including his own system. The simple doubleness of this sentence is essentially the doubleness of Blake's system-making, which in the course of *Jerusalem* becomes a fourfold vision. It is not only a deliverance from the enemy, but also a deliverance from itself. All of us—Los, Blake, and reader—must live through this process.

The major difference between Los's work and that of the Sons of Albion is in revelation and definition. Los's work gives shape to truth and error, good and evil, pleasure and pain, and does not try to deny or conceal either apparent side of an opposition. The fight is against all denial, concealment, and doubt. All that exists must be revealed (the basic meaning of the word "apocalypse") so that error can take on its clearest and most powerful shape, in particulars and in the aggregate, and finally fall away under its own dead weight (see 12.13). Like the Bible, Los's art reveals everything:

> All things acted on Earth are seen in the bright Sculptures of
> Los's Halls ...
> All that can happen to Man in his pilgrimage of seventy years
> Such is the Divine Written Law of Horeb & Sinai:
> And such the Holy Gospel of Mount Olivet & Calvary.
>
> (16.61-62, 67-69)

If all is to be revealed, then nothing can be absolutely prohibited. Total revelation contains the impossibility of exclusion. Even the foolish aspect of Los's approach must be explored. Indeed, in chapter 2 Los finds that it is not possible to separate the correct from the incorrect and eliminate the latter, to separate the victim from the punisher and execute the latter. In fact, if he were able to separate and punish as he seems to want to do, he would be making a mistake like that of the Sons of Albion, would be making a rival system just as destructive of vision as theirs. Blake does not wish, nor does he present or advocate, a rival system which simply counters and negates the first system. Such is not possible anyway. Such a process, such a method, will not work in the poem, and it will not work for us as readers or critics or human beings.

The longest and most confusing single example of Los's frustration in simply carrying out his explicit goals occurs in chapter 2 when he tries to force Reuben to cross over the Jordan. These episodes (on plates 30 and 32) are crucial to understanding the complications and simplicities of Blake's systems. Blake bases the episodes on the story in Numbers 32 in which Reuben chooses to settle on the east side of the Jordan instead of crossing over and settling on the west with the other tribes of Israel.[17]

Blake's Reuben stories emphasize system-breaking (crossing the Jordan, destroying the Canaanites) and system-making (setting boundaries, establishing the state of Israel). Both tasks must be carried on simultaneously, and are not always easy to distinguish from each other. Los wants to break through the limits of perception which the Jordan represents, into the land of Canaan which Reuben perceives as a terror, and reorganize Canaan and Britain according to new categories and limits. Los's attempts to send Reuben are absolutely necessary, even if they are a mistake. Without those attempts, Vision can never be attained, but Los finds that the actions in and of themselves simply do not work.

When Reuben refuses Los's commands to cross over, he sleeps "Between Succoth & Zaretan beside the Stone of Bohan" (30.45). The first part of this phrase is taken from Solomon's building of the Temple:

> In the plain of Jordan did the king cast them [vessels for the Temple] in the clay ground between Succoth and Zarthan. (I Kings 7.46 [an identical passage occurs in II Chronicles 4.17])

This casting marks the culmination of the building of the Temple before the ark of the covenant is brought into the Holy of Holies (which, as pointed out above, Blake invokes in 10.15-16 when he describes the abstractions of the Sons of Albion). *The New English Bible* translates the words for "clay ground" as "foundry,"[18] and that is certainly Blake's meaning in his only use of the phrase "clay ground" when Los works earlier in *Jerusalem*:

> With great labour upon his anvils, & in his ladles the Ore
> He lifted, pouring it into the clay ground prepar'd with art;
> Striving with Systems to deliver Individuals from those Systems.
>
> (11.3-5)

It will be recalled that this last line is crucial to understanding the purpose of Los's system building. By their shared allusion to the clay ground between Succoth and Zaretan, these two passages from *Jerusalem* (30.45 and 11.4) reveal that the imaginative site of Los's artistic action is identical with the site of Reuben's sleepy recalcitrance. That is, the forging in the foundry happens at the very same place where Reuben lays his head on the rock and refuses to move. Trying to build and trying to force Reuben over Jordan are essentially the same action. But trying to build Golgonooza is clearly a visionary act; trying to force Reuben over Jordan often appears to be a mistake. As is often true in Blake, the site of a fallen action and the site of a Visionary action are identical. And in fact the actions themselves are identical. As Los discovers in the Reuben episodes and again later when he descends into the interiors of Albion's bosom, he is making a terrible mistake when he tries to force his system on others. He cannot simply push Reuben over Jordan, for Reuben simply will not go. Similarly, Los is discovering that he cannot simply oppose his system to that of the Sons of Albion. In other words, such abstract brutal morality, like that of the Sons of Albion, remains at a standstill. At the same time, Los's insistent hammering away at what he believes is the only way into Vision. Thus system building is both a mistake and a necessary part of redemption.

The main issue of constructing systems is where to draw lines: which lines to break and which ones to establish.[19] Both Succoth and Zaretan are located in the valley of the Jordan, the former in the east and the latter in the west, so that this reference locates Reuben on or near the borderline which is so crucial in this passage, the Jordan River. As W.H. Stevenson explains:

> *The valley* [30.43] implies the Jordan rift valley which cuts Reuben off, as stated in [line] 44. *Succoth* and *Zaretan* are in the valley respectively east and west of Jordan.... The *Stone of Bohan the Reubenite* is mentioned twice as a boundary stone (*Joshua* xv 6, xviii 17): B[lake] only seems interested in the association of Reuben with a stone—always, to B[lake], an evil influence, implying rigidity, death and often sacrifice.[20]

Although Stevenson is helpful here, and largely correct, he is misleading in one important way: the Stone of Bohan is not *only* a stone. Surely Blake chose it because it is a *border* stone, and the Reuben episodes concern themselves with the nature of borders and limits. The account in the Old Testament of the Israelites' conquering of the Promised Land is obsessed with borders—whole chapters of the Bible are devoted to spelling out in great detail exactly where the territory of one tribe ends and that of another begins. The Jordan River itself becomes the most important border, and Reuben's refusal to cross it, in Blake and in the Bible, is a rebellion against hopes for redefinition and renewal. But at the same time Los's angry insistence is shown to be inadequate.

Blake is exploring here the nature of borders—the Jordan River which must be crossed (violated, broken) and the tribal boundaries which must be established (fixed, created). Twice in *Jerusalem* (16.1-60; 71.10-53, continued into 72.1-44) he goes to reader-stupefying lengths to detail assignments of geographical areas in imitation of the Bible. I believe Blake is both breaking through old limits and establishing new ones, a process analogous to the melting down and reshaping Los performs in his furnaces, and analogous to constructing systems in their minute details, a process both blessed and disastrous.

All of this leads to frustration in chapter 2, as the futility of mere action is demonstrated. Because Los is so furious to set his systems against those of the Sons of Albion, he descends into "the interiors of Albions/ Bosom, in all the terrors of friendship" to "search the tempters out" (43.3-5). In what Erdman calls "the central *action* of the whole poem,"[21] Los finds the task of destroying the punishers and sparing the victims completely impossible:

> [Los] saw every Minute Particular of Albion degraded & murderd
> But saw not by whom; they were hidden within in the minute particulars
> ... Los
> Searchd in vain: closd from the minutia he walked, difficult.
> ....
> What shall I do! what could I do, if I could find these Criminals
> I could not dare to take vengeance; for all things are so constructed
> And builded by the Divine hand, that the sinner shall always escape,
> And he who takes vengeance alone is the criminal of Providence;
> If I should dare to lay my finger on a grain of sand
> In way of vengeance; I punish the already punishd. (45.7-34)

This awareness of inextricability takes place near the end of a chapter which has been full of such frustrations. Again and again Los finds out that the method of the Sons of Albion does not work because it destroys the very thing the action is designed to preserve.

Some new consciousness is needed. It comes in the forgiveness which is the subject of chapter 3. Self-annihilation through identification with the other, even with the enemy, begins to bring us out of the trap.

We see a strong hint of this solution near the end of chapter 2, a merciful corollary to the frustrating inextricability Los discovers earlier in that chapter. If, frustratingly, victim cannot be separated from punisher, then, blessedly, neither can Savior be separated from death. Once the agonized Albion falls into death,

> the merciful Saviour in his arms
> Reciev'd him [Albion], in the arms of tender mercy and repos'd
> The pale limbs of his Eternal Individuality
> Upon the Rock of Ages. Then, surrounded with a Cloud:
> In silence the Divine Lord builded with immortal labour,
> Of gold & jewels a sublime Ornament, a Couch of repose,
> With Sixteen pillars: canopied with emblems & written verse,
> Spiritual Verse, order'd & measur'd, from whence, time shall reveal.
> The Five books of the Decalogue, the books of Joshua & Judges,
> Samuel, a double book & Kings, a double book, the Psalms & Prophets
> The Four-fold Gospel, and the Revelations everlasting.

> (48.1-11)

This couch of repose, the pillars of which are books of the Bible, is from another point of view the same couch/tomb which the Sons of Albion have just brought for Albion:

> In stern defiance came from Albions bosom ...
> ... Albions Sons: they bore him a golden couch into the porch
> And on the Couch reposd his limbs, trembling from the bloody field.
> Rearing their Druid Patriarchal rocky Temples around his limbs.
>
> (46.10-14)

Once again, the site of disaster is the site of blessing.

As they did on plate 10, the Sons of Albion try to consolidate the reasoning power not in order to reveal it, but in order to hide it and maintain its negating force. However, the splendid irony of *Jerusalem* is that even this work which sets itself against revelation, which attempts to solidify and enshrine an abominable holiness in its center, this essential error, is also a part of the solution. The fallen and the visionary cannot be separated.

The way to proceed is not to try to negate the opposition as Los has been trying to do, but to include it and re-create it, as Jesus is doing. This concept of inclusion becomes the key to the forgiveness of chapter 3. It breaks through the stand-off of simple contradiction in which one is pitted against one, and begins to create the fourfold wholeness all of *Jerusalem* strives toward. I am not hereby denying Blake's insistence on creating systems which will dispel error, but I am insisting on a method that does not allow itself to fall into the destructive morality of the Sons of Albion. The morality of Jesus, which is based on forgiveness, is simultaneously a method of exclusion and of inclusion.

As long as the holy secretiveness at the center, whether that of the original tabernacle and Temple or that of the usurping Abomination of Desolation (which is the same force to a higher power), tries to maintain itself, it is caught in the tomb of death-in-life. But even this tomb reveals itself to be also the site of the resurrection, life-out-of-death. Its force consolidates itself until it must reveal the self-destructive negation which reverses it. If the fool would persist in his folly he would become wise—with a merciful vengeance.

From the fallen perspective the tomb/couch is a tomb of despair, but from the eternal perspective the couch/tomb is a restful couch of hope. It is both at the same time. The eternal does not cancel the fallen, but operates with it as its contrary. The work of redemption is carried on with the same raw materials as is the work of destruction. The tomb of Albion, which is analogous to the tomb of Jesus in the Bible, is a nadir, evidence of absolute despair. At the same time, partly precisely because it is the lowest point, it is also the point of the beginning of renewal. It is the point where the worst and the best meet, are, in fact, simultaneous, inextricable.

The doubleness in these co-existent contraries does not consist merely in seeing the same thing in two different ways. The event is simultaneously fallen and eternal, sinful and redemptive, accepted and rejected at the same time. In the well-known optical illusion where one can see either two profiles or a vase, it is possible to see both things at the same time with the proper mixture of concentration and relaxation. Similarly, if the reader can bring to *Jerusalem*'s paradoxes the same inextricable mixture of activity and passivity the poet brings, and Los learns to bring, then he can perceive things which he thought were mutually exclusive, and he will be seeing no illusion, but Vision.

As a more complete version of his virtuoso couch carpentry, Jesus in chapter 3 creates himself as the ultimate Christian artist. He becomes the other, the enemy, the Satanic Selfhood.

Imaginative acts must take definite shape; if they remain undefined, then man is forever lost in the void. (This is part of the idea of the merciful limits described on plate 31, between the two plates containing the Reuben episodes: Adam, the limit of contraction, prevents the body from falling into more disorder; Satan, the limit of opacity, similarly protects the spirit.) Fallen vision does not perceive the eternal, and so tries to create a substitute of concealment and mystery. Eternal Vision perceives the essential coincidence of opposites which fallen vision divides, and so it fully enters into the definite shapes, the minute particulars where the center and the circumference of Eternity meet. Jesus is born, gives himself a definite shape, for the same reason that Los sets limits and Blake engraves lines: to break through the false abstract categories which fallen vision tries to maintain, to create new definite forms and thereby to reveal the eternal in the temporal. Jesus submits to the fallen world in order to reveal it for what it is: the eternal perversely reflected.[22] However, in order to do this, he must accept his opposite, take on his Satanic Selfhood, make a terrible error. The Incarnation is not a gimmick, as in *Paradise Lost* where the heroic Jesus knows he will win, but is instead a complete descent into dark otherness. Paradoxically, embracing that error is the only way to escape its terrors, the only way to fight it. To be taken on (combatted) it must be taken on (assumed).

The event of Incarnation, which is the ultimate extent of falling away from divinity because spirit has become flesh, is the beginning of re-unification. Just as the stars of the created universe are both evidence of the Fall and a merciful holding structure, just as the Bible as a work of art reveals the disastrous extent of the Fall and at the same time urges Regeneration, so the birth of Jesus occurs only because man has fallen so far away, but at the same time it assures his re-unification with God. God becomes as we are so that we may become as he is. The birth of Jesus is a way that the infinite becomes finite, becomes its opposite, the absolute other. Instead of trying to eliminate otherness or defend against it or deny its existence, Jesus forgives by becoming that other. This is the very movement of Spirit.[23] Forgiveness does not assume sin on the part of the other and therefore exclude the other, but assumes and creates a fundamental identity between self and other and is therefore a forgiveness of self as well as other. Constructing a system must thus be not only a way of protecting the artist from the destructive errors of the others, but also at the same time must be a becoming of the other, an acceptance of the sin of the other, which is in effect a redefinition of that sin.

The Incarnation of Jesus is an act of forgiveness in the deepest sense because it accepts completely the fallen world while at the same time transforming it through the resurrection which follows the crucifixion. The death of Jesus in the fallen world allows him to pass through the apparent limit of death (see *Jerusalem* 62.18-20) into a resurrection which absolutely reverses the power of death and the Fall even while appearing to succumb to it.

This is the way to solve the problem, by breaking through apparent limits, taking on (in both senses of the term) the Selfhood. The purpose of Jesus in being born, crucified, and resurrected is precisely to convert religious/sexual energy into redemption:

> Hence the Infernal Veil grows in the disobedient Female.
> Which Jesus rends & the whole Druid Law removes away
> From the Inner Sanctuary: a False Holiness hid within the Center,
> For the Sanctuary of Eden. is in the Camp: in the Outline,
> In the Circumference: & every Minute Particular is Holy:
> Embraces are Cominglings: from the Head even to the Feet;
> And not a pompous High Priest entering by a Secret Place.
> (69.38-44)

The birth of Jesus, which has already been shown on plate 61 to have arisen from a sexual act, is here revealed to be another sexual act, because not only does it penetrate the veil at the mysterious center, but it also embraces all the minute particulars of existence. Just as it destroys female falsehood, so it destroys the male falsehoods the Sons of Albion create when they abstract good and evil and set up the Abomination of Desolation in the Holy of Holies. The rending of the veil of the Temple, a New Testament type for the redefinition of God's Old Testament law by Jesus, serves as a sexual and a religious metaphor.

Even after several reassurances, Los fears that if he immerses himself too much in the fallen world, in other words, if he builds systems too well, if he allows himself to become completely fallen as Jesus has done, he will lose eternity:

> But pangs of love draw me down to my loins which are
> Become a fountain of veiny pipes: O Albion! my brother!
> Corruptibility appears upon thy limbs, and never more
> Can I arise and leave thy side, but labour here incessant
> Till thy awaking! yet alas I shall forget Eternity!
> Against the Patriarchal pomp and cruelty, labouring incessant
> I shall become an Infant horror. (82.83-84; 83.1-5)

Not realizing how close he is to seeing Albion awaken, Los here doubts the very principle of action—immersion in the fallen world—which will help bring about the desired result. He forgets that complete descent into the horror of infancy is precisely what Jesus accomplished in chapter 3. He fears that the constant work which is absolutely necessary may lead to the opposite of what he intends. But he has forgotten that apparently direct action, on the model of that of the Sons of Albion, does lead to a result opposite to what he intends. Thus he is still trapped somewhat in the original error of *Jerusalem* 10.7-16, only resisting the error and not also becoming it. However, to say so is not to distance that voice of superior knowledge. I can judge Los in that way, but I am no less caught in the trap, and neither is Blake. Blake's ironies do not take a superior attitude toward his poem's characters, but a sympathetic, self-implicating one. To take the superior, snide attitude would be once again to fall into the original problem of false, abstract self-righteous error.

There is a special poignancy in Los's fear if we read it as Blake's own. What is to be done when one cannot vigorously and optimistically build systems? After proclaiming on plate 77 that the essence of Christianity is constant striving without idleness, Blake here reveals that this very striving may entangle him helplessly in the fallen world. A story told by Alexander Gilchrist about the aging Blake illustrates perfectly Blake's own solution to the problem of losing eternity:

> 'Never,' [says] Mr. Richmond, 'have I known an artist so spiritual, so devoted, so single-minded, or cherishing imagination as he did.' Once, the young artist finding his invention flag during a whole fortnight, went to Blake, as was his wont, for some advice or comfort. He found him sitting at tea with his wife. He related his distress; how he felt deserted by the power of invention. To his astonishment, Blake turned to his wife suddenly and said: 'It is just so with us, is it not, for weeks together, when the visions forsake us? What do we do then, Kate?' 'We kneel down and pray, Mr. Blake.'[24]

Los's method of praying, undoubtedly like Blake's, is not a cessation of action, but a continued hammering while he cries for divine aid. Los seems to learn, however, that not everything can be achieved through active percussion:

> The land is markd for desolation & unless we plant
> The seeds of Cities & of Villages in the Human bosom
> Albion must be a rock of blood: mark ye the points
> Where Cities shall remain & where Villages; for the rest!
> It must lie in confusion till Albions time of awaking.
>
> (83.54-58)

Not only does Los admit that some parts of the world cannot be organized by him by force, no matter how hard he tries; he also changes his mode of action: instead of being only a blacksmith and a builder, he becomes also a farmer. That is, he engages in an activity which demands both action and waiting, not just action.

This realization has already been adumbrated in plate 3. The poet informs us, "When this Verse was first dictated to me I consider'd a Monotonous Cadence...," but he decides to produce variety instead. Several critics find a problem in this passage. Many ignore either the passive inspiration or the active choice. But we ignore the paradox at our own peril. The poet and the blacksmith and the reader must combine within themselves the freedom of individual choice and the passivity of the divine unity, the construction of systems and the acceptance of confusion.

The essential solution finally is to allow annihilation of the fixed and jealous self.[25] The Christian artist must become his opposite, instead of trying to exclude it. Only through this apparently paradoxical activity, which is the action of forgiveness, can the dead-end be broken through. Anything more sensible fails because it keeps us in the endless round of reprisal, most vividly sung in "The Mental Traveller." Jesus, as the self-creating artist, becomes the horrible Satan to which he seems the antithesis. He does not, as do the Sons of Albion and as Los seems to be trying to do at first, try to separate off evil, but he recreates it, in the sense of accepting and becoming it, so that he can recreate in both senses: he imitates it and he changes it. This is, in fact, the essence of forgiveness.

It is also the essence of Blake's systems. Systems, like bodies, like tribal boundaries, must take particular shape, even at the risk of falling into sin. Trying to avoid evil or sin or the fall as abstractions keeps us in the trap. Jesus does not shrink squeamishly from sin. He is the Friend of Sinners, and in Blake's re-writing of the birth of Jesus in plate 61 even becomes the product of sin. The result of a human sexual embrace, he re-enacts another by penetrating the veil, reversing center and circumference, finding thereby a new way of seeing:

> He who would see the Divinity must see him in his Children
> One first, in friendship & love; then a Divine Family, & in the midst
> Jesus will appear; so he who wishes to see a Vision; a perfect Whole
> Must see it in its Minute Particulars; Organized & not as thou
> O Fiend of Righteousness pretendest ...
> You accumulate Particulars, & murder by analyzing, that you
> May take the aggregate; & you call the aggregate Moral Law:
> And you call that Swelld & bloated form a Minute Particular.
> But General Forms have their vitality in Particulars: & every
> Particular is a Man; a Divine Member of the Divine Jesus.
>
> (91.18-22, 26-30)

This recommendation for new vision culminates in a scene of transfiguration:[26]

> Then Jesus appeared standing by Albion as the Good Shepherd
> By the lost Sheep that he hath found & Albion knew that it
> Was the Lord the Universal Humanity, & Albion saw his Form
> A Man. & they conversed as Man with Man, in Ages of Eternity
> And the Divine Appearance was the likeness & similitude of Los.
>
> (96.3-7)

The movement of systems which I see in *Jerusalem* provides an interesting way to look at Blake's conception of his fourfold vision. Single vision, called "Newton's sleep" in the letter to Butts, 24 November

1802 (E720), is in this scheme the negating vision of the Sons of Albion. It is imposed vision. Double vision is the realization, through the attempt to separate, that "good" and "evil" are inseparable. It is the attempt to create a rival system, which finds that the contraries are inextricable. Since, after this realization, double vision cannot simply blindly oppose the other, it must learn to accept and reject simultaneously through the power of forgiveness, and thereby become threefold vision, the vision which sees through the doubleness of oppositions and contraries. The birth of Jesus brings this third dimension to the opposition of the sexes. Threefold vision, by self-implication through self-annihilation, even comes to the point of becoming the other, the Satanic Selfhood. The movement from twofold to threefold is the realization that simple opposition is a dead-end and that only joining with the other provides escape. Fourfold vision reciprocates the movement of the infinite into the finite and transfigures limited existence into infinity.

When all human forms are identified in 99.1-2, the word "identified" contains a similar fourfold meaning: in single vision, each individual is identified as an ego, unique as in an identification card; in twofold vision, each individual sees the separation of the other which is caused by single vision, identifies it as other and begins to oppose it; in threefold vision, by becoming the other, the individual identifies with the other, in a way that we call sympathy, and all human forms become the same; in fourfold vision, we see clearly, identified as what we are, both individuals and parts of the whole of humanity, neither extreme compromised, expanding and contracting at will.

The conclusion of *Jerusalem* shows us this absolute end which is paradoxically also an ongoing process:

> Driving outward the Body of Death in an Eternal Death & Resurrection
> Awaking it to Life among the Flowers of Beulah rejoicing in Unity
> In the Four Senses in the Outline the Circumference & Form, for ever
> In Forgiveness of Sins which is Self Annihilation. it is the Covenant
>   of Jehovah. (98.20-23)

The "Covenant" of the Old Law, which established the abstractions that made Los so angry in the first place, becomes identical with forgiveness.

Like the Bodhisattva of Mahayana Buddhism, this ultimate vision of unity also remains in the real world. There seems to be a happy oscillation which includes both the large and the small view:

> the all tremendous unfathomable Non Ens
> Of Death was seen in regenerations terrific or complacent varying

According to the subject of discourse & every Word & Every
    Character
Was Human according to the Expansion or Contraction, the
    Translucence or
Opakeness of Nervous fibres such was the variation of Time &
    Space
Which vary according as the Organs of Perception vary & they
    walked
To & fro in Eternity as One Man reflecting each in each &
    clearly seen
And seeing: according to fitness & order. (98.33-40)

In the twentieth century, the theologian Rudolf Bultmann has defined a similar Christianity of an absolute end which is also an open continuation:

> According to the New Testament, *Jesus Christ is the eschatological event*, the action of God by which God has set an end to the old world.... It is the paradox of the Christian message that the eschatological event ... is not to be understood as a dramatic cosmic catastrophe but as happening within history, beginning with the appearance of Jesus Christ and in continuity with this occurring again and again in history, but not as the kind of historical development which can be confirmed by any historian.... [A]lthough the advent of Christ is an historical event which happened "once" in the past, it is, at the same time an eternal event which occurs again and again in the soul of any Christian in whose soul Christ is born, suffers, dies and is raised up to eternal life.... [E]very instant has the possibility of being an eschatological instant and in Christian faith this possibility is realised.... In every moment slumbers the possibility of being the eschatological moment. You must awaken it.[27]

Thus Blake's system, while insisting upon an absolute end, at the same time goes on in the world. To choose absolutely either an end or a continuation is to recapitulate the horrors of the Sons of Albion.

It is appropriate to conclude this study with a statement from Blake's greatest critic, who approaches this problem from the question of whether Blake's art is complete or not:

> It is clear that the argument over whether art is complete in itself or suggests something beyond itself ... is dealt with by Blake as he

deals with all questions that are cracked down the middle by a cloven fiction.... The work of art suggests something beyond itself most obviously when it is most complete in itself.[28]

Similarly, the question of whether Blake does or does not construct a system is a cloven fiction. Blake is constructing systems most coherently when he is smashing systems; Blake is smashing systems most vigorously when he is constructing systems.

Notes

1. Much of the work on this paper took place in the summer of 1985, during which I studied at Stanford University in a seminar for college teachers sponsored by the National Endowment for the Humanities. I thank the NEH for that opportunity.

Several other members of the seminar, particularly Patricia L. Skarda, encouraged me in discussions; above all, the leader of the seminar, Michael Cooke, gave me suggestions and courage. His *Acts of Inclusion: Studies Bearing on an Elementary Theory of Romanticism* (New Haven: Yale Univ. Press, 1979) had already proved valuable to me before the seminar. His "Romanticism and the Paradox of Wholeness," *Studies in Romanticism*, 23 (1985), pp. 435-53, which appeared during the summer of 1985, stimulated me with its similarities to and differences from my own views.

I would also like to thank Michael Tolley, whose groundbreaking work in his unpublished dissertation, *William Blake's Use of the Bible* (London, 1974), revealed much to me.

No words can acknowledge the debt I owe David Erdman, who guided my doctoral studies at Stony Brook and who made suggestions to improve this article.

2. Friedrich Schlegel, *Schlegel's Lucinde and the Fragments*, trans. Peter Firchow (Minneapolis: Univ. of Minnesota, 1971), Atheneum Fragment #53.

3. *A Blake Dictionary: The Ideas and Symbols of William Blake* (1965; rpt. Boulder, Colo.: Shambhala, 1979).

4. *Fearful Symmetry: A Study of William Blake* (Princeton: Princeton Univ. Press, 1969).

5. *Symbol and Truth in Blake's Myth* (Princeton: Princeton Univ. Press, 1980). For example, writing of Emanations, Damrosch admits that they must be understood "as a mystical attempt to keep what we have and yet transform it utterly" (240). However, on a similar subject, he refuses this mysticism: "the body is at once a merciful 'limit of contraction' and a trap from which we must escape. But it is easier to say that it is both at once than to understand how it

can be" (175). Finally, Damrosch has a definition of sense which excludes him from Blake's vision: "I do not deny that analogues to Blake's position [concerning the paradoxes of sexuality] may be found in Boehme and elsewhere; I deny that they make sense" (238).

6. Review of Damrosch in David V. Erdman, ed., *The Romantic Movement: A Selective and Critical Bibliography for 1981* (New York: Garland, 1982), pp. 79-80.

7. *The New Apocalypse: The Radical Christian Vision of William Blake* (Lansing: Michigan State Univ. Press, 1967), p. xvi.

8. *Philosophy of the Literary Symbolic* (Tallahassee: Univ. Presses of Florida, 1983). Adams writes: "from poetry's point of view the poem makes a language, which creates and contains its signified and allows it to emanate into the world to be devoured; though I shall recognize that from the opposite point of view, which I shall call 'antimyth,' it copies or signifies only and cannot contain or radically form. And I shall hold that *both views are necessary fictions*—Blakean contraries from which a desirable culture can, but admittedly may not, emerge. This book is an attempt to build a language that expresses this situation of contraries as fundamental and necessary" (28) [italics mine].

9. *Literal Imagination: Blake's Vision of Words* (Berkeley: Univ. of California Press, 1983).

10. "Blakean Zen," *Studies in Romanticism*, 24 (1985), p. 196.

11. Steven Shaviro, "'Striving With Systems': Blake and the Politics of Difference," *boundary 2*, 10 (1983): pp. 229-50.

12. Christine Gallant, *Blake and the Assimilation of Chaos* (Princeton: Princeton Univ. Press, 1978), pp. 10-15.

13. For abbreviations, see above, pp. ix-x.

14. See 69.44 (quoted later in this essay), Blake's improvement on Hebrews 9.7-15, in which Jesus is described as the new high priest.

15. Biblical scholars are not sure exactly what the Abomination was thought to be, but Daniel seems to expect some kind of Babylonian idol to be set up in the Temple.

Blake similarly equates the Abomination of Desolation and the Temple's secrecies in his annotations to Watson: "The Bible or Peculiar Word of God, Exclusive of Conscience or the Word of God Universal, is that Abomination which like the Jewish ceremonies is for ever removed & henceforth every man may converse with God & be a King & Priest in his own house" (E615).

16. The first words on plate 3 of *Jerusalem* (the first words in the poem after Blake effaced the words on plate 2), in white-line etching in the black

border above the clouds, are "SHEEP" and "GOATS." Because "SHEEP" appears on the reader's left and "GOATS" on his right, it seems as if Blake is inviting the reader to be judged by the text which he sees before him. As Erdman puts it, "the judging-forgiving Christ would be sitting just above the page (his name appears in top center, Plate 4)" (*IB* 283).

17. Useful discussions of Reuben can be found in Karl Kiralis, "A Guide to the Intellectual Symbolism of William Blake's Later Prophetic Writings," *Criticism*, 1 (1959), pp. 190-210; James Ferguson, "Prefaces to *Jerusalem*," in Michael Phillips, ed., *Interpreting Blake* (Cambridge: Cambridge Univ. Press, 1979), pp. 164-95; and W.H. Stevenson, ed., *The Poems of William Blake* (London: Longmans, 1971).

18. *New English Bible, with the Apocrypha* (Oxford Univ. and Cambridge Univ., 1970), p. 383.

19. Of course Blake's statements about the wiry bounding line in his drawing and painting make an interesting juxtaposition here.

20. Stevenson, p. 686.

21. *Blake: Prophet Against Empire*, 3rd ed. (Princeton: Princeton Univ. Press, 1977), p. 469.

22. For a brilliant discussion of this concept see Northrop Frye's explanation of "the central point of the argument of *Jerusalem*" in terms of reflection (*Fearful Symmetry*, pp. 383-90).

In addition, this idea of the reversed relationship of the visionary and the fallen finds a fascinating analogue in Blake's physical production of his illuminated poems. The raised surfaces on copper are literally the *type* of the finished product on paper. But the entire physical process of printing is figuratively a *type* of the spiritual process of regeneration. Although it has its own identity as a physical process, it fulfills itself only in its reversal into a spiritual or mental product.

Furthermore, the printmaker can complete his task only in an action of physical reversal. That is, when he prints on paper, his design is reversed. For detailed explanations of Blake's probable methods, see Robert Essick, *William Blake, Printmaker* (Princeton: Princeton Univ. Press, 1980), *passim*, especially pp. 89-92. Throughout *Jerusalem* Blake indicates that the attainment of eternal Vision can come only through a reversal of the fallen world.

In a profound sense, to find the eternal world is to reverse the fallen world, just as the printmaker must reverse his design in order to print it onto paper. But he cannot reverse the plate until he has fully shaped it, in all its minute particularity. Furthermore, the design on paper is identical in every detail to the design on copper, except that it has been completely reversed, transformed in its perspective as well as in its medium. It is entirely different, even while it is the same, and both the sameness and the difference have been radically redefined from their original connotations.

Just as the printmaker's work must be fulfilled by a process of reversal, so the Christian artist's task must be fulfilled by a process of reversal, a reversal which completely accepts the fallen world and at the same time utterly transforms it.

"The poet himself must be able to write his script in reverse, so that it should appear in legible form through the second inversion in the mirror of art" (Jean Paul Richter, *Vorschule der Asthetik* #39, quoted in Lillian Furst, *Fictions of Romantic Irony* (Cambridge: Harvard Univ. Press, 1984), p. 121). This wonderful little statement encapsulizes the process of reversal. See also the illustration on *Jerusalem* 81, in which Gwendolyn's secret is displayed in mirror writing.

23. "The full meaning of the Incarnation is that the Incarnation is a dual and dialectical process whereby God empties Himself of Himself and becomes man and man empties himself of his historical particularity and his individual selfhood and becomes God: 'Therefore God becomes as we are, that we may be as he is.'... Spirit *is* this eternal movement of absolute self-negation" (Altizer, pp. 74-75).

24. *Life of William Blake* I (1880; rpt. Totowa, N.J.: Rowman and Littlefield, 1973), pp. 342-43.

25. For a brilliant explanation of the annihilation of the self in Blake's *Milton* see Mark Bracher's *Being Form'd: Thinking Through Blake's Milton* (Barrytown, N.Y.: Station Hill Press, 1985), esp. pp. 243-44.

26. I argue elsewhere that the whole of *Jerusalem* is framed by a transfiguration scene, analogous to that found in Matthew and Luke, which is set up on plate 4 and completed in this passage on plate 96.

27. *History and Eschatology* (New York: Harper, 1957), pp. 151-55.

28. Frye, p. 418.

Blake as an Eighteenth-Century Hebraist

Sheila A. Spector

It is generally recognized that despite his assertion to the contrary, Blake knew small Latin and even less Hebrew.[1] The only direct evidence we have of his familiarity with the Holy Tongue is his sporadic use of Hebrew letters in some of the drawings, and, as Arnold Cheskin has demonstrated, these examples are fraught with error, exhibiting at best only a rudimentary acquaintance with the language.[2] So, if we view the subject from the perspective of linguistic accuracy, there is no question but that Blake was incapable of using Hebrew with any measure of competence. To impose standards of linguistic accuracy, however, on the eighteenth-century Christian, who (as far as we know) did not know Latin, is anachronistic; for two centuries ago, Christian Hebraism in England was undergoing profound changes as a result of a number of historical factors which, in effect, produced a state of linguistic anarchy in relation to Hebrew, so that the free-thinking Englishman could have felt justified in manipulating Hebrew in virtually any way he chose.[3] Therefore, in order to comprehend Blake's use of Hebrew, we must explore the state of Christian Hebraism at the time, rather than expect the poet to conform to our own standards of grammar.[4]

I
The Intellectual Context

Eighteenth-Century Hebraism

The eighteenth-century controversies over the language of the Old Testament were directly related to the upheaval over Christianity itself, for virtually all attitudes toward religion were justified by interpretations of the Bible which were predicated on the basis of linguistics, though frequently those making pronouncements on Hebrew themselves had little or no knowledge of traditional Hebrew grammar.[5] If today we first study grammar and vocabulary before attempting to evaluate a text, the reverse was frequently the case two centuries ago. Christians espousing a number of religious and social theories frequently sought linguistic justification for what otherwise might be considered prejudicial beliefs and, in turn, produced grammars and dictionaries that would validate those theories. Consequently, not only could the eighteenth-century Englishman find, from among the myriad of linguistic studies published, a rationalization for virtually any abuse of the language he chose, but the purist would be hard put to determine the true nature of Hebrew from the sources available to him.[6] Primarily four historical considerations influenced these studies of Hebrew grammar: Anti-Semitism, Linguistics, Mythology, and Mysticism.[7]

Although difficult for someone of the twentieth century to comprehend, the most significant aspect of eighteenth-century Christian Hebraism was its anti-Semitism.[8] While today we recognize that religion is a study distinct from linguistics, in the eighteenth century anti-Semitism proved to be a useful explanation for a number of contradictions facing believers in the Divinity of the Bible who were being attacked from within by Sectarians, and from without by Deists. Historically, even though the Jews were considered to be the authorities on Hebrew grammar, having spoken the Holy Tongue and having preserved the Old Testament, the Church generally attempted to discredit the validity of Jewish exegesis in favor of the writings of the Church Fathers. In the Renaissance, however, with the general awakening of knowledge came a renewed interest in Hebrew, and with it a need for instructors. While many of the teachers were apostates, almost all based their instruction on the work of medieval Jewish grammarians so that Christians who studied Hebrew were at least indirectly introduced to the scholarship of the Jews. Later, when the Reformers rejected the Church teachings, they, too, had to rely on Jewish scholarship, at least until Protestants became adept enough in Hebrew to approach Scriptures on their own.[9] In the eighteenth century, when Christians no longer needed Jewish exegetes to explain the text, they again had to face the contradiction inherent in relying on the Jews, who, having rejected Christ, must have misconstrued Scriptures, for rules on how to read the Bible. Thus, in the Age of Enlightenment, anyone who read the Book had to account for the people of the Book, as well.[10]

Virtually all eighteenth-century Christians who wrote about Hebrew took a stand on the Jewish question, and not surprisingly, the attitudes tended to be closely related to the writer's relationship to Christian orthodoxy: those who accepted traditional exegesis based on the work of Jewish grammarians had to justify relying on such "unreliable" authorities, while those who proffered new interpretations of the Bible had to undermine the basis for the older exegesis.[11] Few English writers of the time agreed with Anthony Purver who, in his *New and Literal Translation of All the Books of the Old Testament* (2 vols.; London, 1764), asserted that "their Rabbies too were good Grammarians of the Hebrew tongue" (I.ii). Rather, the consensus seemed to be that the Jews were ignorant, the only difference of opinion being whether or not they deliberately mutilated the text.[12] In his *Dissertation concerning the Antiquity of the Hebrew-Language* (London, 1767), John Gill explained that the Jews are

> very ignorant of divine things, and therefore the more to be pitied. Even though many of them are, no doubt, very immoral persons; but have we not such of both sorts among ourselves? yet, as bad as the Jews are, the worst among them, I believe, would sooner die, than wilfully corrupt any part of the Hebrew Bible. (8)

More neutral is Thomas Sharp who, in his *Discourses Touching the Antiquity of the Hebrew Tongue and Character* (London, 1755), advises objectivity since even though "the Rabbinical Jews" produced grammars "not only without any authority, but, I think, irrationally," still

> I should rather chuse to judge of [the Hebrew tongue] with impartiality, and to speak of it with caution, according to the best intelligence we can get concerning it, and according to the most rational conclusions, or most probable inferences we can make from thence. (81-82)

Not all Christians, however, were willing to accept Sharp's advice. Alexander Geddes offers his *Prospectus of a New Translation of the Holy Bible* (Glasgow, 1786), in part because "with the first elements of Hebrew learning, were propagated in the Christian schools the most ridiculous notions of the Rabbins; and no one called in question their bold assertions, because no one supposed he could know anything of the matter but through them" (6).

The most virulent attacks came from Sectarians. To John Hutchinson, "a half-educated and fanciful man of boundless vanity" (*D.N.B.* X.342), worse than ignorant, "the Jews are Corrupters of the Text, thieves and Lyars."[13] Hutchinson's follower Julius Bate, a Hebraist of far greater accomplishment and reputation than the founder of the sect, seems unable to let pass an opportunity to attack the Jews. In his treatise on *The Integrity of the Hebrew Text* (London, 1754), Bate claims that Jews "knew but little, very little in the Matter, Hebrew having been a dead Language near 700 Years when the first Christian Translation was made" (7). Similarly, in his *Reply to Dr. Sharp's Review and Defence of His Dissertation on the Scripture Meaning of Aleim and Berith* (London, 1755), Bate asserts that "If we are forced to go to the apostate Jews to construe the Hebrew Bible for us, we had better have been without it" (171), since "though the language itself came from God, the rules by which they have construed the writings in it came from the Synagogue of Satan" (28). Bate is most explicit in his *Critica Hebraea, or, A Hebrew-English Dictionary, without Points* (London, 1767):

> Strange, strange infatuation, that any man should ever think that those who crucified the Messiah, through ignorance of the Scriptures, should be able to teach others to find the Christ in them! (iii)

Most of Bate's work is intended to support Hutchinsonian doctrines and to defend the Sectarian's interpretation of Hebrew from attacks by more traditional Christians, and the anti-Semitism seems to be a means of questioning the authority upon which more orthodox interpretations of the Bible are predicated while, at the same time, providing a ready scapegoat for Christian misinterpretations of the Bible.[14]

While Bate's intention in denigrating the Jews was to bolster Hutchinsonian arguments then under attack by non-Sectarians, in fact he contributed to the position of the Deists who denied the Divinity of the Bible itself. In undermining Jewish authority, Bate drew what he considered to be the logical conclusion that because the extant text was preserved by the Jews, and because the Jews corrupted the text, then we could not possibly have any authoritative copy of the Old Testament:

> So that the Scriptures, unless we get a better Set of them, by the Help of a Corrupted, interpolated Copy; and a vague, loose, irregular, and in many Places unintelligible Version, are lost; and we have no Scripture at all since the Jews have played such Tricks with it, and made a new Scripture for themselves, not us. ... who can give us any Security that they have not done unto them [Scriptures] whatsoever they listed? and where then will their Credit be? (*Integrity of the Hebrew Text*, 48)

While to Bate this means that Hutchinson's manipulation of the text is an attempt to derive the Divinity's true intention, to Deists it means that there is no text. After all, as Thomas Paine explains in his letter to the Honorable T. Erskine, "Yet we take the word of a restless, bloody-minded people, as the Jews of Palestine were, when we would reject the same authority from a better people. We ought to see it is habit and prejudice that have prevented people from examining the Bible."[15] Paine's attack takes us full circle, for he has forced literalists like Bishop R. Watson, who assert the Divinity of the Bible, in turn to defend the Jews as the chosen people. As a result, as Blake indicates in his "Annotations to Watson," "To defend the Bible in this year 1798 would cost a man his life" (E611).[16]

The anti-Semitism found in eighteenth-century Christian Hebraism, more than the historical response to a "stiff-necked people," had a linguistic basis as well, for the Jews themselves, two centuries earlier, had begun the controversy over the vowel points which by Blake's time was to turn Jew against Jew, Christian against Jew, Catholic against Protestant, and Sectarian against orthodox Christian. In order to understand the linguistic controversy which developed around Hebrew in the eighteenth century, it is necessary to consider the nature and history of the language itself. The Hebrew alphabet consists of twenty-two letters, five of which have different forms when they are the final letters of a word, making a total of twenty-seven characters. While several of these letters can serve as vowels, vocalization is usually indicated by a series of points affixed to the letters, though in printed texts points are often omitted so that one must be quite proficient to read correctly. The accepted text of the Old Testament, the source of interest in the language, was not codified until the post-talmudic period (roughly the second through the tenth centuries), when the Masoretes, those engaged in the preparation of a critical text, recorded the accepted version of the Bible.

Until the Renaissance, the Masoretic text was viewed as the received version of Revelation. In addition to the biblical text, the Masoretes included critical notes and points for vocalization, as well as diacritical marks to indicate cantillation for chanting at religious services. Since the diacritical marks indicate pauses, accents, and stresses, they also serve as punctuation marks; and even though the logic underlying their order is still not fully understood, they usually coincide with grammatical punctuation and are useful for reading, as well as chanting.

In the sixteenth century, the grammarian Elias Levita published *Massoreth Ha-Massoreth* (Venice, 1538), in which he argued that the points of the Masoretic text were not coeval with the letters, and that while they do aid interpretation, they cannot be considered part of the originally received text.[17] While today we universally accept Levita's assertion, for centuries following his original argument the religious communities were divided over which to accept as the received text.[18] Gill summarizes the dimensions of the controversy in the fourth chapter of his *Dissertation*, "Of the Antiquity of the Vowel-Points, and Accents":

> There have been divers opinions concerning them. Some think they are of a divine original; and others, that they are of human invention. Some suppose that they were first invented by *Ben Asher* and *Ben Naphtali*, about the year 1037; others, that they were devised by the Jews of *Tiberias*, 500 years after Christ at least, or however were invented after the *Talmud* was finished; others ascribe them to *Ezra* and the men of the great synagogue; who they suppose, at least revived and restored them, and fixed them to the consonants, which before were only delivered and used in a traditionary way; and others are of opinion, they were given to *Moses* on mount *Sinai*, as to the power of them in pronouncing and reading, though not as to the make and figures of them in writing, but were propagated by tradition to the times of *Ezra*; whilst others believe they were *ab origine*, and were invented by *Adam* together with the letters, or however that they were coeval with the letters, and in use as soon as they were: (136-37)

Once the authority of the text was undermined, exegetes granted themselves a number of liberties in interpreting the Bible; so in his treatise Gill attempts to demonstrate the antiquity of the points primarily in order to constrain the excesses of sectarians who manipulated the Bible to support their own interpretations.[19] But by Blake's time, the conservatives had lost out to the more radical Christian Hebraists, the most radical being John Hutchinson who justified his manipulation of the language as being a countermeasure against Jews, whom he accused of adding the points and thereby manipulating the text in order to hide the true meaning:

> And it is also of use, to find that wherever there is a *Hebrew* Word, which opposed the Scheme of these Apostates, and which no Construction, nor any Stories they could forge about it, could secure them so, but that it might be construed to destroy their System, that they took to their last Shift of reading it otherwise than it was writ, by adding a Mark, which they call Pointing, to insert a Let-

ter, and make it a Word different from what it was, or of another
Root, or of another Signification, than the Word would have been
without pointing, in that Context. (*Covenant in the Cherubim*,
153-54)

If Hutchinson lacked the background in Hebrew to support his con-
tentions, his followers Julius Bate and John Parkhurst were sufficiently
skilled to sway many Englishmen of the time. Both produced works
which proudly announce their position on the controversy: Bate, *Critica
Hebraea* (cited above; see fig. 1), and Parkhurst, *Hebrew and English
Lexicon, without Points*, to which is prefixed *A Methodical Hebrew
Grammar without Points* (London, 1762, 1778, 1792). As Tannenbaum
notes, Parkhurst's *Lexicon* was "the most widely read and respected
Hebrew Lexicon of the time" (100), going through four editions during
the century (315-16, n. 56). A glance at Roth's *Magna* indicates that the
eighteenth-century Christian had a wide variety of grammars and
dictionaries from which to choose, with most titles indicating the author's
stand regarding the controversy over points; there is no way of predicting
which side of the controversy any individual would have taken.

A third factor influencing Christian Hebraism in eighteenth-century
England was the growing interest in ancient mythology. As long as it
was generally believed that Hebrew was the language of Adam, and that
the Bible was the earliest extant Hebrew text, Christian grammarians
generally accepted the dicta of Jewish grammarians who, as the descendants of the people of the Book, were considered the authorities on the
language. But discoveries in both linguistics and ancient mythologies
forced Christians to re-evaluate their attitudes toward both Hebrew as a
language and the Bible as the primary example of that language.

The most conservative position, reflected in Gill's *Discourse*, was
that Adam was taught Hebrew by God, so that Hebrew is the language of
God, and the Old Testament an authentic text delivered by God. To support this position, Gill relied on the classical Hebraists of the past. Other
Christian exegetes relied on the conclusions of linguists and mythologists
whose view was that the antiquity of Hebrew and indeed of "all the
languages spoken in Europe, all Asia, ... and some part of Africa" identified them as all "dialects of one parent-language," which, to James Burnet
at least, was "probably invented in Egypt."[20] Or, as Jacob Bryant explained more fully in his *Ancient Mythology*,

There was once but one language among the sons of men. Upon
the dispersion of mankind, this was branched out into dialects; and

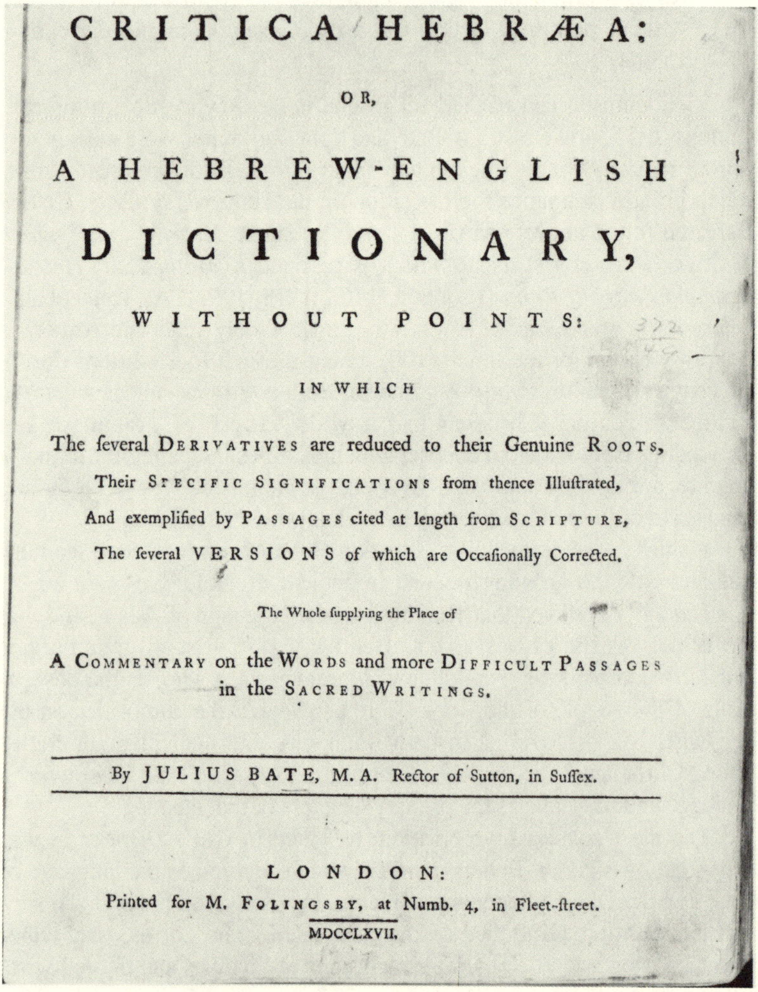

CRITICA HEBRÆA:

OR,

A HEBREW-ENGLISH

DICTIONARY,

WITHOUT POINTS:

IN WHICH

The feveral DERIVATIVES are reduced to their Genuine ROOTS,

Their SPECIFIC SIGNIFICATIONS from thence Illuftrated,

And exemplified by PASSAGES cited at length from SCRIPTURE,

The feveral VERSIONS of which are Occafionally Corrected.

The Whole fupplying the Place of

A COMMENTARY on the WORDS and more DIFFICULT PASSAGES
in the SACRED WRITINGS.

By JULIUS BATE, M.A. Rector of Sutton, in Suffex.

LONDON:

Printed for M. FOLINGSBY, at Numb. 4, in Fleet-ftreet.

MDCCLXVII.

Figure 1. Title page of Julius Bate's *Critica Hebraea: or, A Hebrew-English Dictionary, without Points* (London, 1767) —*Library of Congress*

those again were subdivided: all which varied every age; not only in respect to one another; but each language differed from itself more and more continually. It is therefore impossible to reduce the whole of these to the mode, and standard of any one.[21]

As a result of these theories, the Divinity of the Bible, and concomitantly its language, was being questioned from yet another perspective. To Deists, like Voltaire, who denied the Divinity of the Bible, Hebrew was viewed as the simplistic language reflective of the barbarians who spoke it;[22] while to Gill and G. Gregory, the translator of Robert Lowth's *Lectures on the Sacred Poetry of the Hebrews* (2 vols.; London, 1787), it was manifest that Hebrew must be, as Gill asserts, "the pure dialect, which the others are a derivation of and not so pure" (6). To Bate, a Hutchinsonian to whom the debate gave license to manipulate the language, the Hebrew of the Jews is derivative, a corrupted form of the original language of God:

> The Hebrew language was formed by God himself, who taught Adam to speak, and to speak in this Language. It continued to be the Language of the Church of God till the Babylonish Captivity, through the best Part of 4000 Years; one Half of which Time it depended upon Memory, Letters not having been revealed, till Moses received them from God in the Wilderness, and gave an Account in writing, in this Language, and the now revealed Character, of those hieroglyphical Figures, Rites, and Ceremonies, which had kept up the Faith of Believers, and the Form of Religion in the patriarchal, or holy Line, till the Egyptian Bondage had well nigh confounded the Truth of Religion with the Errors of Idolatry ... (*Integrity of the Hebrew Text*, 1)

And to Parkhurst,

> Since the *Hebrew* Grammar, unsophisticated by *Rabbinical* Points, is so very easy, simple and concise, ... it is evident that the most natural and rational method of teaching the learned languages would be to begin with the *Hebrew*. I now argue only from the greater easiness of the grammatical part, and do not urge, that *Hebrew* is certainly the common Mother of *Greek* and *Latin*, if not all other languages. Those, at least, of which I have any knowledge, retain a manifest resemblance of their *original* Parent: And the nearer the fountain, the purer the stream; the more ancient and uncompounded the language, the more similar it is to the *Hebrew*. (Preface to the

Methodical Hebrew Grammar, without Points, published with the *Lexicon*)[23]

The search for the parent language went far beyond the boundaries of biblical scholars, for the growing interest in primitivism led many non-Hebraists to posit theories about the origin of Hebrew. Linguists like Burnet freely admitted that "I do not understand the Hebrew" (I.612), yet had no qualms about developing theories of its origin. In England especially, Hebrew linguistics was closely linked to theories of mythology by those who wished to posit the British as the direct descendants of the Patriarchs. In his *Celtic Researches on the Origin, Traditions & Language, of the Ancient Britons* (London, 1804), Edward Davies attempts to demonstrate that

> the *Irish* names unite with corresponding terms, in *Hebrew*, and *Greek*. This union of the import, conveyed by similar sounds, in the names of the letters, demonstrates to me the original identity of the languages, and of the conceptions entertained by the several nations, respecting their elementary character, or *symbols* of sounds. (334)

In order to demonstrate the antiquity of English, Davies included in the *Celtic Researches* an "Essay on the Celtic Language: in which its radical principles, are appreciated and compared with primitives, and simple terms, in Hebrew, Greek, and Latin" (347-561), showing the commonality of Hebrew and English.[24]

By the end of the eighteenth century, one could find justification for the belief that Hebrew was or was not the language of Adam; that the Old Testament was or was not the authentic Revelation of God; and that Hebrew was or was not the parent language. In addition, one could find linguistic studies "demonstrating" that all languages, including Latin, Greek, and English, derived from Hebrew, or that Hebrew and the other ancient languages, or that Hebrew and English, derived from a common source now lost.[25] In asserting that "All had originally one language, and one religion, this was the religion of Jesus, the everlasting Gospel" (*DC*, E543), Blake concurs with mythologists like Bryant, whom he cites in the same paragraph, who believe in a parent language which precedes Hebrew, since "The antiquities of every Nation Under Heaven, is no less sacred than that of the Jews." But by placing the assertion in his discussion of "The Ancient Britons," Blake implies that "English, the rough basement," is a direct descendant of the parent, since "Los built the stubborn structure of the Language" (*J* 36.58, 59, E183), and that, therefore, there is a direct linguistic relationship between English and Hebrew.

The final element influencing eighteenth-century Hebraism is mysticism. Many Christians accepted the Jewish belief that the Hebrew alphabet, as well as the language itself, was delivered by God; hence the characters in which Scriptures were rendered became as important as the words themselves, each letter being accorded mystical properties.[26] Any variation of a letter was viewed as significant, down to the addition of a single serif, and the reversal of a letter was said to convey a special meaning.[27] Historically, the Hebrew script, like that of any other language, underwent numerous stylistic changes which themselves were accorded mystical significance. For example, in the third of his *Three Books of Occult Philosophy* (London, 1651), Cornelius Agrippa notes three different styles of Hebrew calligraphy, each significant in its own way. Compare the traditional *alef* (a) to that of Celestial Writing (b), The Writing called Malachim (angels) (c), and The Passing of the River (d) (439-44):

(a) א (b) 𐤍 (c) ⊟ (d) ∖

In the eighteenth century, as with language, the original alphabet was also being sought; different styles of Hebrew letters, similarities between Hebrew and Greek, as well as other ancient alphabets, were being explored in the search. Bate claims: "It seems, out of doubt, that we have borrowed our *letters* and *numerals* from the Hebrew alphabet" (*Critica Hebraea*, iv). Also, William Milns includes several different styles of calligraphy in his *Penman's Repository* (London, 1787; see figs. 2 and 3).

Mystics were interested not only in calligraphy, but in the combinations of letters as well. To Kabbalists, the literal meaning of the Bible was considered to be merely the "outer garment" or "shell" which the adept had to remove before he could perceive the truth of Revelation; hence both Christian and Jewish Kabbalists practiced what is broadly known as *Gematria*, the non-linguistic manipulation of letters to derive the real meaning of the text.[28] The word *Gematria* is also used to refer specifically to the numerical evaluation of letters. Since each letter is assigned a specific number, practitioners of *Gematria* considered words of equal quantitative value to be linguistically equivalent, and substituted them for each other. Since all sorts of mathematical operations can be performed on the numbers, the possibilities, obviously, are endless; thus, while Christians used *Gematriot* to demonstrate the Divinity of Christ,

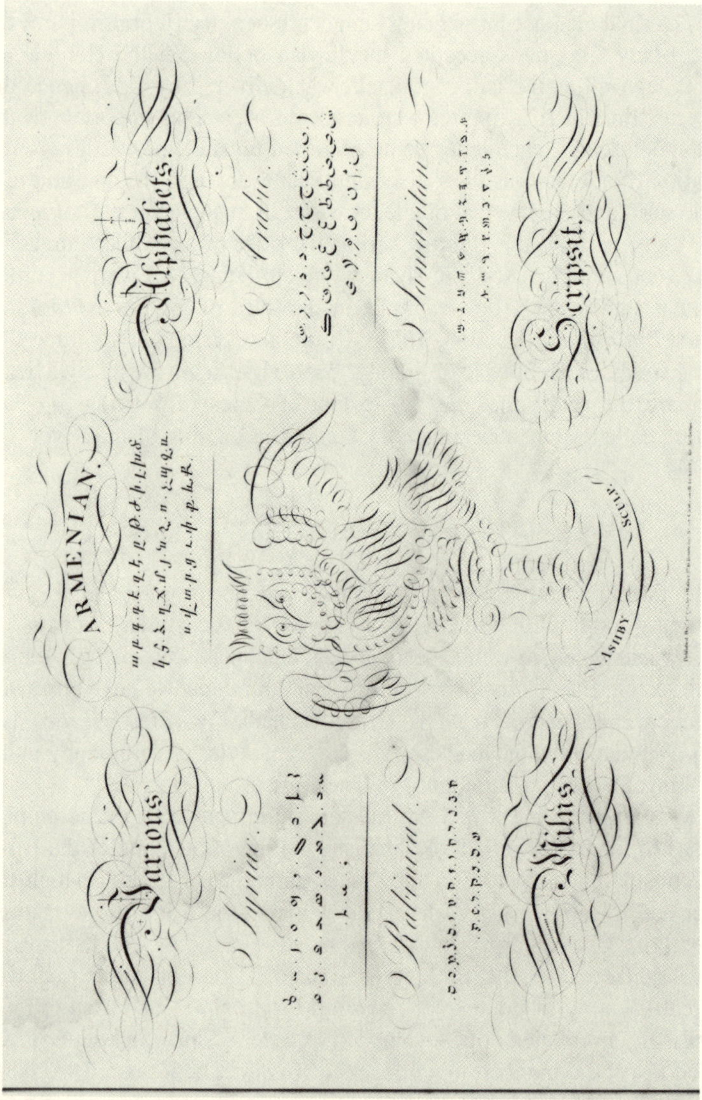

Figure 2: Rabinical, p. 22, lower left

Figures 2 and 3. Alphabet charts from William Milns' *The Penman's Repository, containing Seventy Correct Alphabets, a Valuable Selection of Flourishes and a Variety of New Designs* (London, 1787)—*Library of Congress*

Figure 3: "The Letters of the Running hand of the Jews of Germany," p. 35, upper left, and "The Letters of the Running hand of the Jews of Spain," p. 35, upper right.

Jewish computation derived the opposite result. *Notaricon*, the second form of *Gematria*, involved the formation of new words from the initial letters of words in phrases or sentences; and *Temurah* was the practice of substituting letters for each other, such as replacing all *alef*'s (the first letter of the alphabet) with *tav*'s (the last) to form magical combinations. Through these practices, mystics derived "words" which defy interpretation. Although the *Gematriist* presumably included method in his madness, others could go mad figuring these processes out.

The last influence of the mystics involves terminology. Even though English mystics knew very little Hebrew, they frequently incorporated kabbalistic terminology in their English works, so that texts of Rosicrucians, for example, are replete with Hebrew, either in Hebrew characters or transliterated, though often erroneously translated. This caused an even greater problem for the eighteenth-century Englishman because the Hebrew-English lexicons were devoted to Scriptures and did not include much of this specialized terminology. Therefore, there was no way to check the accuracy of sources. Even today, this terminology is usually excluded from dictionaries so that Hebraists unfamiliar with Kabbalah may overlook the significance of Hebrew words frequently included in the texts and drawings of the Rosicrucians.

Linguistic Abuses

These factors combined to produce a number of abuses of the language. Would-be Hebraists who rejected the authority of traditional grammar, both as produced by Jews and by traditional Christians, created a milieu in which virtually any distortion of the language became acceptable, and while one could usually identify the bias of a given Hebraist, one could not necessarily determine just how extensively the bias influenced a particular interpretation of the language.

The primary abuse involved pronunciation. Those who agreed with Bate that "As the Hebrew is a dead Language, it is not necessary to our *understanding* to be able to give the same Sound to it" (*Hebrew Grammar*, 4) gave themselves license to pronounce and transliterate as freely as they chose. In fact, Bate believed that the only importance of pronunciation is for instruction since "one common Pronuntiation is exceeding useful, and in some Measure necessary, betwixt *Master* and *Scholar*, yet we may learn it without a Master, or hearing it pronounced" (*Hebrew Grammar*, 4).[29] While we recognize the same kind of problem with Latin, classicists insisting on pronouncing *circa* "kirka" rather than "sirka," because Hebrew script and phonetics differ from those of English, the numerous possible variations of Hebrew could lead the speaker to erroneous linguistic associations and through (mis)transliteration, the production of combinations of sounds having little to do with the original words. And because David Levi's *Lingua Sacra* contained the only English-Hebrew glossary, it was very difficult, especially for those who rejected traditional Hebrew, to check back to the original.

The peculiarities of the alphabet also contributed to the confusion. Of the twenty-two letters, seven are "double," being pronounced differently depending on pointing, and since many eschewed points, different sources provided various English equivalents for letters: *beth* was said to be pronounced *b* or *v*; *gimel, g* or hard *g*; *daleth, d* or *th*; *caph, c* hard, *h*, or *ch*; *pe, p, f*, or *ph*; *shin, sh* or *s*; and *tav, t, th*, or *s*. In addition, *alef* was transliterated *a* or nothing; *he, h, e*, or nothing; *vav, v, u*, or *w*; *zayen, z* or *s*; *heth, ch* or *h*; *teth, t* or *th*; *yod, i, j*, or *y*; *ayin, o, ng*, or *ngn*; *tsadi, ts, t, s, z, j*, or *g*; and *kuf*, hard *c, q*, or *k*. In his *Compendious Hebrew Lexicon, Adopted to the English Language, and Composed upon a New, Commodious Plan; To which is Annexed A Brief Account of the Construction and Rationale of the Hebrew Tongue* (London, 1776), Samuel A. Pike denies the complexities of pronunciation entirely:

> It is remarkable, that in this alphabet each letter has a distinct simple sound: and that all of them together express *all* the simple articulations (save one) that are found in any of the learned languages, and perhaps in any other language whatsoever; which is much more than can be said in favour of any other alphabet. (171)[30]

Since vocalization was usually indicated by points and since many words lacked any of the letters which these Hebraists considered to be vowels, syllabification was whimsical, to say the least. Bate advises his readers that

> by supplying any Vowel you please, and more or fewer, according to the Number of Consonants in a Word, you would pronounce, but always pronouncing *short* or *quick* those you so supply, and *long* every Vowel you find in a Word, which will keep up the Distinction without any Confusion; tho' I think one would not chuse to make more Syllables than necessary in a Word. (*Hebrew Grammar*, 5)[31]

Not only does confusion result from these explanations, but so, too, does error. Take, for example, Bate's explanation from his *Critica Hebraea*:

> Thus [SHIM] and [SHIMaH] may be distinguished, as we should *shim* and *shime*; and do *tim* and *time*. The [heh], at the beginning of a verb, may be joined, where it can, to the first syllable: thus [HaSHaMaYiM] reads *Eshmin*; and [HaAReTZ] *earj*, as one syllable, like *earth, earn, earl*; and [VeHaAReTZ] either as one syllable, as *veal*, and *veer*; or else, as [vav] is a conjunctive *particle*, and no part of the word, *u-earj*; though, before another vowel, I think we always make a consonant of it: a rule which euphony, or ease, as well as brevity, recommends. (v)

Bate's first example is a good illustration of the problem. The initial *shin* is a double letter, pronounced *sh* or *s*, depending on the location of the point. Spelled as Bate has it in his dictionary, *shin, yod, mem*, the word could only mean "to place," pronounced "sim." With a *he* at the end, the word could mean either "the act of placing," *SIMaH*, or with a *shin* rather than a *sin*, "assessment, estimate," *SHIMaH*. Bate has no entry for *SHIM* in his *Critica Hebraea*, including these as well as other meanings under *SHM*.

Not only was pronunciation ignored, but grammar was oversimplified to the point of inaccuracy, as can be seen in John Parkhurst's one-page *Hebrew Grammar, at One View* (fig. 4), an "Epitome" which, he believed, "not only shows in how narrow a Compass the most necessary Rules of the Hebrew Language may be comprised, but also may well serve as a Grammar to be learned by *heart*...."

According to all eighteenth-century Hebraists, including Levi, the twenty-two letters of the alphabet could be divided into two groups: roots, those letters used to form the roots of words; and serviles, affixes to indicate grammatical function or relation, although, as all grammarians explained, serviles could sometimes serve also as roots while roots could never serve as serviles. Thus, the *s* of "walks" is servile, indicating either tense or number, but in other instances, it could also serve as a root— "sing." In order to decipher Scriptures, the would-be Hebraist was advised to eliminate all serviles from a word in order to derive the root, which he could then look up in a dictionary, much the way that we would look up "walk" rather than "walks."[32]

If the theory seems acceptable, in practice it led to great distortions of the language. First, the application of affixes is not the only way to indi-

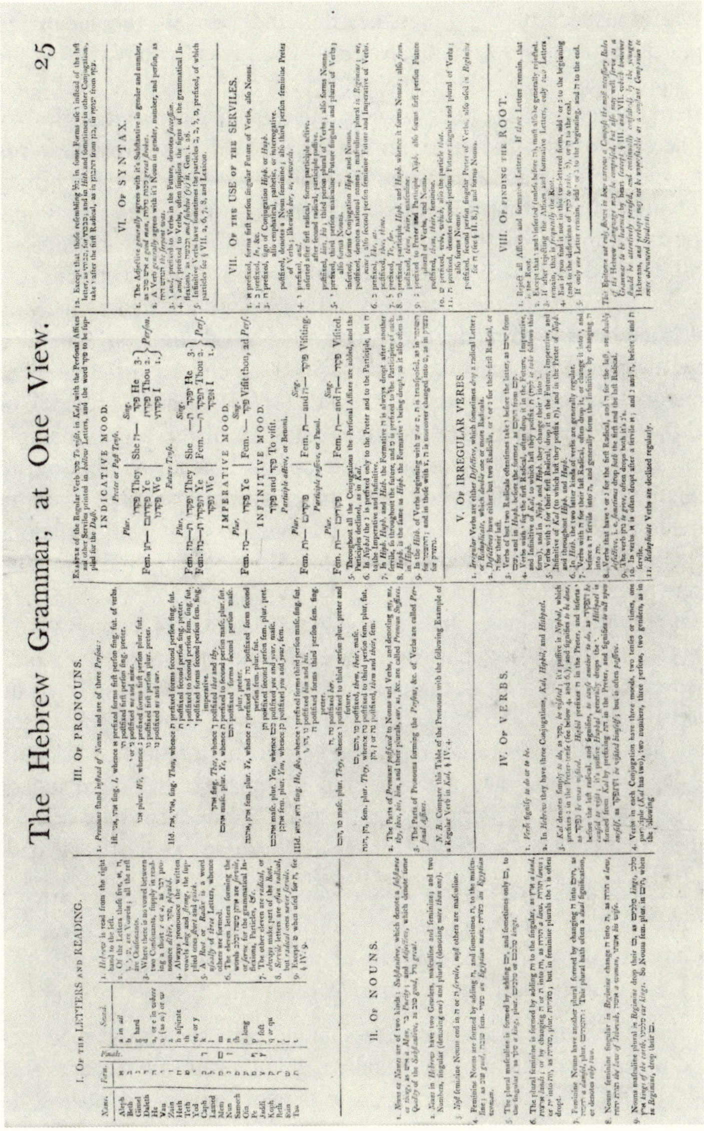

Figure 4. John Parkhurst's *The Hebrew Grammar, at One View,* included in *An Hebrew and English Lexicon, without Points,* 4th ed. (London, 1799)—*Library of Congress*

cate grammatical function in Hebrew. As in English, vowels are often used, so when the Hebraist denied the validity of the points, he eliminated an integral aspect of the language, denying himself the means to distinguish between, for example, *NoTeN*—"he gives," and *NaTaN*—"he gave" (like "sing" and "sang" in English). In addition, some Hebraists considered several letters to be vowels and treated them as though they were the equivalent of points, ignoring them at will. As a result, words sharing the same phonic base were all lumped together as though they were etymologically related. For example, the first word Bate cites in the previous example of pronunciation, *SHIM*, does not exist in Hebrew. With the *yod* (*I*) included, the only possible word is *SIM*, "to place," the distinction between the *shim* (or *shin*) and *sin* being indicated by the way in which the letter is pointed. After eliminating this distinction, Bate then "throws away" the internal *yod*, to derive *SHM*, an entirely different word meaning, depending on the vowels, "name" (*SHeM*), "there" (*SHaM*), or Shem, the son of Noah; Bate then combines all of these into a single entry in his *Critica Hebraea*, which is comparable to combining all combinations of *RD*—ride, rood, etc., under a single heading. Then, in addition to mixing the roots, he expands the entry to include all variations constructed through the affixation of serviles, like including "redolent" and "arduous" with "red."

Having thus eliminated the etymological distinctions among words, Bate is free to substitute such words for each other, the means by which "The several versions" of Scriptures "are occasionally corrected," as he proclaims in his title. This is like substituting "night" for "knight" in the opening line of Spenser's *Faerie Queene*: "A gentle [night] was pricking on the plain"—we now have a weather report in place of the initial action; or "a gent[i]le knight was pricking on the plain"—our hero could now be a heathen. In cases like these, Bate directs the reader to examine context:

> examine all the passages a word occurs in, and consider the different roots it *may* come from, and what different powers the *serviles may* have in the word; and then he may understand the original, and judge of the translation. (*Critica Hebraea*, vi)

But if all of the words in a sentence (assuming that a sentence can be recognized without punctuation) are equally ambiguous, then a reader is free to impose any convenient translation to support any interpretation he wishes.

In addition to this confusion of Hebrew grammar, those who believed Hebrew to be the original language derived Hebrew etymologies for words in other languages. While in the first edition of his *Lexicon* Parkhurst tentatively offered only a few suggestions about Hebrew etymologies, they were so well received by his readers that by the second edition he expanded his study to include more English, as well as Greek, Latin, and Northern words. For example, *AiSH*, the Hebrew word for "fire," is cited as the original of the English "ashes"; *BaHan*, "watch-tower," became in English "beacon" or "beckon"; *BaLA*, "to swallow," is "belly," in Celtic "Bulg," in Welsh "bal, bola, boly," in Latin, "Bellua, a great beast or fish," and so on (a possible etymology of Blake's Bowlahoola?), and *Boor*, "a brutish person," corresponds to its English equivalent.[33]

In the light of these rules, Hebrew orthography becomes a game of draw poker. Useful letters are retained as roots, while "serviles" are drawn as needed, placed where most useful. Oddly enough, though, virtually all of the Hebraists emphasized the importance of final letters because with only two exceptions, they are used consistently in the biblical text (Pike, 171).

Calligraphy, too, was considered important; Bate instructs his reader that "Writing over the Characters several times is the best Way to make them familiar to the Reader" (*Hebrew Grammar*, 6), while Parkhurst explains that "Hebrew ought always to be written broad and Strong." Although styles vary to the point of ambiguity, as can be seen in the different calligraphic charts found in William Milns's *The Penman's Repository, containing Seventy Correct Alphabets, a Valuable Selection of Flourishes and a Variety of New Designs* (London, 1787; see figs. 2 and 3, pp. 190-191 above), the letters, believed to have been given to Moses, were not willfully tampered with, as were the grammar and punctuation, thought to be later alterations of the text.

In the eighteenth century, Blake's possible sources of Hebrew were as varied as the exegetical traditions which they were used to support. In David Levi's *Lingua Sacra*, he could learn "Jewish" Hebrew, with points. In traditional grammars, he could find rabbinic Hebrew modified to accommodate more orthodox Christian points of view. And from books published throughout his lifetime, he could have been introduced to innumerable linguistic innovations, ranging from texts predicated on the belief that Hebrew was the parent language, to those postulating an ur-language from which Hebrew descended, all manipulating Hebrew roots to support their approaches. And if, indeed, Blake did know Hebrew, his attitude toward the language was likely as eclectic and inconsistent as that toward the text itself.[34]

II
Blake's Hebrew

When viewed in the light of eighteenth-century Christian Hebraism, the question of Blake's Hebrew becomes far more complex than has hitherto been believed. Although we are most likely relieved of the necessity of demonstrating that Blake knew traditional Hebrew grammar, we are left with the problem of assessing his knowledge within the context of a virtually limitless field, one in which any anomaly could conceivably be significant. Therefore, before we can begin to evaluate Blake's Hebrew, we must make several assumptions about Blake as an artist.

Basic to any analysis is the belief that Blake was a careful artist. If he was careless, then any inconsistency could be accidental, and therefore could not be used as a basis for drawing conclusions. However, Blake believed his work to be inspired by the Poetic Genius, and he tells us in *Jerusalem* that he is an extremely careful artist: "Every word and every letter is studied and put into its fit place" ("To the Public," E146); also, we know from textual evidence and historical account that he continually reworked plates to perfect them. Therefore, we should explore the possibility that even if his judgment and sources of information about Hebrew were faulty, he did have specific reasons for doing everything that he did, including "willfully subverting" the Hebrew.[35] So it would be more profitable for us to try to account for the anomalies than attribute them to ignorance or carelessness.

We must also consider Blake's purpose for using Hebrew, assuming that he did incorporate the Holy Tongue into his work. As a prophet, Blake deliberately obscured his work in order to promote careful contemplation on the part of his audience, so that the Hebrew, a language unfamiliar to most Englishmen, should be treated symbolically and not as literal discourse.[36] To reduce Blake's erroneous use of Hebrew either to ignorance or willful subversion is to overlook the numerous possibilities inherent in the symbolic use of language, especially in light of the multifarious theories about Hebrew prevalent during his lifetime. Rather than judge Blake against a standard which he more than likely would have rejected, we must "read between the lines" in order to decipher his "hieroglyphics."

The best place to begin an analysis of Blake's Hebrew is with the obvious, his use of Hebrew letters in marginalia and drawings. The many examples of linguistically accurate Hebrew tell us that Blake was capable of executing perfectly recognizable letters and could locate appropriate Hebrew words to complement his work. For example, in *Milton* 32, he includes the Hebrew word *RaBIM*, as well as the correct English, "multitudes," and Latin, "vox populi," in the margin.[37] The first and last letters of the word, the *resh* and final *mem*, could cause problems for the tyro, the *resh* being similar to a *daleth*, and the final *mem* to a *samech*. Not only does Blake make these letters easily distinguishable, but he also includes the final letter, a form wholly alien to the English speaker. Similarly, as Cheskin points out, it is the critics and not Blake who erred in mislabeling "Job in Prosperity," a drawing which, as Blake indicates by the word written in the book held up in the foreground, is really about Enoch; and the Hebrew phrase meaning "And he was no more because God took him" (Gen. 5.24) quite appropriately is found on the scroll in the background, as the biblical description of Enoch's death. Thus, we can infer that when he so desired, Blake could provide us with correct Hebrew lettering.

Since Blake was capable of rendering Hebrew accurately, we have to consider the possibility that he did have a reason for producing inaccurate examples in his work; but when analyzing the irregularities, it is best to limit our inquiry to those instances which clearly violate the rules of language. While, upon closer scrutiny, unintelligible letters could, conceivably, be found to resemble those of the standard alphabet, we cannot tell whether their obscurity was deliberate or the result, for example, of a technical error in the etching process; in other words, they make a poor basis for analysis. Similarly, series of letters which form no known Hebrew words could represent some private form of *Gematria* which we will probably never be able to decipher. Therefore, we should consider only those examples of calligraphic and orthographic irregularities which clearly contradict a Hebrew text.

A good example of Blake's lettering, the one upon which Cheskin bases much of his argument, occurs in "Job's Evil Dreams," no. 11 of the Butts watercolor illustrations to the Book of Job (no. 11 of the later series omits the Hebrew) (fig. 5). For the most part, the Hebrew is correct, though there are two anomalies, a reversed *alef* and the absence of a final *nun*. To Cheskin, both irregularities suggest ignorance on Blake's part, but an examination of their context indicates at least the possibility that Blake deliberately altered the text for his own purposes.

From the correct portions of the drawing, it is possible to infer that Blake had a version of the Hebrew Scriptures before him as he worked. Visually, the Hebrew is contained within arcs suggestive of the tablets

Figure 5. "Job's Evil Dreams," no. 11 of the Butts Job illustrations—*Library of Congress*

used in Jewish ceremonial art, and as Cheskin notes, Blake's text comes from the biblical passage containing the Decalogue. But the Jewish depiction generally contains abbreviations of the Commandments, and Blake's inscription contains words found not in the abbreviation but in the biblical text. Since most of Blake's drawing is unpointed, it is significant that he vocalizes one letter to correspond accurately to the biblical source, because ceremonial art tends to be unpointed and because the word which he vocalizes is generally not included in the abbreviation. The two words which Blake adds, as Cheskin notes, are part of the last phrase preceding the Sixth Commandment, but they are not the last two words of the sentence. The completed phrase reads: "Your God gives (to) you."[38] The possessive is indicated in the Hebrew by the vocalized final *kaph*; and the object is the last word of the verse. In the transcription, it is not likely that Blake simply "mistook the end of the fifth Commandment for the beginning of the sixth," a possibility raised by Cheskin, for then the Hebrew would have read "gives to you," but instead, we have "Your God gives," the subject and verb of the clause. Since Blake probably had a Hebrew text before him as he worked, had he wished, he could have reproduced this source exactly. The picture's irregularities, then, are probably deliberate rather than accidental.

The first inconsistency in the picture is the reversed *alef* in the negation of the Seventh Commandment, "Thou shalt *not* commit adultery." Since three of the four *alef*'s in the plate are correct, we can assume that Blake knew how to form the letter; and since the incorrect *alef* is directly beneath a correct one, we can also assume that had the reversal been accidental, Blake would have noticed it and, as a careful artist, would have corrected it. Therefore, we have to consider the possibility that the reversal was deliberate and try to infer an explanation for the inconsistency.[39]

Given Blake's attitude toward the "Shalt not's" and toward chastity, it seems not insignificant that the error should occur in the Seventh Commandment, rather than the Sixth, which also contains an *alef*, or the phrase from the Fifth, which begins with an *alef—Elohecha*, from the root *Elohim*. Actually, there are two *alef*'s in the Seventh Commandment, another one in the word *TiN'AF*, "thou shalt commit adultery." It is possible that Blake deliberately corrupted the negation in order to suggest ambiguity toward the subject. To copy the Commandment exactly would indicate endorsement of its intent; to eliminate the negation would read as total endorsement of adultery; but an ambiguous reversal of a letter in the negation could signify that the subject is too complex to be reduced to a simple either-or, as he indicates in his *Visions of the Daughters of Albion*.

While the same reasoning can be applied to the other anomaly of the illustration, its implications are less suggestive. In the phrase, "Your God gives," Blake declines to use the final *nun* form for the verb "gives." Again, we can assume that Blake knew about final letters since the plate contains other examples: the final *mem* of *SHaMaYiM*, "the heaven," the only word on the right-hand tablet; the final *kaph* of *ELoHeCHa*; and the final *fe* of *TiN'AF*. And again, it is possible to infer that Blake deliberately chose to distort his text since "he gives" comes from the biblical phrase which he adds to the traditional abbreviation. But explanations for the anomaly are less clear. Since Blake deliberately points the possessive affix of *"Your* God" and then deliberately corrupts the Hebrew in the drawing as a whole—what "Your God" gives—perhaps he is suggesting ambiguity about either the act of giving or the gift itself, that either it is an incomplete act (no final letter) or, since it is the Elohim who is giving, that the gift is suspect.

Blake's work is full of such inconsistencies, not only within single drawings, but among individual drawings as well. For example, at the top of "The Laocoön" is the heading "The Angel of the Divine Presence," followed by a corrupt Hebrew version in which the *alef* of the word "angel" is reversed—*MaL'ACH* (fig. 6). In contrast, the identical phrase heads the second Job illustration, but here, Blake omits the *alef* entirely, leaving us with *MeLeCH*, the Hebrew word for "king" (fig. 7). If we assume that Blake did not simply forget to include the *alef*, especially since he knew the word, then we must conclude that the corruption was deliberate, though the explanation for the alteration may defy our powers of analysis.[40]

These few examples suggest not only that Blake could execute the letters of the Hebrew alphabet, but also that to some degree, at least, he was capable of recognizing Hebrew words and, if he chose, of using them symbolically. While he apparently did not attempt to compose his own phrases or sentences, he does seem interested in using Hebrew to expand the symbolic references of his pictures; so it is possible that the inclusion of Hebraisms in the poetry can also be viewed symbolically, though as we proceed, our inferences must become more and more tentative.

The most certain conclusions can be drawn from the inclusion of Hebrew names in the prophecies. To eighteenth-century linguists, names provide the clearest evidence we have of the original Hebrew, before it became corrupted over the years; and to Hebraists, the names of biblical

Figure 6. "The Laocoön": above him is the heading "The Angel of the Divine Presence," followed by a corrupt Hebrew version in which the *alef* of the word "angel" is reversed (*MaL' ach*)—*Library of Congress*

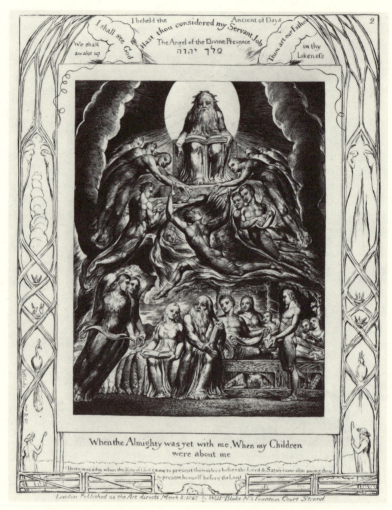

Figure 7. "Satan before the Throne of God," the second Job illustration—*Library of Congress*

places and characters are allegorical. Since most Bible dictionaries include definitions of names, Christians tended to be familiar with at least some of the meanings; so it is possible that when Blake included biblical names in his "Bible of Hell," he, too, allegorized.[41]

It is generally noted that in developing his myth, Blake worked the geography of the Holy Land into his prophecies, having the rivers Jordan and Thames, the cities Jerusalem and London, etc., correspond. And since biblical place names were usually allegorical, any Christian familiar with the Bible could allegorize geographically.[42] For example, in *Jerusalem*, Blake has "Jerusalem lay before the Gates upon Mount Zion" (78.21, E234), a literal statement since Zion is another name for Jerusalem. However, the same word (both spelling and pronunciation) could also mean "a desolate place" or "a wilderness," or as Blake completes the passage:

> Naked Jerusalem lay before the Gates upon Mount Zion
> The Hill of Giants, all her foundations levelld with the dust!
>
> (78.22-23)

Blake's description of Mount Zion as a wilderness could be a coincidence, except that in the next plate, Jerusalem laments: "I melt my soul in reasonings among the towers of Heshbon" (79.3), Heshbon being a geographical location, but also a Hebrew word meaning "accounting" or "reckoning"—"reasonings." And sixty lines later, we find her "Shrunk to a narrow doleful form in the dark land of Cabul" (l. 63, E235), a geographical location whose name means "fettered," "chained," "bound." At the very least, we can infer that Blake was most likely aware of the literal meanings of place names in the Bible.

If Blake used Hebrew for geographical locations, then it is possible that he used Hebrew for the names of characters as well. Florence Sandler has noted the possibility that the name Rahab, in addition to the biblical character, could also signify "breadth," an allegorical meaning which "could contribute to his concept of the Female Space."[43] Similarly, Blake's character Tirzah, the daughter of Rahab, though generally associated with either the youngest daughter of Zelophehad or the ancient Canaanite city, could also be a transliteration of "thou shalt kill," the key word of the Sixth Commandment, which appears in "Job's Evil Dreams."[44] As the "Mother of my Mortal Part" ("To Tirzah," l. 9, E30), Tirzah symbolizes death, and along with Rahab could constitute the coordinates of the physical world, Time and Space, since Leutha in dreams

... bore the shadowy Spectre of Sleep, & namd him Death.

In dreams she bore Rahab the mother of Tirzah & her sisters
In Lambeths vales; in Cambridge & in Oxford, places of
    Thought
Intricate labyrinths of Times and Spaces unknown.

(M 13.40-43, E107)

And at the Last Judgment, "Rahab & Tirzah wail aloud in the wild flame; they give themselves up to Consummation" (*FZ*, n. 9, 118.7, E387), as the cosmos returns to the purely spiritual state which obtained before the "fall into the Generation of Decay & Death" (*FZ*, n. 1, 4.5, E301).

The association of Tirzah with both the Sixth Commandment and the biblical character suggests the possibility that Blake could have located an unusual root for a biblical name. Although the etymologies of the two roots are different, to some eighteenth-century Christian Hebraists, the practice was encouraged as the only means of deriving the true meaning of Scriptures. And if we accept the possibility that Blake derived new roots for already existing Hebrew words, then it is possible that, like the mythologists, he derived Hebrew roots for words of other languages in the attempt to derive the parent tongue.

A good possibility is the name Sotha, identified by Northrop Frye as Sothis, the Egyptian name for Sirius, the basis of Egyptian Chronology[45]—a suggestion Kathleen Raine develops: "'the Star Sothis, which the Greeks call the Dog, is near to Cancer'—that is, to the northern gate of generation. Is Sothis the original of Blake's 'Sotha,' who 'in the North' gave to Odin 'a Code of War'?"[46] Given Bryant's assumption that "There are in every climate some shattered fragments of original history; some trace of a primitive and universal language" and that these "may be observed in the names of Deities, terms of worship, and titles of honour, which prevail among nations widely separated" (*Ancient Mythology*, III.600-1), it is possible that Blake noted the similarity between the two names and assumed a common root. But in that case, it is equally possible that, believing he had found "a shattered fragment of original history," he located a Hebrew root to coordinate with the others.

In Hebrew, the name Sotha could refer to *Sota*, a Hebrew word meaning "adulteress," and the title of the Talmudic tractate devoted to the laws dealing with women suspected of adultery. In the eighteenth century, one way that Christians rationalized anti-Semitism while still retaining belief in the Scriptures was to separate the biblical and post-biblical periods. The ancient Israelites of the biblical period were idealized into a perfectly ordered society in the midst of barbaric non-believers. In the post-biblical period, however, rather than accept Christ's abrogation of the

Law, the misguided Jews chose, instead, to codify ("bonify"?) the law in the form of the Talmud which became to Christians the symbol of Jewish obstinacy. The "Code of War" which Sotha gave to Odin in *The Song of Los* could therefore be associated with the Talmud, Christ being peace and, by contrast, the Talmud being war. It is also possible that of all the Tractates, Blake deliberately chose *Sota* to suggest a relationship between codified chastity and war, especially since in *Milton*, Sotha stands "in the Gate of Luban anxious" (28.21, E126), Luban signifying, according to Damon, the vagina (253).[47]

The next logical step in this hypothetical chain of reasoning is to explore the possibility that Blake derived Hebrew etymologies from names which he had already formed from non-Hebraic roots. We generally accept the English etymology of "Your Reason" as a pun for the name Urizen, as well as the Greek root "horizon," to suggest the limitations of the overly rational quality of the character.[48] But in *The Four Zoas*, Blake begins to refer to the character as "prince" (Hebrew, *RaZoN*) of "light" (Hebrew, *UR*, one of Bryant's roots), so it is possible that some time after coining the English-Greek pun, Blake derived Hebrew roots which underscore the conflict between Urthona (*UR*, "light"; *TaNaH*, "one who gives or teaches"), the Christ-figure who through the end of *The Four Zoas* remains dark, and the usurping "prince of light" who declares himself God.

If Blake was capable of deriving Hebrew roots from words in other languages, then he could also have coined his own words by combining Hebrew roots. Since, according to Bate, Hebrew "is the only language, all whose words are affixed to Ideas" (*Hebrew Grammar*, vii), "names are definitions of descriptions in one word, and sometimes two compounded" (*Reply to Dr. Sharp*, 184). A good example of the danger inherent in the procedure is the name Ulro. Easily identifiable as an aggregate of *AL*, "negation," and *Ro'EH*, from the root "vision," Ulro could literally signify darkness, "deepest night" (*J* 42:17, E189), symbolically the loss of vision, "dreams ... dark delusive" (*FZ*, n. 7, 85:21, E360), or both:

Thus Satan rag'd amidst the Assembly! and his bosom grew
Opake against the Divine Vision: the paved terraces of
His bosom inwards shone with fires, but the stones becoming opake!
Hid him from sight, in an extreme blackness and darkness,
And there a World of deeper Ulro was open'd, in the midst
Of the Assembly. In Satans bosom a vast unfathomable Abyss.

(M 9.30-35, E103)

But when spelled differently, the root for "ul" could also suggest "God," and "ro," "evil," making Ulro the realm of the God of Evil, Satan, or, if the roots are interchanged, the "God of Vision," or the "Negation of Evil."[49] In addition, the name could also refer to the twelfth-century false messiah David Alroy, a figure whom Blake could have learned about in Basnage's *History of the Jews*. While the etymology "negation of vision" seems appropriate in context, so could some of the others, and we have no way of knowing which, if any, Blake intended.

According to Joshua Trachtenberg, new names for angels were "constructed of a root term and a theophrous suffix," like "Kochbiel, who governs the stars (*kochab*)."[50] Analogously, Tiriel, which is not original with Blake, could have been comprised of *TaRaH*, "admonition or warning." and *EL*, God, as the character who embodies the mark of Cain throughout his poem; Zazel, described as the type of the wanderer ("Chusing to wander like a Son of Zazal"), [*Tiriel*, 1.38, E277]), could be derived from *ZaZ*, "to move," and *EL*, God.[51] This procedure could also be applied to non-angelic names. For example, in *Milton*, Ozoth, the character assigned the task of producing the optic nerve, could be "a symbol of strength or power," *OZ* meaning "strength," and *OTH*, "sign," since he "builds walls of rocks against the surging sea," and all of his creatures, "The speckled Newt, the Spider & Beetle, the Rat & Mouse,/ The Badger & Fox: they worship before his feet in trembling fear" (28.39, 42-43, E126).[52]

A final possibility, one more hypothetical than any of the others mentioned thus far, is that Blake translated English into Hebrew. Even though there was only one English-Hebrew lexicon available to him (David Levi's *Lingua Sacra*), it is possible that Blake was familiar enough with some key Hebrew roots to construct aggregates which would in a somewhat crude manner render English into the language of the Bible. The best example to illustrate this possibility is the name Leutha, occurring in a line borrowed almost directly from *Paradise Lost*: "and call'd me Sin, and for a Sign/ Portentous held me" (II.760-61).[53] The name can be broken down into three parts: *le*, *uth*, and *tha*. As all eighteenth-century Hebrew-English dictionaries and grammars explain, the letter *lamed* is a servile signifying "to," "for the use of," or "for the purpose of." *UTH* or *OTH* (the two are interchangeable if the word is not pointed), as seen in the discussion of Ozoth, means "sign." And THa'AH means "to err." Together, the roots comprise the phrase "for a sign of sin," an inversion of the line in the Bard's Song in which Leutha is identified as a sign of sin: "And call'd me Sin, and for a sign portentous held me" (*M* 12.39, E106).

Were the line original to Blake, we could assume either coincidence or translation from Hebrew to English, that Blake first coined the name and then wrote the line; but since the line is Milton's, even if we are not willing to grant Blake this degree of proficiency, we must at least consider the possibility of intentionality rather than coincidence.

From this examination of individual words, it is possible to infer that Blake knew more Hebrew than he has been given credit for. But that is not the real issue. As readers of Blake, we need to know how significant the language was to Blake, or from our perspective, whether or not the Hebrew will contribute to our understanding of the poetry. Therefore, we have to explore the possibility that the Hebrew words interrelate with each other in associational clusters which might produce hidden levels of meaning. Given the protean nature of Christian Hebraism, we could conceivably derive meanings to support virtually any interpretation, comparable to the Hutchinsonians' interpretations of the Bible; but we must explore the limits of improbability before we can define those of the possible.

Because of the numerous ways in which Hebrew words can be transliterated, it is best to use a passage like *Jerusalem* 32.1-13 (E178), which contains biblical names whose spellings and meanings are fixed:

> Reuben return'd to his place, in vain he sought beautiful Tirzah
> For his Eyelids were narrowd, & his Nostrils scented the ground
> And Sixty Winters Los raged in the Divisions of Reuben:
> Building the Moon of Ulro, plank by plank & rib by rib
> Reuben slept in the Cave of Adam, and Los folded his Tongue
> Between Lips of mire & clay, then sent him forth over Jordan
> In the love of Tirzah he said Doubt is my food day & night—
> All that beheld him fled howling and gnawed their tongues
> For pain: they became what they beheld[.] In reasonings Reuben
> returned
> To Heshbon. disconsolate he walkd thro Moab & he stood
> Before the Furnaces of Los in a horrible dreamful slumber,
> On Mount Gilead looking toward Gilgal: and Los bended
> His Ear in a spiral circle outward; then sent him over Jordan.

Of the six geographical locations, three have generally accepted etymologies: Jordan means "the descender," the river descending to the Dead Sea; Heshbon, as already noted, means "accounting"; and Gilead, "a hard, rocky region." The other three, not translated, are defined in terms of characteristics associated with them: Tirzah is noted for its beauty; Moab is arid, given its location near the Dead Sea; and Gilgal is located on a hillock or rising ground. Since Blake defines only two of the locations, referring to "beautiful Tirzah" (descriptive), and Reuben's "reasonings" when he returns to Heshbon, we can conclude that Blake is not constructing a geographical allegory.

But if we assume that the names were chosen deliberately rather than simply for their metrical value in the poetry, we should next explore the possibility that Blake was, perhaps, referring to words which, though vocalized differently, shared what the eighteenth century would consider to be the same root. Pronounced differently, Gilgal becomes *GaLGaL*, "a wheel or cycle," apparently an appropriate meaning since "Los bended/ His Ear in a spiral circle outward," and Reuben's wanderings back and forth across the Jordan do constitute a cycle. Also, as seen earlier, in addition to its biblical associations, Tirzah can also mean "thou shalt kill," the key word of the Sixth Commandment. While this meaning of Tirzah is not directly indicated, as is the alternate meaning of Gilgal, it can be inferred from context. The Jordan leads to the Dead Sea, near which Moab is located; Reuben is "in a horrible dreamful slumber"; and at the end of the plate, we learn that there are "those in Great Eternity who contemplate on Death" (l. 50, E179). The key to the passage seems to be the concept of death.

Death suggests a third possibility for the name Gilgal, *GiLGul*, the kabbalistic theory of the transmigration of the soul.[54] According to Kabbalists, the function of life is the perfection of the soul, but since no soul can be perfected in a single lifetime, it must undergo a series of revolutions until it is purified of any sin. At the end of each revolution, an accounting is taken of the state of the soul, known as *HeSHBoN HaNe-FeSH*, "reckoning of the soul," to determine whether or not the soul must undergo yet another cycle.

From this perspective, Reuben, synechdochically the twelve tribes, is, as we learn later in the poem, the body, in which case Tirzah ("thou shalt kill") could signify mortality, death being the definition of mortality.[55] Los labors "Sixty Winters," the life span, while Reuben sleeps (state of mortality) in the Cave of Adam (mortality). Los "folded his Tongue/ Beneath Lips of mire & clay," creates the physical body, and sends Reuben "forth over Jordan," the river (life) which leads to the Dead Sea, "In the love of Tirzah," mortality. "All that beheld him fled" because "they became what they beheld"—mortal. "In Reasonings Reuben returned/ To Heshbon, disconsolate," at the necessity of another revolution "thro Moab," near the Dead Sea, "On Mount Gilead," the horrible rocky place, "looking toward Gilgal," another revolution. It is possible, then, to read the passage as an allegory of the life cycle, "Of the Sleep of Ulro," the loss of vision, "and of the passage through/ Eternal Death! and of the awaking to Eternal Life" (4.1-2, E146).

When read from the perspective of the Hebrew allegory, the passage is strongly reminiscent of Spenser's description of the Garden of Adonis in the third book of *The Faerie Queene*, that "ioyous Paradize" governed by the Old Genius who "letteth in, and he letteth out to wend,/ All that come into the world desire" (32.1-2).[56] Like Los, the Genius "clothes with sinfull mire,/ and sendeth forth to liue in mortall state," all souls who then "returne backe by the hinder gate" (32.7-9). In Spenser's description of the life cycle, souls are sent back and forth "So like a wheele around they runne from old to new" (33.9).

In *Jerusalem* Blake transforms Spenser's description of Paradise into the process of perfecting the fallen world. Both believe in the eternality of the soul which undergoes these revolutions. To Spenser, "The substance is not chaunged, nor altered,/ But th'only the forme and outward fashion;/ … For formes are variable and decay" (38.1-2, 6); while in Blake,

> Albion hath enterd the State Satan! Be permanent O State!
> And be thou for ever accursed! that Albion may arise again:
> And be thou created into a State! I go forth to Create
> States: to deliver Individuals evermore! Amen.
>
> (31.13-16, E177-78)

But while Spenser views the process as the descent into the world of "Fleshly corruption" and "mortall paine" which all will forget when they return again to the Garden, Blake views the "Fleshly corruption" and "mortall paine" as the process of purification which culminates in physical death, i.e., Eternal Life, when the Lamb will "take away the remembrance of Sin" (51.30, E200). Thus, while to Spenser the "Great enimy/ … Is wicked *Time*, who with his scyth addrest,/ Does mow" down all life (39.1, 3-4), Blake's Reuben actively seeks "beautiful Tirzah," but in vain because he cannot have physical death until the entire cycle is completed.

If read with the Spenserian model in mind, *Jerusalem* can be viewed as the dramatization of the process of mutability delineated in *The Faerie Queene*. When Albion turns his back on the Saviour (to Albion the "shadow of immortality!" [4.24, E146]), he causes the world to fall into the state of mutability, and become subject to physical decay: "O that death & Annihilation were the same!" (23.40, E169). His friend Los then organizes mutability into the process of regeneration through which mankind will be delivered:

> All human Forms identified even Tree Metal Earth & Stone. all
> Human Forms identified, living going forth & returning wearied
> Into the Planetary lives of Years Months Days & Hours reposing
> And then Awaking into his Bosom in the Life of Immortality.
>   (99.1-4, E258)

The conclusion of *Jerusalem* is the achievement of the State of the Garden. If Spenser is describing the Eden of Genesis, Blake focuses on the New Eden, the New Jerusalem, a dynamic form of unity in multiplicity, or eternality in mutability.

While the Spenserian associations are evident throughout the poem, it is possible that both Spenser and Blake drew from a common stock of imagery. There are enough parallels, however, between Spenser and the Hebraic allegory of plate 32 to suggest a close relationship, assuming the validity of this interpretation of Blake. As readers, though, we are faced with a circular argument. If we assume that the Hebrew is accurate, we can then postulate a Spenserian model for the passage, but we can only justify the Spenser through the Hebrew. Still, we do know that Blake used Spenser in other works, and we do have examples in which Blake indicates some sort of knowledge of Hebrew, so the possibility should not be discounted.

The implications of this examination of Blake's Hebrew are, admittedly, not much more precise than those of its predecessors. We still cannot assert with certainty that Blake deliberately incorporated Hebrew into his work. But we can establish some guidelines for further inquiry. Most important, we must reject traditional Hebrew linguistics as the only standard against which to measure Blake's use of Hebrew. Not only was his access to traditional instruction limited, but, given the linguistic attitudes of his day, most likely he would no more have relied on orthodox approaches to the language of Scriptures than he would have on the exegesis of high criticism. Also, we should not expect consistency from Blake. There were a number of different theories concerning Hebrew two centuries ago, and as with exegesis, Blake probably familiarized himself with most of them. We know that he read Bryant, Fludd, Agrippa, Paine, and Watson, and each of these writers presented a completely different view of Hebrew to his reader. Finally, we should not expect Blake's Hebrew to be directly accessible to us. As a writer of prophecy, he deliberately obscured his work to make it intelligible only to the most persistent of readers, and multi-lingual acrobatics are already recognized to be one of his methods for preventing "idiots" from perceiving his truth.

In exploring Blake's Hebrew, we must be extremely cautious. We know that he knew the alphabet and we know that he was capable of incorporating biblical words and phrases in to his work. But we have no evidence that he could do more than use a dictionary. He apparently did not attempt Hebrew composition with any kind of linguistic accuracy, and seems to have limited himself to the formation of aggregates of roots with, perhaps, the occasional affixation of a "servile." The examples cited in this paper are only isolated instances which suggest the possibility that Blake could have used some Hebrew in his work. But before we can draw any conclusions, we must examine the Hebraic aspects of the entire corpus in order to determine whether he used the Hebrew with any kind of consistency, or whether the isolated cases are merely coincidences. We shall never know with certainty just how much Hebrew Blake knew, but further investigation should provide us with a better sense of probability. At this point, we can only discard the conclusion that "Blake knew little or no Hebrew"; rather, we must further consider the possibility that Blake knew a different kind of Hebrew, for if we ignore the subject entirely, we may be limiting our access to a poet who overtly placed himself in the biblical tradition of prophecy.

Notes

1. In a letter to his brother James (30 January 1803), Blake claims to "go on Merrily with my Greek & Latin: am very sorry that I did not begin to learn languages early in life as I find it very Easy. am now learning my Hebrew" (E727).

2. The only study devoted to the subject of Blake's Hebrew is Cheskin's "The Echoing Greenhorn: Blake as Hebraist," *BIQ*, 12 (Winter 1978-79), 178-83. While in *Jerusalem and Albion: The Hebraic Factor in Seventeenth-Century Literature*, Harold Fisch explores "the 'Hebraic factor' as a deeper and more pervasive influence," he is "not concerned with Hebrew learning as such" (New York: Schocken Books, 1964), 15, n. 2. In "The Echoing Greenhorn," Cheskin refines Fisch's assertion in the *Encyclopaedia Judaica* that Blake "knew little or no Hebrew" (see Fisch's article on "William Blake" [Jerusalem: Keter Publishing House, 1971]), into Blake "was not entirely without Hebrew."

3. The logical assumption is that the Jews were Blake's source for knowledge about Judaica, or, as S. Foster Damon assumes in his *Blake Dictionary: The Ideas and Symbols of William Blake*, that Blake studied

"probably with some local rabbi, who must have been a remarkable person, as the information he gave Blake was a tremendous stimulus" (1965; Boulder: Shambhala, 1979), 215. But just as Blake most likely had no access to Jewish sources for Kabbalism (see my "Kabbalistic Sources—Blake's and His Critics'," *BIQ*, 17 [Winter 1983-84], 84-101), so, too, with Hebrew, for not only was the Anglo-Jewish community of the time noted for its paucity of Jewish learning, but most of the rabbis were imported from the Continent and did not know English (see Charles Duschinsky, *The Rabbinate of the Great Synagogue, London, from 1756-1843* [1921; rpt. London: Gregg International Publishers, 1971]). There was only a handful of English-speaking Jews educated enough to teach Hebrew, and given the attitudes toward Jews prevalent at the time, they are known more for defending the Jews against anti-Semitic attacks than for ecumenicism. Also, in the eighteenth century, most Jews knowledgeable in Judaica tended to be strict construction-ists of the Law and, therefore, would likely have found Blake's attitude toward the Bible anathema, as he would have found theirs. While Blake could have learned Hebrew from David Levi's *Lingua Sacra* (5 vols. [1785-87; London, 1803]), the most comprehensive Hebrew grammar and dictionary of the time, Blake had access, as we shall see, to Christian sources which he would have found more compatible with his own views. Finally, as will be seen, unlike Christians both before and after the eighteenth century, many in Blake's time rejected the Jews as authorities on the language, believing, instead, that the Jews perverted Scriptures in order to distort what Christians believed to be the true message. Consequently, in order to locate Blake's source of Hebrew, one should turn to Christian Hebraists, and not some "local rabbi." Cecil Roth, *History of the Jews in England*, 3rd ed. (Oxford: Clarendon Press, 1964) is the standard history of Anglo-Judaica; and Todd M. Endelman's *The Jews of Geor-gian England: Tradition and Change in a Liberal Society* (Philadelphia: Jewish Publication Society of America, 1979) focuses on eighteenth-century Anglo-Jewry.

4. One legacy of seventeenth-century Christian Hebraism, according to David S. Katz, was the popularization of Hebrew (*Philo-Semitism and the Readmission of the Jews to England, 1603-1655* [Oxford: Clarendon Press, 1982], 66-67). It was fashionable in the century before Blake's to place Hebrew with the other learned languages, Latin and Greek; and Hebraists attempted to make the Holy Tongue generally available by producing Hebrew-English grammars which would not require Latin as the intermediary to the Bible. While in the seventeenth century, the debates over and studies of the language were conducted by the major intellects of the day, in the eighteenth, the language had been popularized to the extent that the more scholarly treatments were overshadowed by the myriad of original approaches being

devised at the time. Thus, while Blake could conceivably have confined himself to traditional studies of Hebrew, for several reasons he probably did not: (1) various sectarians derived new approaches which would have appealed to the non-conformist; (2) the most popular dictionaries and grammars were those of sectarians; (3) several of these original approaches were accorded validity by well-respected scholars; and (4) some authors with whom we know Blake was familiar used Hebrew in unusual ways. Therefore, it is more likely that if Blake did study Hebrew, it was non-traditional, although, of course, he still could have encountered some of the more standard approaches to the language.

Because the purpose of this study is to explore the possibility that Blake used Hebrew in a non-traditional fashion, the survey of eighteenth-century Christian Hebraism is weighted toward the more unusual linguistic theories of the period, though I have tried to balance the treatment by including examples from all sides of the various controversies surrounding the language. This paper, however, should in no way be construed as an exhaustive study of eighteenth-century Christian Hebraism in England. Since the focus is on Blake, I do not explore theories, especially those written in Latin, to which Blake would not have had access.

For a general survey of Christian Hebraism, see Raphael Loewe's "Hebraists, Christian" in the *Encyclopaedia Judaica*. Although Loewe omits eighteenth-century Hebraists, he does provide a good overview of the subject. On Christian Hebraism in Renaissance England, see G. Lloyd Jones, *The Discovery of Hebrew in Tudor England: A Third Language* (Manchester: Manchester Univ. Press, 1983). And the second chapter of Katz's *Philo-Semitism*, "Babel Revers'd: The Search for a Universal Language and the Glorification of Hebrew," discusses Christian Hebraism in seventeenth-century England (43-88). The only references to eighteenth-century Christian Hebraism in England that I have found are in Christian D. Ginsberg's translation of *The Massoreth Ha-Massoreth of Elias Levita, Being an Exposition of the Massoretic Notes on the Hebrew Bible or the Ancient Critical Apparatus of the Old Testament* (1867; rpt. New York: Ktav, 1968). In his biographical sketch of Levita, Ginsberg discusses the attitudes of eighteenth-century Englishmen to the controversy over vowel points (Ginsberg covers the controversy in general on pp. 44-61, eighteenth-century England in particular on pp. 59-60; see above, pp. 183-85).

5. The best study of Blake's attitude toward eighteenth-century biblical criticism is Leslie Tannenbaum, *Biblical Tradition in Blake's Early Prophecies: The Great Code of Art* (Princeton: Princeton Univ. Press, 1982). Since Tannenbaum's purpose is to explore exegetical trends of the eighteenth century, he does not consider Hebraism per se.

6. For a bibliography of works by Christian Hebraists in England, see the sections on "Christian Hebrew Scholarship" and "Grammars and Dictionaries," in Cecil Roth's *Magna Bibliotheca Anglo-Judaica: A Bibliographical Guide to Anglo-Jewish History* (London: Jewish Historical Society of England, 1937), 343-71.

7. In his survey, Loewe cites six major reasons why Christians studied Hebrew: (1) Recognition that the Latin Vulgate did not correspond exactly with the original Hebrew; (2) Interest in the religious experience of Jesus— "The Christian student thus regarded his Jewish informants as an organically living, though theologically fossilized specimen of the personal, domestic, social, jurisprudential, ethical, and speculative realities of ancient" Israel; (3) Desire to convert the Jews; (4) Anti-Semitism; (5) Renewal of learning in the West; and (6) "Incipient orientalism." While all six reasons are represented in eighteenth-century English works about the Jews, not all are reflected in language studies, the specific focus of this paper.

8. In the eighteenth century, attitudes toward anti-Semitism were undergoing a radical transformation. Since prejudice was antithetical to the rationalistic beliefs of enlightened Christians, Deists such as Voltaire and Paine rationalized their dislike of the Jews on the basis of the irrationality of a religion which was predicated on the Bible and a nation which rejected the tenets of the Enlightenment. They also distinguished between contemporary and ancient Jews, faulting the ancient civilization for being primitive in the sense of uncivilized. Non-Deists made a further distinction between biblical and post-biblical Jews: the former, as the people of the Book, symbolizing the ideal of primitivism in its pristine state; the latter, as those who rejected Christ, representing the ignorant, stiff-necked impediment to the Second Coming. The best study of eighteenth-century anti-Semitism is Arthur Hertzberg's *The French Enlightenment and the Jews: The Origins of Modern Anti-Semitism* (1968; New York: Schocken Books, 1970); Endelman includes a chapter on "Anti-Jewish Sentiment—Religious and Secular" in his *Jews of Georgian England* (86-117). Since my purpose is only to demonstrate how anti-Semitism affected attitudes toward Hebrew, the discussion is, perforce, incomplete.

9. In his Introduction, Jones discusses "Early Christian Hebraists (A.D. 200-1350)" (7-16), and the first section of the book surveys the development of Christian Hebraism through the Renaissance (18-83).

10. While the contradiction itself was not new to the eighteenth century, this paper will focus only on responses in Blake's time. For example, in his *Treatise upon the Authenticity of the Scriptures, and the Truth of the Christian Religion*, Jacob Bryant demonstrates the way in which Christians argued the

authenticity of Scriptures while, at the same time, denying the validity of Jewish interpretation: "But above all others the Jews themselves afford the strongest proof to the present purpose. For they remain a standing miracle, being, as was foretold, scattered over the face of the earth; and every where retaining those sacred records, in which their future rejection was denounced. Nothing but a judicial infatuation can prevent their seeing, what so nearly concerns their happiness. But this cloud must remain, till they have fulfilled the high purposes of the deity.... In consequence of this blindness the Jews, who are the greatest enemies to Christianity, have preserved the strongest proofs in favour of the Gospel. They shew to a demonstration, that the Christians have not altered the books of Moses and the Prophets" (1791; Cambridge, 1793; 29-30).

11. See Chapter VIII of Hertzberg, "Churchmen and the Jews" (248-67), for a summary of French attitudes toward the Jews. While France, a Catholic country, was different from England, elements of the French controversy crossed the channel via the Deists and translations of French works. In England, according to Endelman, there was also "a religious tradition largely absent elsewhere, one that wished to appease rather than persecute the Jews" (85).

12. According to Thomas Paine, "As to the Jews, there is not one single improvement in any science or in any scientific art, that they ever produced. They were the most ignorant of all the illiterate world. If the word of the Lord had come to them, as they pretend, and as the bishop [R. Watson] professes to believe, and that they were to be the harbingers of it to the rest of the world; the Lord would have taught them the use of letters, and the art of printing; for without the means of communicating the word, it could not be communicated; whereas letters were the invention of the Gentile world; and printing of the modern world" ("Extract from a Reply to the Bishop of Llandaff," in *The Complete Religious and Theological Works*, 2 vols. [New York: Freethought Press Association, 1954], I.355-56). Blake disagreed with Paine's examples of Jewish ignorance, asserting in "To the Public" that it was "God from whom [*all books are given,*]/ Who in mysterious Sinais awful cave/ To man the wond'rous art of writing gave" (E145).

13. The full title of Hutchinson's treatise is enough to demonstrate his attitude toward the Jews: *The Covenant in the Cherubim: So the Hebrew Writings Perfect Alterations by Rabbies Forged. Shewing the Evidence for the Scriptures; That Christianity was Exhibited to Adam; Invisibles by Visibles, Past and to Come by Types; By Cherubim, Urim, Tumim, Sacrifice, Cloud &c. That Jews and Gentiles Understood Them; That Tradition was of the Things Typified, That though They Understood the Tradition, Even of the Covenant*

before the World, They had Perverted the Intent of It That the Alterations and Stories of the Jews, After They Had Lost Them Types and Hebrew; Are Not Traditions, but Studied Evasions, To Expositions of Inspired Christians, &c. And to Support Their Apostasy, That the Grammatical Formation of the Hebrew, which is Descriptive, so Gives Proper Names, Cannot Admit VOWEL POINTING; nor Mr. Masclef's Method (in his *Hebrew Writings* [London, 1749], Vol. VII). Since Hutchinson supported his version of Christianity by devising unique methods of interpreting Scriptures, he defended his exegesis by attacking the Jewish basis of high criticism. Also see Edward Larrissy, "Blake and the Hutchinsonians," *BIQ,* 20 (Fall 1986), 44-47.

14. Most of the sources cited in this section are representatives of the Hutchinsonian controversy. Among his other beliefs, Hutchinson asserted that many words of the Bible have been mistranslated, for example, that "Elohim" means not God but "curse" or "denunciation." Hutchinson provoked Thomas Sharp to write *Two Dissertations concerning the Etymology and Scripture-Meaning of the Hebrew Words Elohim and Berith* (London, 1751), which, in turn, provoked a relatively large interchange: Benjamin Holloway, *Remarks on Dr. Sharp's Pieces on the Words Elohim and Berith* (Oxford, 1751) and *Originals Physical and Theological, Sacred and Profane, or, An Essay towards a Discovery of the First Descriptive Ideas in Things, by Discovery of the Simple or Primary Roots in Words* (Oxford, 1751), which traces Hebrew etymologies, and his *Primaevity and Preeminence of the Sacred Hebrew* (Oxford, 1754). Sharp followed with *A Review and Defence of Two Dissertations concerning the Etymology and Scripture-Meaning of the Hebrew Words Elohim and Berith* (London, 1754), and was answered by Bate's *Reply to Dr. Sharp's Review and Defence of His Dissertations on the Scripture Meaning of Aleim and Berith* (London, 1755). In the midst of the fray were Bate's *The Integrity of the Hebrew Text, and Many Passages of Scripture* (London, 1754); David Aboad's *Remarks on Dr. Sharp's Two Dissertations concerning the Etymology and Scripture-Meaning of the Hebrew Words Elohim and Berith* (London, 1751); and Benjamin Kennicott, *A Word to the Hutchinsonians; or Remarks on Three Extraordinary Sermons* (London, 1756), among others. Tannenbaum implies an affinity between Blake and "the Hutchinsonians, a sect that shared Blake's dislike of Isaac Newton" (315-16, n. 56). For a more complete discussion, see Larrissy, "Blake and the Hutchinsonians."

15. I.284. Paine is a primary example of the Deistic attitude toward the Jews. While he does not overtly attack them in his public discourse, *The Age of Reason,* his criticism of the Bible implies criticism of the people; and obversely, those who wished to defend the authenticity of the Book frequently had to defend the Jews as well. This quotation of Paine's is a response to R.

Watson's *Apology for the Bible* (London, 1797), which is a response to
Paine's original attack.

16. In the "Annotations to Watson," Blake avoids the logical trap which
snared both Paine and Watson by distinguishing between the Bible and the
"Jewish Imposture" (E614). While it is tempting to infer from this and other
passages in the "Annotations," as well as in *The Marriage of Heaven and Hell*,
that Blake was an anti-Semite, it seems more likely that the Jews qua Jews
were irrelevant to Blake, other than as the antagonists of his personal myth of
the Christian dialectic. If he criticizes the Jews in the "Annotations," a
Christian would say that he praises them in "To the Jews": "If Humility is
Christianity; you O Jews are the true Christians" (E174). Damon's assertion
that "Unfortunately, Blake disliked the London Jews" (215-16), based on passages from "The Everlasting Gospel," does not account for the fact that ev-
eryone fares badly in this satire.

17. While Levita was not the first to assert that the vowel points were
later additions, having been preceded most notably by Abraham Ibn Ezra
(twelfth century), he was the first to present a fully delineated argument based
on ancient texts. Truly a Renaissance man, Levita (1468 or 1469-1549) was a
Hebrew philologist, grammarian, and lexicographer who taught Hebrew
language and grammar, as well as Kabbalism, to the major Christian Hebraists
of his day, and also wrote grammars, compiled dictionaries, and adapted and
translated medieval romances for a popular, Yiddish-speaking audience. On
Levita, see Gerard E. Weil, *Élie Lévita, Humaniste et Massorète, 1469-1549*
(Leiden: E.J. Brill, 1963); Weil discusses the controversy over points in his
section on "Azaryah de Rossi" (314-22).

18. According to Weil, resistance to Levita's thesis resulted from the fear
that he had opened the door to a movement which would oppose the orthodox
tradition accepted by the Jews (317). The defense of the orthodox Jewish position came from Azariah de Rossi (c. 1511-c. 1578) who, in his *Me'or
Einayim* (1573-75), offered a refutation of Levita's argument based heavily on
passages from the *Bahir* and the *Zohar*, two mystical works believed to have
been of ancient origin, although they were, in fact, written in the Middle Ages
(on the *Bahir*, see Aryeh Kaplan, trans., *The Bahir: An Ancient Kabbalistic
Text Attributed to Rabbi Nehuniah ben HaKana, First Century C.E.* [New York:
Samuel Weiser, 1979]; on the textual history of the *Zohar*, see Gershom G.
Scholem, *Major Trends in Jewish Mysticism* [New York: Schocken Books,
1954], 156-204).

In the sixteenth century, according to Ginsberg, Christians used Levita's
argument to buttress their positions regarding the Reformation. Protestants,
who had already accepted earlier assertions that the vowel points were not co-

eval with the biblical text, saw Levita's argument as a further denunciation of
the traditions of the Church Fathers who had relied on the points for their interpretations of the Bible. In contrast, Catholics viewed Levita's argument as
justification of their belief that in ancient times, only a few spiritual leaders,
those familiar with the points, were capable of reading the text correctly so
that the masses, who were ignorant of the vowels, had to rely on the Church to
interpret Scriptures for them. But when Protestants realized that they were using the same arguments—though to support different interpretations—as the
Church, the Reformers, under the leadership of Johann Buxtorf the Elder, then
reversed their position, asserting that both the letters and vowel points were
of Divine origin.

In eighteenth-century England, the only Jewish contribution to the debate was David Levi's *Lingua Sacra*, written because "although some attempts
have been made towards a *Hebrew* grammar in English, yet none have hitherto
been produced, that are clear and explicit enough to enable a person to attain a
thorough knowledge of the language: Besides, they are generally without
points, on which account, can be but of little use to those who wish to approach as near as possible to the true pronunciation of the Hebrew" (I.viii).
Levi includes a section "On the Necessity of Points" in his Hebrew grammar
(I.20-36), in which he refutes the arguments of those who deny the authenticity and utility of points. David Jennings includes a summary of the controversy from the traditional Christian point of view in his *Jewish Antiquities;
or, a Course of Lectures on the Three First Books of Godwin's Moses and
Aaron. To which is Annexed, a Dissertation on the Hebrew Language* (2 vols.;
London, 1766). In addition to points, Jennings discusses the original language and the confusion of languages.

19. In 1624, Lewis Cappellus anonymously published *Arcanum puncta-
tionis revelatum*, a defense of Levita's original position, though carried one
step further. Levita believed that even though the vowels were later additions
to the text, they represented the authentic reading of the Old Testament. After
accepting Levita's assertion that the vowels were later additions, however,
Cappellus then concluded that the entire Masoretic text had been corrupted.
Having studied at Oxford for two years, Cappellus brought the controversy to
England where in the seventeenth century the Levita/Cappellus interpretation
was represented by Brian Walton, the De Rossi/Buxtorf by John Lightfoot. In
the eighteenth century, Lightfoot's position was adopted by P. Whitfield (*A
Dissertation on the Hebrew Vowel-Points, Showing that They are an Original
and Essential Part of the Language* [Liverpool, 1748]), and by Gill, in his *Dissertation*. The anti-vowelists of eighteenth-century England were divided into
two groups, those who believed that the biblical text was corrupt but could be
rescued through emendation (the most prominent of this group was Robert

Lowth), and those who believed that the Jews deliberately corrupted the text (this is the position of the Hutchinsonians).

20. James Burnet, Lord Monbodo, *Of the Origin and Progress of Language*, 6 vols. (Edinburgh, 1772-92; rpt. New York: Garland Publishing, 1970), I.655.

21. *A New System, or, an Analysis of Ancient Mythology*, 3 vols. (London, 1774-76), I.54. The *Ancient Mythology* contains "A Mythological, Etymological, and Historical Dictionary" (published separately in 1793), which lists and defines what Bryant perceived to be the extant roots of the ur-language. In his *Dictionary*, Bryant traces the etymologies of these roots, many of which are Hebrew, and demonstrates their manifestations in the various ancient languages.

22. As Voltaire explains in his *Philosophy of History* (London, 1766), "But what wisdom was necessary to distinguish the different senses? How came we to express the different gradations *I would, I should have willed*, the positive things and those that are conditional? It could only have happened among those nations that were already most polished, that by dint of time they expressed with compound words, those secret operations of the human mind; so we find among the Barbarians, there are but two or three tenses: the Hebrews made use of only the present and future tenses. And after all, notwithstanding all the efforts of man, no language comes near to perfection" (45). To David Levi, Voltaire demonstrates not the paucity of the language, but the ignorance of the writer (I.vi-viii).

23. In the preface to his *Critica Hebraea*, Bate claims that "The Hebrew grammar is more conformable to the English, than the Latin or Greek" (v).

24. The attempt to derive Hebrew roots for English words was not new in the eighteenth century. In 1649, John Sadler explained in his *Rights of the Kingdom* that he found "a New Etymology, for the names of *Brittain*: which (notwithstanding *Brith*, for Colour or Painting; and *Bretas*, in some Greek poets, for a *Picture* or a *painted Brat*;) he would have, to be called, by the *Phoenicians*, *Berat Anac*, or the *Field of Tyn and Lead*" (47). And in his *Court of the Gentiles* (Oxford, 1672), Theophilus Gale takes the Phoenician back to its original—Hebrew (46): "As for the other European Languages, the Italian, Spanish, French, German, English &c. its evident, that they are, as to their present constitution, made up, for the most part, of the Latin, and so originally from the Hebrew" (84).

Sadler, the first to proffer the doctrine of the Anglo-Israelites, claimed that the British were descended from the Ten Lost Tribes and hence were the true chosen of God, the Jews being usurpers. As descendants of Noah's son Japhet, ancient Britons were to have spoken the true Hebrew dialect, that of the Jews being a later corruption. While, in Blake's time, the movement gained popularity through the prophecies of Richard Brothers, the self-proclaimed nephew of God, Brothers himself did not employ linguistic justification in his prophecies, though later Anglo-Israelites did: "we find a large portion of our Saxon tongue having the Hebrew as its roots and stems" (W.H. Poole, *Anglo-Israel or The Saxon Race Proved to be the Lost Tribes of Israel* [Toronto: William Briggs, 1889], 319). On parallels between Blake and Brothers' prophecies, see Morton D. Paley, "William Blake, The Prince of the Hebrews, and the Woman Clothed with the Sun," in *William Blake: Essays in Honor of Sir Geoffrey Keynes*, ed. Paley and Michael Phillips (Oxford: Clarendon Press, 1973), 260-93.

25. In *Remnants of Japhet: Being Historical Enquiries into the Affinity and Origin of the European Languages*, James Parson explores the thesis that "those who speak the dialects of the *Japhetan* language to this day, which are the *Gomerian* and *Magogian*, or *Scotish* languages; and yet these are the only unmixed remains of the children of *Japhet*, upon the Globe; and the King of *Great Britain*, the only monarch upon the earth who rules the remains of that original people"; Parsons does refer to "a suspicion of its being related to the *Hebrew*, among some ingenious gentlemen, either as a mutilated dialect of it, or as a sister-dialect with that of some more ancient antediluvian tongue.... However this may be, since we cannot think that *Japhet's* people, or those of *Shem*, were at all concerned in the affair of *Babel*, we must suppose them both to have been languages of the antediluvian world, and both in the house of *Noah*" ([1767; rpt. Menston, England: Scolar Press, 1968], x, xix-xx).

26. As noted, Bate claimed that "Moses received [the alphabet] from God" (*Integrity*, 1). In contrast, Sharp felt that "it is very supposable at least, that neither the character now called *Hebrew*, nor that called *Samaritan*, is the true original character in which the Lawe was first written, but are characters, which, like others, have gradually changed according to the genius, industry, elegance, and taste, of the persons who used them, and improved them in different ages" (*Discourses*, 224).

27. In the section on "Letters," Augustin Calmet explains that "The cabalistical Doctors have refined much upon the Letters of the Hebrew alphabet. Other Rabbins, though more serious than the Cabalists, have likewise found some Mystery in certain Letters of the Hebrew Text, some of which are turned topsy turvy, others suspended, others closed; all which according to these Doctors is mysterious, and deserves particular Consideration; but whether this is done designedly or by Chance, we may affirm, that the Letters in themselves, taken separately from the Word which they compose, have no sense, and include no Mystery" (*An Historical, Critical, Chronological, and*

Etymological Dictionary of the Holy Bible, trans. Samuel D'Oyly and John Colson, 3 vols. [London, 1732]. II.58). In his *History of the Jews* (London, 1708), Jacques Basnage includes a section on the "Mysteries of the Letters" (189-90). It is interesting to note that in the Preface to *Jerusalem*, Blake claims that "Every word and every letter is studied and put into its fit place" (E146).

28. Because of Agrippa's influence, in the popular mind Kabbalism was believed to consist almost entirely of *Gematria*. As a result, those eighteenth-century texts which dealt with Kabbalah usually included discussions of Hebrew numerology, the most extensive being that of John Peter Stehelin in *The Traditions of the Jews* (London, 1732-34; 2nd ed. 1742-43, II.142-66). Two other sources of possible significance are William Enfield, *The History of Philosophy from the Earliest Periods: Drawn up from Brucker's Historia Critica Philosophiae* (London: Joseph Johnson, 1792), 408-18, noteworthy because Blake engraved at least one illustration for another of Enfield's works, *The Speaker* (1780-1820?); and Ephraim Chambers, *Cyclopedia, or an Universal Dictionary of Arts and Sciences*, 2 vols. (London, 1728), which was later expanded and revised by Abraham Rees—Blake did some engraving for the Rees edition as well.

29. In contrast, in his *Grammar*, David Levi explains: "And, as the proper pronunciation of the language is one of its most essential qualities, I have, for that reason, immediately after the *Hebrew*, placed the true pronunciation in *English*; by which means (and the plain rules laid down in the grammar) any person may be enabled, without the help of a master, to attain a competent knowledge of the Sacred Language" (I.vii).

30. Pike et al. ignore the fact that Hebrew contains sounds not found in English. Instead, each arbitrarily assigns phonic values to letters, not necessarily the same, so that, for example, Bate pronounces *tsade* "J or G soft," while Levi transliterates the letter *ts*. In addition to Bate and Parkhurst, who stay "relatively" close to traditional Hebrew, there were grammarians who devised entirely new methods for reading the Sacred Tongue. John Robertson's *True and Antient Manner of Reading Hebrew without Points* (London, 1751) uses Greek models for pronunciation, and Latin and Greek models for poetics. And John Brikell asserts that "The Hebrew Alphabet had a competent number of Vowel-Letters (or, which is the same thing, in effect, Letters that served instead of Vowels) to render the Hebrew Scriptures sufficiently intelligible at the first, without the Points, and as legible as any writings in other languages" (*An Essay on the Hebrew Tongue, being an Attempt to Shew That the Hebrew Bible might be Originally Read by Vowel-Letters without the Vowel-Points* [London, 1758], 7).

31. In order to comprehend the magnitude of error which can arise, imagine a foreign speaker applying Bate's rule to the English word "knight." For the convenience of non-Hebraists, wherever possible I will supply English examples to illustrate the abuses fostered by some of these eighteenth-century Hebraists. Also, because so many of the abuses arise from the elimination of the vowel points, in transliterating the Hebrew I have not followed the accepted formations of the words. Instead, I have signified the letters actually found in the Hebrew word with upper-case Roman letters, and indicated the vowel sounds derived from pointing with lower case.

32. As Bate explains: "To find out a word in the Dictionary, throw away the serviles from the beginning or ending of a word, and [*vav*] or [*yod*] out of the middle, if you can't find it with them; and the remainder will generally be the root: if not, add [*he*], [*yod*], or [*nun*], and the word will be found" (*Critica Hebraea*, vi).

33. Etymologies of this sort were a commonplace in eighteenth-century England. John Williams provided his readers with *A Concordance to the Greek Testament; with the English Version to Each Word; the Principal Hebrew Roots corresponding to the Greek Words of the Septuagint; and an Index for the Benefit of the English Reader* (London, 1767). And Edward Davies' "Essay on the Celtic Language" coordinates Hebrew, Greek, and Latin, with Celtic. Jacob Bryant's *Mythological, Etymological, and Historical Dictionary* coordinates roots from ancient languages to indicate, for example, that the word "Ees, rendered As and Is, like [*ESH*] of the Hebrews, related to light and fire; and was one of the titles of the Sun." *Esh*, in turn, "is often found combined with Or.... It is often combined with El, and Il.... In short, from the Amonian terms, Al-As, came the Grecian [*a'los, a'las*], as from the same terms reversed (As-El) were formed the Latine Sal, Sol, and Salum" (*New System*, I.26-30). Could this be an intricate etymology of Los?

34. According to Tannenbaum, "Thus biblical tradition in the eighteenth century consisted of a variety of strands that provided sources of or contexts for Blake's ideas and artistic practice. As we would expect, Blake was frequently attracted to the more imaginative and radical elements of that tradition, but he also adopted, modified and transformed the ideas of more orthodox and conventional schools of thought. Inheriting the influence of a number of exegetical schools, Blake never completely adhered to any of them" (23).

35. According to Cheskin, "The unmethodical character of the irregularities [in Blake's Hebrew] leaves us with two possible explanations: willful subversion or ignorance. But the case for willful subversion ... is simultaneously unsupportable and irrefutable" (182). Cheskin seems to assume

that Blake would have wished to duplicate traditional Hebrew, but as we have seen, that is not necessarily true.

36. Blake explains in his letter to Dr. Trusler (23 August 1799) that "What is Grand is necessarily obscure to Weak men. That which can be made Explicit to the Idiot is not worth my care" (E702). In *Visionary Poetics: Milton's Tradition and His Legacy* (San Marino: Huntington Library, 1979), Joseph A. Wittreich, Jr. discusses "obscurity, a veil that can be penetrated by the spiritual eye," as one of the strategies of prophecy (30). And in "Opening the Seals: Blake's Epics and the Milton Tradition," he applies the strategy to Blake (in *Blake's Sublime Allegory: Essays on The Four Zoas, Milton, Jerusalem*, ed. Stuart Curran and Wittreich [Madison: Univ. of Wisconsin Press, 1973], 23-58).

37. In "Blake's Comme-bined Cherubim: A Note on *Milton*, Plate 32," Leslie Brisman explores the possibility that the Hebrew in *Milton* 32 is also a pun on the word Cherubim (*BIQ*, 21 [Winter 1987-88], 95-98).

38. Cheskin mistranslates the phrase as "your God has given," rather than "gives."

39. Cheskin compares the reversal of the *alef* to the arabic numeral 4, the top of which can be either closed or open, and assumes that, as with the number, Blake believed that either form of the letter would do. A closer analogy would be with the letter "N" which, while often reversed by those still learning English, is never considered correct in that form.

40. Stephen Mitchell points out this inconsistency in his "Postscript on Blake's Hebrew Lettering" to David V. Erdman's "Redefining the Texts of Blake (another temporary report)," *BIQ*, 17 (Summer 1983), 14.

41. Probably the best dictionary available to Blake was Calmet's. The 1732 edition contains not only extensive entries on the major aspects of the Scriptures, but also detailed appendices on editions and translations of the Bible, as well as biblical scholarship. The revised edition of C. Taylor (3 vols.; London, 1797-1801) contains different indices and less information about Judaica.

42. According to Bate, "The Hebrew is an ideal language; and names are definitions or descriptions in one word, and sometimes two compounded" (*Reply to Dr. Sharp*, 184).

43. "The Iconoclastic Enterprise: Blake's Critique of 'Milton's Religion,'" *Blake Studies*, 5 (1972), 37. In order to derive her etymology, Sandler substitutes a *he* for a *heth*, an acceptable practice since both receive the same transliteration. While her translation is correct, her transcription of the Hebrew is inaccurate.

44. Without vocalization, the name of the city is transliterated *TRZH*, the last letter being a *he*, comparable to our *h*; and the word from the Sixth Commandment is also *TRZH*, the last letter being *heth*, a guttural sound with no English equivalent, though transliterated with an *h*. Vocalized, both the name and word would be transliterated as Blake spells his, *TiRZaH*. Since writing this article, I have completed a more extensive study of the "Sources and Etymologies of Blake's 'Tirzah,'" forthcoming in *BIQ*.

45. "Notes for a Commentary on *Milton*," in *The Divine Vision: Studies in the Poetry and Art of William Blake*, ed. Vivian de Sola Pinto (1957; rpt. N.Y.: Haskell House, 1968), 126, n. 1.

46. *Blake and Tradition*, Bollingen Series xxxv.11, 2 vols. (Princeton: Princeton Univ. Press, 1968), I.398, n. 19.

47. D.J. Sloss and J.P.R. Wallis locate the source of the name Luban in Bryant's *Ancient Mythology* (III.21), where Luban is identified as the "Ararat of Moses: here I imagine that the Patriarch resided, and ... gave instructions to his children and vanished from the sight of men" (*Prophetic Writings of William Blake*, 2 vols. [Oxford: Clarendon Press, 1926], I.258). Built "Upon the Limit of Translucence" (*FZ*, n.5, 60.4, E340), Luban also suggests the Hebrew root *LaVaN*, "white," or in its verb form, "to make white," "to purify."

48. Joseph Wicksteed derived Urizen from "your reason" (*William Blake's "Jerusalem"* [London: Trianon Press, 1954], 34); and Dorothy Plowman first located the Greek source "meaning 'to bound' or 'limit,' with the cognate form 'Uranus,' signifying The Lord of the Firmament" (in her edition of *The Book of Urizen* [London: Dent, 1929], 17). A more complete discussion of Urizen's Hebraic etymologies can be found in my article "The Reasons for Urizen" (*BIQ*, 21 [Spring 1988], 147-49); and my "Hebraic Etymologies of Proper Names in Blake's Myths" (*Philological Quarterly* 67, 3 [1988]: 345-63) considers possible Hebraic etymologies for Ariston, Enitharmon, Los, Ocalythron, Orc, Rintrah and Urthona. [*And once Blake had coined a name, he liked to pun on it—e.g., fitting "Tharmas" into "doubting Thomas" and "Thomas Paine."—Ed.*]

49. To compound our confusion, Blake created several different states of Ulro in *Milton* (34.8-19, E134):

And the Four States of Humanity in its Repose,
Were shewed them. First of Beulah a most pleasant Sleep
On Couches soft, with mild music, tended by Flowers of Beulah
Sweet Female forms, winged or floating in the air spontaneous
The Second State is Alla & the third State Al-Ulro;
But the Fourth State is dreadful; it is named Or-Ulro:

The First State is in the Head, the Second is in the Heart:
The Third in the Loins & Seminal Vessels & the Fourth
In the Stomach & Intestines terrible, deadly, unutterable
And he whose Gates are opend in those Regions of his Body
Can from those Gates view all these wondrous Imaginations
But Ololon sought the Or-Urlo & its fiery Gates

Alla, the next-to-the highest state, resembles the traditional Hebrew verb "to ascend or mount upwards," while the Al of Al-Ulro, the state between the "ascending" Alla and the dreadful lower Or-Ulro, suggests Parkhurst's inventive transformation of the Hebrew *el* (meaning God) into "interposer, intervener," or in its verb form, "to interpose, intervene, mediate, come or be between, for protection, prevention." Finally, the prefix for Or-Ulro seems to be a combination of the traditional meaning of *or*, "light" ("the Or-Ulro & its fiery Gates"), and Parkhurst's more innovative coinage, "curse." Hence the "dreadful" fourth state.

50. *Jewish Magic and Superstition: A Study in Folk Religion* (1939; New York: Atheneum, 1979), 260-61. While Trachtenberg cites the *Sefer Raziel*, a magical-kabbalistic text, his examples demonstrate that the practice was widespread throughout the Middle Ages.

51. The name Tiriel was originally used by Agrippa. Harold Bloom derives a multi-lingual etymology, considering Tiriel to be a combination of the Greek "tyrant," and the Hebrew "El," God. Zazel, also found in Agrippa, could be, according to Bloom, a version of the Hebrew *Azazel*, "scapegoat" (*Blake's Apocalypse: A Study in Poetic Argument* [New York: Doubleday, 1963], 30, 32).

52. To Frye, Ozoth comes from "azoth," an alchemical term used by Paracelsus (126, n. 1), while Raine sees the name as a combination of "Azoth" and "Optic" (II.302, n.36).

53. *Paradise Lost: A Poem in Twelve Books*, ed. Merritt Y. Hughes, new ed. (New York: Odyssey, 1962). Leutha has been derived from: a combination of Luvah and Lilith (Peter F. Fisher, *The Valley of Vision: Blake as Prophet and Revolutionary*, ed. Northrop Frye [Toronto: Univ. of Toronto Press, 1961], 197, n. 16); and Macpherson's Lutha (H.M. Margoliouth, *William Blake* [London: Oxford Univ. Press, 1951], 15).

54. In England, *gilgul* was one of the more written about kabbalistic concepts and was at least alluded to in most sources through the eighteenth century. However, the most comprehensive discussions are found in the works of a seventeenth-century Christian Kabbalist, Franciscus Mercurius van Helmont, several of which were translated into English: *A Cabbalistical*

Dialogue in Answer to the Opinion of a Learned Doctor in Philosophy and Theology that the World Was Made of Nothing (London, 1682); *Two Hundred Queries Moderately Propounded concerning the Doctrine of the Revolution of Humane Souls* (London, 1684); *The Paradoxical Discourses of F.M. Van Helmont* (London, 1685); and *Seder Olam; or the Order, Series, or Succession of All the Ages, Periods, and Times of the Whole World* (London, 1694). For a more comprehensive bibliography on Blake's kabbalistic sources, see my "Kabbalistic Sources—Blake's and His Critics'" and, on the development of Kabbalah in England, my *Jewish Mysticism: An Annotated Bibliography on the Kabballah in English* (New York: Garland Publishing, 1984).

The association of Gilgal, the city, *GaLGaL*, "wheel," and *gilgul* would not be original to Blake, for in *Seder Olam*, van Helmont explains in his discussion of the wheels of Ezekiel's chariot (the biblical text uses the word *ofanim* for "wheels"): "Which Wheels and Faces signifie nothing else than four great Revolutions of Souls.... Those four Wheels are called Gilgal or a Wheel, because they make but one great Wheel, to wit, the vast Revolution of 4000 years" (72).

55. And above Albions Land was seen the heavenly Canaan
      As the Substance is to the Shadow: and above Albions
          Twelve Sons
      Were seen Jerusalems Sons: and all the Twelve Tribes
          spreading
      Over Albion. As the Soul is to the Body, so Jerusalems
          Sons,
      Are to the Sons of Albion (*J* 71.1-5, E224)

The concept of *gilgul* suggests another meaning for Golgonooza, the city of Los. In addition to Golconda (Frye, *Fearful Symmetry: A Study of William Blake* [1947; Princeton Univ. Press, 1969], 445, n. 43), Golgotha (Wicksteed, 137, n. 1), and "golgos"—skull (Raine, II.321, n. 37), Bloom notes that "It is possible (though with much twisting) to find Hebrew roots in the name which would make it mean 'the hidden hub'" (337). If we observe eighteenth-century rules, the etymology requires less twisting than Bloom thought. *GNZ* is a root for "hidden" or "secret," *GeNooZa* being the adjectival form. And *GLGL* is the root for "wheel, cycle," etc. Kabbalistically, the name would signify the hidden location where the soul is purified (*gilgul*), especially since "travellers from Eternity. pass outward to Satan's seat,/ But travellers to Eternity. pass inward to Golgonooza" (*M* 17.30-31, E111); and Golgonooza is where Enitharmon weaves "the Web of Life/ Out from the ashes of the Dead" (*M* 6.28-29, E100).

56. *Spenser: Poetical Works*, ed. J.C. Smith and E. de Selincourt (1912; London: Oxford Univ. Press, 1970), III.vi.29-49. The most extensive study of Blake's debt to Spenser is Robert F. Gleckner's *Blake and Spenser* (Baltimore: Johns Hopkins Univ. Press, 1985).

Index

231